AF778615

Women's Social and Legal Issues in African Current Affairs

Women's Social and Legal Issues in African Current Affairs

Lifting the Barriers

Victoria M. Time

LEXINGTON BOOKS
Lanham • Boulder • New York • London

Published by Lexington Books
An imprint of The Rowman & Littlefield Publishing Group, Inc.
4501 Forbes Boulevard, Suite 200, Lanham, Maryland 20706
www.rowman.com

Unit A, Whitacre Mews, 26-34 Stannary Street, London SE11 4AB

Copyright © 2017 by Lexington Books

All rights reserved. No part of this book may be reproduced in any form or by any electronic or mechanical means, including information storage and retrieval systems, without written permission from the publisher, except by a reviewer who may quote passages in a review.

British Library Cataloguing in Publication Information Available

Library of Congress Cataloging-in-Publication Data
The hardback edition of this book was previously catalogued by the Library of Congress as follows:

Names: Time, Victoria M., 1962- author.
Title: Women's social and legal issues in African current affairs : lifting the barriers / Victoria M. Time.
Description: Lanham : Lexington Books, 2017. | Includes bibliographical references and index.
Identifiers: LCCN 2016034879 (print) | LCCN 2016035389 (ebook) | ISBN 9781498538787 (cloth : alk. paper) | ISBN 9781498538794 (electronic)
Subjects: LCSH: Women—Africa—Social conditions—21st century. | Women—Legal status, laws, etc.—Africa. | Women—Africa—Economic conditions—21st century. | Patriarchy—Africa. | Sex discrimination against women—Africa.
Classification: LCC HQ1787 .T56 2017 (print) | LCC HQ1787 (ebook) | DDC 305.42096—dc23
LC record available at https://lccn.loc.gov/2016034879

∞™ The paper used in this publication meets the minimum requirements of American National Standard for Information Sciences Permanence of Paper for Printed Library Materials, ANSI/NISO Z39.48-1992.

Printed in the United States of America

In loving memory of my father, John Edie Time, who passed away on April 1, 2014; my brother Ewane Time who went to be with the Lord on August 28, 2016; and to my mother, Marie E. Time.

Contents

Foreword

Few books have forewords these days. Unlike the preface or introduction that alerts the reader to a book's subject matter, the foreword provides background or a context for the author, and makes the connection between the writer and how or why the book emerged when it did. Simply stated, it is helpful to know a little something about the author before reading a book. Thus, forewords are written by someone other than the author, it being somewhat unseemly for a writer to speak of their own accolades. As a lead-in to this significant treatise on the plight of women in Africa, and with the caveat that there may be some overlap between a foreword and an introduction, a few words are in order about Dr. Victoria M. Time.

I came to know Dr. Time, referred to as Vickie by friends and some colleagues, two decades ago. She was applying for a PhD program in criminology at Indiana University of Pennsylvania, and at that time I happened to be the contact person for recruitment into the doctoral program. Email was yet to become conventional, and our correspondence required old-fashioned paper and stamped envelopes. From the start, Vickie was distinctive by already holding four university degrees. Two law degrees were received with honors (LL.B and LL.M), from the University of Cameroon, and two graduate degrees from Washington, DC-based universities: George Washington University (Masters of Comparative Law) and American University (Masters of Science in Justice, Law and Society).

Not surprisingly, Vickie sailed through our PhD coursework. One Friday afternoon she expressed some apprehension about a direction for her dissertation and remarked she was just going to go home and engross herself in a few of Shakespeare's plays. I clearly recall quipping "why don't you write a dissertation on Shakespeare"? I think the idea caught both of us by surprise, but a year or so later she published one of the few, and perhaps the most imaginative work ever written on Shakespeare's criminals. I recall in her early years as an academic, her paper presentations at national conferences aroused audiences as she enlightened the listeners on how Shakespeare's verse pondered all the major theoretical themes in criminology in the mid-sixteenth century, long before the birth of Cesare Beccaria. Victoria M. Time enjoys living on the edge as a researcher and educator. I was not surprised for a moment when she was bestowed the title of University Professor by Old Dominion University even a few years before being awarded the academic rank of professor.

It is a natural sequence of events that Victoria M. Time pens this book. In a sense, her life has been in its preparation. Four reasons come to mind. First, since graduate school, Professor Time's writings and presentations at numerous national and international conferences concerned issues of comparative justice, most, but not all, emphasizing affairs of Africa. Second, Victoria M. Time's journeys have taken her to most of the continents of the world on research and teaching expeditions providing a keen sense of cross-cultural awareness. Periodically (five times in a decade), she has supervised a class of students for university credit to Europe, providing them a taste of international justice issues outside the classroom. Such a transnational emphasis on teaching, including instruction for a semester in Japan, contributed to her multiple teaching awards.

Third, her academic preparation combines law, criminology, and social sciences, allowing approaches to her subject matter of African women from multidisciplinary outlooks. For instance, noticeable from the start is that this book encompasses anthropological perspectives by tackling such topics as the origins and dysfunctions of patriarchy, bride prices, levirate marriages, and female circumcisions. The underpinning sociological and theoretical issues impacting African women, to include poverty, education, economy, and human trafficking, are addressed with separate chapters. Victoria M. Time comfortably wears the hat of the criminologist and lawyer as she offers a full chapter on policy implications. She argues that outdated laws, and the way laws are sometimes written to subjugate and victimize African women must be addressed. Here, the author is in her bailiwick by presenting one of the most detailed chapters of the book on recommendations—how do we fix the problems of African women?

Finally, being reared in Africa, she can remain subjective in her understanding and appreciation of the problems in the continent even while objectively analyzing research findings pertinent to African women. This is not an easy task, but Dr. Time's approach and final outcome is exemplary. Although this relatively small book captures the human interest story of the life struggle for African women, it is perhaps foremost a scholarly work, filled with 400 or so citations.

This book is unquestionably timely. The world is getting smaller and Africa is no longer the forgotten continent it once was. This is a double-edged sword. Today, we know of Africa with 24/7 news coverage, surely a positive development. Yet, at the same time, the problems of Africa and especially its women, now seen up close and personal, still remain unsolved. The book ought to be at arm's reach of both beginning and seasoned scholars of Africa and comparative issues.

Timothy Austin, professor
Indiana University of Pennsylvania

Preface

This volume explains the difficulties that beset African women in the twenty-first century. These problems as later discussed inhibit women from excelling in many walks of life on the continent. Asymmetrical relations in society position women in subjugated and marginalized roles. This is not just because of customary practices that over time have left women in vulnerable and subsidiary positions; also to blame are statutory provisions that fester this process.

Despite its richness in raw materials and mineral resources, Africa remains retarded when compared to other continents. The economy of most African countries is severely anemic; corruption is rife; poor governance is pervasive; and wars, conflicts, famine and diseases abound.

Even though men also suffer from the scourges of conflicts, diseases, and natural disasters, a stalled economy disproportionately affects women in that as nurturers women have the extra responsibility of taking care of children and members of the extended family. In times of want, women are more likely to give up the little they have so that their children and others may survive.

African customary practices have always projected men as leaders, heads of families, and law enforcers, and this phenomenon has remained rigid over time. As a result, girls are less likely to be sent to school. This impedes their upward mobility. As well, they are more likely to be commoditized for bride price when family circumstances are dire; and since they have had little or no formal education, they remain completely dependent on their purchasers—"husbands," for livelihood. Many of these women live to experience hopelessness either in a nightmarish and cruel life with a stranger of a husband or as a wife of a polygamous husband. Seldom is any attention paid to them.

Much has been written about the plight of African women, with some highlighting specific case studies, some concentrating on a particular country, and some on particular issues. This study brings together many of the most pressing issues that inhibit women from upward mobility in African societies. Occasionally, a country or countries that best exemplifies or exemplify a particular issue is or are introduced.

In this volume, the author outlines a series of recommendations that have been put forth by professionals in the field, and by women themselves as possible solutions to relieve women from their impoverished and secondary roles in African societies. It is contended that without reforms—legal, social, economic, and customary, things are likely to remain the same. Two main questions are answered in this book: first, what issues impede women from upward mobility in Africa? Second, what can be done to improve women's conditions in Africa?

Acknowledgments

My utmost gratitude goes to Ms. Kathryn Tafelski, Ms. Carissa Marcelle, and Ms. Marie-Claire Antoine of Lexington/Rowman & Littlefield Publishers who, without reservation, found value in this work. Thank you.

I wish to thank Dr. W. Timothy Austin, who was my professor and now is a mentor, and a very close friend. He wrote the foreword. Many thanks also to Dr. Ronald Shafer, one of my former professors and now an avid cheerleader of mine. I wish to thank Drs. Chandra de Silva, Roderick Graham, and Mengyan Dai for meticulously reviewing the substantive content of this work and for their various comments and suggestions. Hearty thanks go to Dr. Funwi F. Ayuninjam and Ms. Dianne Berger-Hill for scrutinizing my writing style, correcting grammatical and typographical errors and making adjustments where necessary, and to the anonymous reviewer whose comments on both content and style reshaped this work. Thanks also to my personal friends Andre Mbounda and Allen Evershed for cheering me on.

Finally, my gratitude goes to the rest of the team at Lexington Books, including Ms. Madhumitha Koduvalli, and others who shouldered the responsibility of seeing this manuscript turn into a book.

Any shortcomings of this book remain my full responsibility.

Introduction

My early research about female victimization explained criminology using fictional characters. Then, it did not occur to me that I would extend my inquiries to empirical understanding of female victimizations, and of more significance, in inquiring how customs, politics, the economy, natural occurrences, among other factors, perpetuate female subjugation.

In this book the word "marginalization" is used to explain deprivation of women from opportunities and resources that men have. "Victimization" relates to certain acts that constitute bad or cruel treatment, for example, forced marriages, domestic violence, and trafficking among others. However, at times, as Davies et al. (2007) explain, and as obvious in this book, there is an overlap of the origins of crime, victimization, and inequality. While marginalization and victimization have different definitions, and represent different things, marginalization and disempowerment of a class of people may thrust them into victims. As well, victimization of a class of people may lead to social exclusion or marginalization. In essence, marginalization and victimization converge, at least in the ensuing chapters of this book.

Many have written about the plight of African women, some referencing specific case studies, and specific acts of victimization and deprivation. Much of the literature on victimization and relative deprivation of African women come as journal articles, book chapters, or books devoted to specific issues, or particular countries. That so much attention is paid to the issue emphasizes a dire need to understand and curb the problem

This volume is different in that it attempts to bring together a common understanding of the reasons women have yet to arrive at a level in society that men are readily placed and enjoy in African societies. In this endeavor, not only is reliance placed on a series of sociological/criminological theories, the study is also informed by a variety of variables drawn from politics, economics, history, and other disciplines. As the discussion reveals, it is not the lack of effort, and at times, it is not even the absence of educational opportunities that retard women's progress; sometimes, why women do not move forward remains an enigma that can be understood only through a cultural lens. That women remain severely marginalized in most, if not all, African societies can be summarized in a singular thesis as Dunne (2005) explains:

> Just as one may be distant from the societal center, i.e., the flow of resources to and from the societal center is restricted; this is also true for any local center toward which one may be oriented. Marginality is a multidimensional phenomenon in that a given person may be simultaneously integrated with one or more centers while being marginal from one or more other centers. (15)

Several theoretical perspectives in the field of criminology/sociology are introduced in this volume to help in understanding female victimization and more importantly, to assist policymakers and researchers to fashion out policies and programs that may help disenfranchised and abused women. The book furthers the understanding of female marginalization by exploring why women are far removed from "societal center." This book presents an amalgam of strategies for maintaining order, and uplifting women's position in Africa. Before even addressing the problems that African women face, the reasons why things are the way they are must first be understood.

Easily noticeable, and possibly as significant as other factors in broadening the rift between African men and women, is the absence of laws that provide for an egalitarian society, and even when those laws are in place, there for the most part are absences of enforcement mechanisms. Anderson (2011) explains that failure to apply justice produces "breeding ground for impunity" (p. 787). Literature on deterrence clearly explains that without realistic threats of punishment, the urge to comply diminishes.

In a discussion of how African women can triumph over their plight, one cannot ignore aspects of a healthy life style that promotes progress and prosperity. These factors comprise quality of physical wellbeing, literacy, opportunities to participate in societal functions and activities, and freedom from oppression and crimes specifically targeted at women.

Mackey (2013) discusses three connected procedures to minimize the occurrences and severity of criminal behavior: "primary prevention, secondary prevention, and tertiary prevention" (p. 4). Primary prevention emphasizes proactive and protective measures before one becomes a victim and thus as Mackey explains, is more relevant to the victim. Awareness, education, and self-help programs are also relevant in uplifting self-esteem. Secondary prevention emphasizes persons and environments that are more susceptible to further delinquency. Here, attention is paid to factors that reduce the prevalence, severity, and gravity of offending patterns. Tertiary prevention is focused on curbing continuous criminal behavior through the use of rehabilitative and therapeutic programs.

Regardless of the crime, society ultimately bears the brunt of the cost of crime. Costs of crime are reflected in different ways, including cost of medical care and loss of income. To many African women loss of income entails not going to the farm to harvest crops or to the market to sell them, and loss of other property. Victims also incur intangible costs such as pain and suffering, diminished quality of life, family alienation, psychological instability, or mental disorders, and at times these problems extend to family members. Dependents of victims are adversely affected: orphaned children, or abandoned children, experience a diminished quality of life, and at times, are left to fend for themselves. For children whose parents are severely impoverished, or very ill, or disabled the burden rests on them to take care of their parents. Besides costs to victims, the government and taxpayers have to spend on legal/adjudication services, at times for programs that relate to corrections or to incarceration. Police protection is offered only in rare circumstances in African societies, because of the *lassiez faire* attitude of the criminal justice system agents in some countries.

As a social issue, female victimization does lead to further social problems, like the lack of formal education, and prostitution in order to earn a livelihood. At times, any resistance by victims leads to further domestic violence. Female and children trafficking either as sex slaves or as domestic servants is rife throughout the continent. An obvious social problem particularly in some African countries is that men make the laws, and decide the course of justice thereby absolving themselves of any legal consequences. Nussbaum (2000) sums up these factors:

> Women in much of the world lack support for fundamental functions of a human life. They are less well-nourished than men, less healthy, and more vulnerable to physical violence and sexual abuse. They are much less likely than men to be literate, and still less likely to have professional or technical education. Should they attempt to enter the workplace, they face greater obstacles, including intimidation from family or spouse, sex discrimination in hiring, and sexual harassment in the workplace—all, frequently, without effective legal recourse. Similar obstacles often impede their effective participation in political life. In many nations, women are not full equals under the law: they do not have the same property rights as men, the same rights to make a contract, the same rights of association, mobility, and religious liberty. Burdened, often, with the "double day" of taxing employment and full responsibility for housework and child care; they lack opportunities for play and the cultivation of imaginative and cognitive faculties. All these factors take their toll on emotional well-being: women have fewer opportunities than men to live free from fear and to enjoy rewarding types of love—especially when, as often, they are married without choice in childhood and have no recourse from

> a bad marriage. In all these ways, unequal social and political circumstances give women unequal human capabilities. (219–20)

This book is divided into three main parts. The first part comprises of chapter 1, which explains why African women fall prey to male subjugation. Here several theories are introduced, including those relating to gender and patriarchy, symbolic interactionism, identity, personality, biology, feminist perspective on gender roles, social class and gender role stratification, and the social learning approach or learned helplessness. The intent here is not to give definitive reasons abuses and crimes (subsequently explained in the book) persist. Rather, the intent is to acquaint readers, especially those not attuned to sociological and criminological explanations of behavior, with some of the theories, and to offer those grounded in the theories an opportunity to review and assess them and to examine how they apply in the African context.

The second part explains the problems that African women confront. Here, the discussion is divided into five chapters. Chapter 2 focuses on poverty. Here, time poverty, restricted property rights, poor health care systems, famine, war, violence, disease, and government failure, are discussed as triggers of poverty. Literature on inequality unequivocally reveals that women are disproportionately poorer than men, and as confirmed by Legislative Council Secretariat (2006) and Moghadam (2005), the "feminization of poverty" among Africans is triggered by culture, politics, and gender inequality, among other factors. By citing and discussing perspectives from different sources, this chapter provides clarity on why women in Africa remain poorer than men.

Chapter 3 discusses the absence of education and difficulties women face in enrolling in and staying in school as impediments to upward mobility in society. Customary practices that still prefer boys' education over that of girls, early forced marriages, distance to schools, and abuse at times even in the hands of teachers, among other factors, explain the limited education of many African women. Also as important are the absence of technology in classrooms, poorly stocked libraries if they exist at all, teacher absenteeism due to hardships caused by non-payment of salary or tardiness in disbursement, and student absenteeism precipitated by fears of being waylaid on the way to school.

Chapter 4 explains the impact of the economy on women. Discussions in this chapter center on how a stalled economy or a slow-growing economy constrains women's prosperity. In this chapter, the author explores how low educational attainment, time poverty, reliance on exportation of raw materials, graft, and atavistic methods of tapping natural resources and farming hinder prosperity. While a sluggish economy impacts everyone, women are disproportionately affected because they engage in low-paying jobs, or subsistence work, and in addition bear the brunt of taking care of the family. Of more significance poor governance, misappropriation of funds, unaccountability, and outright ineptitude by some African leaders notoriously cripples many African economies.

Chapter 5 explains another aspect of female subjugation: degrading women through crime. In this chapter the discussion centers on female and child trafficking for the purposes of prostitution, sexual exploitation, slavery in different forms including working on farms or industries, or as domestic workers, or to harvest vital body parts. The discussion reveals how women and children are lured by traffickers through false promises of providing these women and children a better life, or at times through more sinister ways such as kidnapping. The motivations for these despicable acts include poverty (a way of money-making), greed (a primitive and ill-informed assumption that having sex with virgins cures HIV/AIDS), and simply maladjustment in rational thought.

In chapter 6, crimes of culture are discussed. Here, forced marriages, bride price, levirate obligations, female circumcision, and violence against women are discussed. The discussion reveals how these customary practices rob women of their self-esteem, minimize them as persons, and ultimately isolate them from participating in the successes and growth of the dominant group. Further, custodians of law, who for the most part are men, use their positions to further marginalize and disenfranchise women by upholding unconscionable, capricious laws. As well, factors such as poverty, and learned behavior (for example, mother married through one of these customary ways so daughter has to be married in a similar way) that lead parents to acquiesce in the practice are discussed in this chapter.

Part three that comprises just one chapter—chapter 7, explains programs and laws that are in place or that should be in place to alleviate the plight of African women. This chapter relies heavily on recommendations for women's prosperity that experts in the field have laid out either through their published essays, journal articles, or through reports from the United Nations, The World Bank, or any of those global or regional organizations. Recommendations address issues of time poverty, restricted property rights, poor health, famine wars and disasters, government failure, education, impact of the economy, trafficking of women, and crimes of culture.

Several qualitative research strategies inform this study, including document and textual analysis (archival research), observation of settings and people, and interviewing. In order to include many countries in the discussion, much reliance had to be placed on unobtrusive content. Here, discussions incorporated peer reviewed journal articles, and traditional reference and textbooks, and a plethora of documents included in commercial media accounts such as newspapers, magazines, television program transcripts, as well as United Nations documents, World Bank and International Monetary

Fund documents, British Broadcasting Corporation (BBC) documents, and a slew of others. As well, official documentary records such as court records, and speech records were examined. Berg (1995) explains that "qualitative techniques allow the researchers to share in the understandings and perceptions of others and to explore how people structure and give meaning to their daily lives" (7).

Having lived in Cameroon and visited several other African countries, writing about the culture comes foremost from experiential and observational learning. To avoid injecting any skewed observations, and infuse readers with one person's tale, accounts from Cameroonian women in diverse works of life are included. Here, both one-on-one interviews and focus group interviews were performed. Familiarity with how things work in the country, easy establishment of rapport, having connections and creating relationships that facilitated the arrangements of interviews made an otherwise onerous task rather easy. Taking notes posed no problems as the researcher could speak and understand the dialects and languages spoken by interviewees. Most spoke in English, a few in Pidgin, and some in a blend of English, Pidgin, French, and Franglais.

Triangulating methodologies, as Borman et al. (1986) explain, gives researchers the opportunity to introduce to readers the viewpoints of others. More telling is how Denzin (1978) explains is the benefit of triangulation:

> I conclude that no single method will ever meet the requirements of interaction theory. While participant observation permits the careful recording of situations and selves, it does not offer direct data on the wider spheres of influence acting on those observed. Because each method reveals different aspects of empirical reality, multiple methods of observations must be employed. This is termed triangulation. (28)

The experiences of girls are included in the study for three reasons: First, they are of the female gender and this book provides a gendered framework on issues and recommendations. Second, girls even as young as seven are victims of the same kinds of crimes women experience, as discussions in the book will reveal. Third, at times, the problems girls and women suffer from require common solutions, as for example, getting an education, legislating against certain cultural practices, and prosecuting detractors and violators.

Part I

Theoretical Explanations of Female Victimization

Chapter One

Gender and Patriarchy

Following customary practices in Africa, women have felt obligated, if not compelled to be submissive to men. Women are raised to be nurturing, and decades ago priority in getting an education was given to males in the family. This practice still goes on today in many African countries even if it is to a lesser extent. Young girls are brought up to take care of their younger siblings and in some instances to play a parental role. As they grow to be women, depending on family circumstances, the girls may be commoditized through early forced marriages in order for the family to benefit from bride price (Bentheim 2010; Beswick 2001; Monekosso 2001).

On the other hand, boys are groomed to assume manly positions. They are more likely to get an education, to be breadwinners, to be the "man of the house," and thus be the one to lay down the rules of conformity in the household. According to Plan UK, because girls are expected to marry and engage in domestic chores and other kinds of work, the quality of education they obtain may be substandard given that "teachers may give them less attention and poorer access to learning materials than boys. The cost of a daughter's education may not be viewed as a sound investment" (Plan UK). Even those men middling in resources, and those marginalized in other aspects, have a place in society as opposed to a woman (Deegan 2005). Women have to bear children, take care of them, do most of the domestic functions, be a wife, supplement family income through petty trade or some venture, and through all of that exhibit little or no fatigue. Their role limits them to domestic functions as opposed to the plethora of functions available to men in the public arena (Deegan 2005). As Deegan (2005) states, "A defining characteristic of the marginal woman is that she is existential. She is a stranger in her own society" (216). For those who are privileged to get some formal education and a job outside of the home, pay is low relative to that of men, and promotion to higher echelons is often unlikely. Some like Oluwole (1993) contend that contrary to what women of other countries or parts of Nigeria experienced, even before colonization, the Yoruba women of Nigeria played more complementary rather than subjugated roles, and their influence vis-à-vis those of men has not diminished. The Yoruba experience is atypical, and this is a rarity in most societies as well (Bernard 1981; Deegan 2005). Ademiluyi and Adedamola (2010), Omwami (2011) have written about how pervasive female marginalization still is in many parts of Africa, and have blamed this on several factors including relative change theory and patriarchy, among others. Rich (1986) defines patriarchy as:

> the power of the fathers: a familial-social, ideological, political system in which men-by force, direct pressure, or through ritual, tradition, law, and language, customs, etiquette, education, and the division of labor, determine what part women shall or shall not play, and in which the female is everywhere subsumed under the male. (57)

In discussing gender and patriarchy, McIntosh (2009) distinguishes two elements of patriarchy: (1) "an ideology that categorizes women as a distinct (and often inferior) group from men and argues that women should play different and less powerful roles in society; and (2) a set of practices or institutions that serve to limit women's options and create male dominance" (17). Role-playing is a set of gender-based activities that either inadvertently or through socialization a person engages in. These roles may vary from society to society, but for the most part the role women choose to play is that of nurturer. This role at times leads women to obtain just basic education, and consequently to careers that limit their ability to generate income, wealth, and financial assets commensurate to those of men. In order to be competitive with men women have to attain a comparable level of education. Unfortunately, in many societies where customary practices that undermine the worth of women are still commonplace girls are less likely to acquire formal education—a logical ingredient for upward mobility.

Seodi White, a lawyer and advocate for women's rights, explains that Malawian girls are less valued than boys, and this is evidenced by the fact that Malawians prefer sending boys to school, and use girls more as bargaining tools for family profit. Girls as young as 10 years old in the northern part of the country are sold as wives where they thereafter become voiceless, and powerless in their husband's community (LaFraniere 2005).

Based on research in Ethiopia and India, Rose and Al-Samarrai (2001) conclude that the prevailing attitude in those countries is that since women are more likely to be "given away" in marriage, resources should be devoted to males since they will eventually become responsible for the welfare of the family. This mindset remains permissive in many societies today. Sultana

(2010) concludes, "Patriarchal norms has an influence on women's attitudes regarding their privilege, rights and responsibilities towards educating children" (123). According to Taylor (2010), the literacy rate in Africa is 69 percent for women, and 81 percent for men. Literacy is defined as "the ability to read and write at a specific age" (CIA *World Fact Book*, 2010).

Patriarchal norms affect the way women are viewed and treated. Valian (1998) suggests that society develops "gender schemas"—stereotypical perceptions of women. These schemas cultivate society's viewpoints and roles of each gender; and they are also instrumental to self-concept that each person develops, and restrictions or circumscriptions that each one imposes on themselves. These schemas, as Valian (1998) states, are inseminated in humans in three ways: "(1) through how humans react to differences in physical attributes (2) through assigning certain occurrences to a particular gender (3) through regarding women and men as distinct and unique in their qualities" (118).

Some like Kennedy (1972), Grana (2002), and Taylor (2010) expand the discussion of patriarchy with analysis of oppression. Grana (2002) opines

Table 1.1. Literacy Data of African Countries from the *World Fact Book* 2010

Country	Men	Women
Benin	55%	30%
Burkina Faso	29.4%	15.2%
Burundi	72.9%	61.8%
Central African Republic	69.3%	43.2%
Chad	45%	24.2%
The Gambia	60%	40.4%
Liberia	64.8%	56.8%
Malawi	81.1%	68.5%
Mali	43.4%	20.3%
Morocco	68.9%	43.9%
Niger	42.9%	15.1%
Senegal	51.1%	29.2%
Somalia	49.7%	25.8%
South Sudan	40%	16%
Sudan	71.8%	50.5%
Togo	75.4%	46.9%
Uganda	76.8%	57.7%

*Data: Courtesy of Central Intelligence Agency (CIA) *World Fact Book*, 2010.

that oppression encompasses several social and economic aspects, and that it is a catalyst for patriarchy, a premise that is also evident in Taylor's (2010) study. Kennedy (1972) gleans four types of oppression:

1. "Personal/psychological oppression" which refers to a worthless sense of self that conforms to what society thinks of the person.
2. "Private oppression" refers to subjugation that prevails in private settings like work and school, among others. This is when a superior would require personal favors from a woman.
3. "Public oppression" denotes situations whereby powerful institutions in society like the government issues fiats that are detrimental to women's wellbeing.
4. "Cultural oppression" explains a phenomenon whereby contributions of certain groups or class of people are undermined or completely ignored in the annals of a society.

Lako (2004) takes the stance that culture, by and large, dominates people's socialization that it is "a major determinant of the consciousness and experience of the community" (4), and that global development cannot be attained if a culture promotes gender inequality. She further maintains that all societies are guilty of patriarchal domination, and such dominance is evident through female subjugation, "patriarchal relations in paid work," and other despicable ways by which women are suppressed (10). Basing their study on Nigeria, Ademiluyi and Adedamola (2010) find that in order for a woman to excel in politics in Nigeria, she has to be very educated, be placed in a high income bracket, have connections—(which they refer to as having a "godfather") and be very active in community projects (59). More importantly, they contend that because the realm of politics in the country is saturated by men, the "implication is that gender discrimination is a major cause of women abstinence from political participation in Nigeria" (Ademiluyi and Adedamola 2010, 59). Puechguirbal (2010) looks at patriarchy from a different perspective. She scrutinizes United Nations documents in order to better understand female victimization. The documents reveal stereotypical assumptions of women, and those assumptions explain why women are not active in "peace building and conflict resolution" and in essence are responsible for why women's opinions or voices are not heard (Puechguirbal 2010, 173).

Lorde (1984), Hooks (1984), and Obiora (2005) refute the premise of the one-glove-fits-all notion of patriarchy as a basis for women's marginalization. They imply that other factors such as "racism," "class privilege," and a myriad of other factors may explain disparity in women's treatment and position in society. Even small differences in how people are treated in society eventually are magnified in the larger scheme of things and as Valian

(1998) states “it is unfair to neglect even minor instances of group-based bias, because they add up to major inequalities” (3). It follows that even little privileges that may be denied women but given to men may eventually add up to create a glaring difference in their acceptance at the workplace, in politics, within the justice system, and in all facets of the social structure.

Fox (1977) identifies three major forms of control over women:

- Confinement: limits women to just the parameters of their homes
- Protection: women may venture out of their homes only if accompanied by an adult usually, male
- Normative restriction: inculcating certain norms and values to girls from birth. Girls who abide by these values have it relatively easier than those who shun them.

The import of Fox’s discussion is that patriarchy constitutes control, domination, and marginalization. Putting all three together, Grana (2002) states “patriarchy is a social structural arrangement whereby males, just by virtue of being males, have more privilege than women do in society. Moreover, this privilege often leads to greater power, access to opportunity, and better rewards for men” (2).

Much in the discussion of patriarchy revolves around the concept of marginality. Marginality as Dunne (2005) explains, is a phenomenon that removes one from the center of any group, activity, social setting, “flow of resources,” towards a negative rather than an upward position. Adding to the discussion on marginality, Deegan (2005) contends that a marginalized person is one linked to a “minority group,” to a “minority experience,” which experience “justifies further discrimination and hides the social cost of discrimination from the oppressor” (223).

SYMBOLIC INTERACTIONISM

Sense of self as Mead (1934) projects relates to one’s behavior/attitude or deportment toward self as well as toward others. As one of the forerunners of symbolic interactionism theory, Mead’s (1934) premise, like that of others, rests on the fact that humans eventually act in accordance with what they assume others think and expect of them. As children, we begin by emulating behavior of others, and then proceed to role playing and in due course, we adapt to the socialization process whereby we integrate the customs, values, mores transmitted to us by our parents and by the society where we live. The socialization process as Mead (1934) explains begins with children emulating what they see their parents do, and then subsequently progresses into role-playing whereby they act out the activities of those they come in contact with. These activities are played out to others and to themselves, and thus the maturation of "self." As interaction with others become more frequent, children begin to digest the various roles they have to play and how to conform to the expectations of those roles, and these in turn mold their responses toward others. The "generalized other" (the general behavior of those similarly situated) emerges. "Through the generalized other, the community exercises control over its members" (Scanzoni and Scanzoni 1981, 25). Mead also maintains that we (humans) do independently carve out our own traits; and that what those we associate with communicate to us eventually become the labels we identify with.

This phenomenon, as Stryker (2007) comments, is "a formula of symbolic interactionism: society shapes self, and self shapes social behavior" (1089). In identity theory and personality theory, Stryker explains that humans have several identities, and the identity that one projects varies from situation to situation and that those identities placed in a "hierarchy" impact behavior in any situation. Identity/self, as Stryker (2007) further explains, relate to what one conceives as one's role toward others, while personality theory explains traits or distinguishing characteristics that one develops. Simply, one's traits may help explain the role one adopts. As well, behavior is not explained by traits alone; it also requires "role differentiation." Consequently, the more one interacts with the same people even under different circumstances, the more likely role expectations will remain consistent without modification, and the less likely will there be a contrast of trait identity. On the contrary, there will be a variance in trait identity when one's interactions are with people outside one's niche. Perhaps this is what Stets and Burke (2003) allude to when they suggest that one can take on alternative identities. In this regard, the identity is fluid, and depending on the environment, the social context, or the expectations of others, one's identity can be adjusted accordingly.

Herbert Blumer (1986) expounded on Mead's explanation of symbolic interactionism by adding three main concepts: "meaning," "language," and "thought." Meaning relates to a process whereby human reactions reflect what those they deal with have imparted on them, or with regard to objects, what they can deduce from the object. Language is an instrument whereby humans give expression to knowledge, and thereby create a means of discourse with one another. Thought explains each person's understanding of language used, or communication, and how conclusions—right or wrong—can be derived from one's thought. The overall essence of Blumer's essay is that the meanings we draw from others or things are based on our social interaction, and modified through our interpretations of them. Relating Blumer's explanation of symbolic interaction to female marginalization, a woman may define a situation in different ways. One aspect of her definition to a situation may relate to her accepting how she is being treated because she believes that is the way things should be, and in another aspect, may lash out, or be belligerent because she disapproves of her treatment.

IDENTITY AND PERSONALITY THEORY

One's identity can be traced to one's origin and culture. In explaining this theory, Cinoglu and Arikan (2012) note that a person's sense of self reflects the roles that others expect and ascribe to the person. Equipped with these expectations, one begins to act or behave accordingly, and one's identity thereafter is carved out. If the formative self is geared to reflect traditional female roles, then the self will justify and assume that role. McCall and Simmons (1978) also explain identity theory as a behavior or role that one assumes willingly or through societal influence. McCall and Simons identify three sustaining characteristics of self-identity that can be summarized as follows:

1. The extent to which those who shape one's identity influence one
2. The extent to which one accepts and nurtures that identity
3. The benefits one gets for accepting or subscribing to that identity.

Relating these factors to women, if a woman accepts the role she is introduced to in society, and she finds gratification in that role, she will immerse herself in it and maintain the role. This is not to suggest that the woman avoids or is closed to other roles; involvement in such other roles may be constrained from her. People do arrange concepts of themselves in light of what others think and expect of them, and eventually, that concept becomes the identity they adopt.

Stryker (2007) explains that symbolic interactionist theory is the parent of identity theory in that the latter theory is premised as well on the idea that human interactions and actions are directed by how humans define a situation, and those definitions stem from perceptions of their encounters with others. Further, as Stryker (2007) explains, how one thinks of oneself, is instrumental to the actions and reactions that one gets from others. Following the actions and reactions of others, in the long run, one may dictate one's behavior accordingly. How one's sense of self is mirrored in society, and subsequently becomes the way society views the person and reacts to the person may be perpetuated if the social structure stagnates by resisting change.

BIOLOGY

Much has been written about biology and gender roles (Becker and Wagner 2009; Berenbaum, Blakemore, and Beltz 2011; Fishbein 1990; Goldberg 1974; Gove and Carpenter 1982; Jawahar and Raghavendra 2011). Goldberg (1974), for instance, concludes that there is a difference between males and females, and that males are sovereign with regard to exceling in academics, and they are dominant in male-ascribed roles like "aggression." On the contrary, Gove and Carpenter (1982) look beyond biology to consider environmental effects on human composition. While behavior may be triggered by biology, Gove and Carpenter (1982) assert that social and environmental conditions enhance the biological traits that trigger criminal behavior, for instance. Fishbein (1990) however asserts that behavior is not inherited. How we respond to social and environmental stimuli denotes behavior. He states: "As a rule, what is inherited is not a behavior; rather it is the way in which an individual responds to the environment. It provides an orientation, predisposition, or tendency to behave in a certain fashion" (42).

Marini (1990) discusses the role of biology on sex differences and acknowledges that while there may be slight behavioral differences between men and women that may be associated to biology she nonetheless concedes that such differences may be mitigated by socialization. She explains that the socialization process begins right from birth since parents treat boys differently from girls (Seavey et al. 1975; Condry and Condry 1976). This difference in treatment is carried on to grade school where teachers react differently to boys and girls (Leinhardt et al. 1979).

In her writings on hormones and gender roles, Ramey (1973) sends out warning notes that not much emphasis should be placed on research outcomes that project hormonal influences on developmental processes of the brain and the life course behavior of a person. She further cautions that even after analyzing data on the subject, people have to be leery of drawing conclusions that suggest a causal link between hormones and the predispositions of women to "traditional or nontraditional" gender roles (1973, 240–41). Expounding on this, Ehrhardt (1977), surmises that both hormonal and environmental factors affect behavior. Miles et al. (2007) find a nexus between androgens and traits that are physiologically induced and "territorial and courtship."

On the issue of testosterone and gender roles, Ramey (1973) opines that without taking into consideration social factors, it would be naïve to conclude that testosterone is responsible for the roles that either gender assumes. Scanzoni and Scanzoni (1981) subsequently conclude that:

> Perhaps the only thing that can be said about hormones and sex differences is that, while hormonal factors both before and after birth cannot be ignored, they

> should not be viewed as a basis for a fatalistic determinism that seals the destinies of females and males. We must pay attention to the social environment and how human beings of both sexes respond to that environment. (43)

In a later study Hines et al. (2002) find a linear relationship between testosterone and gender roles in pre-school girls, but that was not the case with boys in the same cohort. Their study also revealed that "the presence of older brothers or sisters in the home, parental adherence to traditional sex roles, the presence of a male partner in the home, and maternal education" (1678) had no bearing on "gender role behavior" or on the relation between testosterone and behavior (Hines et al., 1678). In sum, the majority of studies suggest that social setting has a bearing on one's role, and whatever influence biology has is rather slight. Deegan (2005) concludes that women are "on the other side of a biological divide built into an institutionally reflexive reality, a world where minor biological differences between the sexes are augmented, exaggerated, and elaborated" (216). Goffman (1977) has also expressed this viewpoint.

Berenbaum et al. (2011) look at the influence of biology on behavior. They conclude that hormones more so than genes account for the behavioral difference between genders. The authors explain that both social and psychological factors and hormones influence behavior. The authors, however, show as a limitation of their study that findings are limited to western countries and may not be generalized to developing countries. They also advise that because social and environmental factors may influence behavior, biology should not be considered as "destiny." The authors glean some differences between genders. Among the differences are physiological/self-regulation, interests in activities, and spatial ability, but the authors concede that biology plays a role in emotional differences with females being more susceptible to depression.

FEMINIST PERSPECTIVE ON GENDER ROLES

Acker (1992), Ademiluyi and Adedamola (2010), Adler (1975), Chesney-Lind (1989), Mason and Lu (1988), and Omwami (2011), have written about the roles of women in society. As Cullen and Agnew (2011) explain the feminist movement that sprung up following the civil rights movement had two principal outcomes in regards to criminology and civil rights. One outcome was that women became interested in the field of criminology as their life experiences shed light on the discipline. Another result was that more light was shed on power control, socialization, economics, and other disparities between genders. Burgess-Proctor, (2006), Chesney-Lind (1989), Chesney-Lind and Sheldon (2004), Daly (1997), and Miller and Mullens (2009) cast light on the role that inequities, male dominance, patriarchy, and the law have on female subjugation, victimization, and other ways that situate women in repressive circumstances.

Chesney-Lind (1989), for instance, looks into ways through which custodians of the law—law enforcement and the judiciary, advance stereotypical notions of women and their presumed place in society. In this regard, she explains that stemming from a patriarchal premise, women who are constantly exposed to abuse flee from that environment, and instead of law enforcement officers finding out ways of addressing the problem, officers consider them recalcitrant and return them to the very environment where they were abused. The girls once again escape and, having no way else of self-sustenance, they resort to petty offenses and prostitution. They are now seen as "sexual objects." Doener and Lab (1998, 2007) have also discussed the process whereby not much attention is paid to the plight of women. They maintain that abuse of women has been "ignored by the male-dominated criminal justice system and society." The perception that a "man's home is his castle" and the line of thinking "has kept the public outside and the violence inside" (Doener and Lab 1998, 143).

Another ambit of feminist theorizing is Marxist or socialist feminism. The Marxist or socialist feminism viewpoint, as Miller et al. (2008) explain, links female oppression to disparities that are obvious in capitalism. The thrust of socialist feminism is that as a result of capitalist economies that disproportionately enable male dominance, women are put in a tenuous situation that enables men to maintain economic superiority, and with that retain control over other aspects of women's lives.

Adler (1975), whose perspective is classified as liberal and at odds with those of others (see also Chesney-Lind 1997; Steffensmeier 1980), maintains that male dominance is not a consequence of women's inherent compliant nature; rather social and technological changes, and policies that promote power dimensions project men's superior strength.

Omwami (2011) states "according to the feminists' viewpoint, patriarchy undermines the position of women by excluding them from participation in the hierarchical socio-economic structures" (18). Using Kenya as her research *situs,* Omwami sets out to understand why women in the country are not getting the requisite education needed to elevate their statuses in society. Even though she lists colonialism, dependency theory, feminism, relative-change theory, among others as possible explanations, she delves more on relative-change theory. While Omwami (2011) acknowledges that relative-change theory hinges on empowering others, she nonetheless explains:

> Although global bureaucratic institutions encourage social and political empowerment, the separation of the economic and the socio-political dimensions of the lives of the target populations result in economic interests overriding the investment considerations in education. The privileged position of males is

> represented by the asymmetrical empowerment relationship embodied in the patriarchal governance structure in governments around the world, but particularly so in the developing regions of the world. (18–19)

Whichever feminist perspective one embraces, the predicate thesis is that there are social differences between the genders, and these differences define the role that each plays. The society in which a woman lives, not surprisingly, also plays a role in the functions that either gender plays. Oduyoye (1995) poignantly describes how for the most part, in Africa, regardless of what path a woman takes, she is doomed. She states:

> In Africa, the very idea of a "free woman" conjures up negative images. We have been brought up to believe that a woman should always have a suzerain, that she should be "owned" by a man, be he father, uncle, or husband. A "free woman" spells disaster. An adult woman, if unmarried, is immediately reckoned to be available for the pleasure of all males and is treated as such. The single woman who manages her affaires successfully without a man is an affront to patriarchy and a direct challenge to the so-called masculinity of men who want to "possess" her. Some women are struggling to be free from this compulsory attachment to the male. Women want the right to be fully human, whether or not they choose to be attached to men. (4–5)

SOCIAL CLASS AND GENDER ROLE STRATIFICATION

How gender role or gender functions are perceived may be different based on society. In addition, social class may have an impact. Social class, as measured by Christens et al. (2011), includes income and level of formal education, while Lott and Bullock (2010) include prestige and occupation to the list. Now more than ever, gender inequities have dropped somewhat, but huge vestiges are still apparent (Lott and Bullock 2010; Catalyst 2008). As Lott and Bullock (2010) and Langston (1988) explain, social class encompasses several factors, including how one feels, what one owns, where one lives, how one speaks, who one's acquaintances are, and even what one eats. Access to resources is usually based on power distribution; it follows that the rich are more exposed to resources. The converse is true for the poor, and thus limits their upward mobility in society.

As reported, women are more likely than men to stay at the bottom echelon of society, and more likely to experience a tumble should they move upwards (PEW Charitable Trusts 2010). How class and gender interact provides a clearer picture of women's experiences and roles in society. Even in the United States, which is considered to be the most industrialized country in the world, for commensurate jobs, women earn less than men (Lott and Bullock 2010). A multitude of problems besets women, particularly those of the lower class—not being able to find affordable housing in safe neighborhoods, not being able to pay for utilities, skipping meals, or providing unhealthy meals to children just to get by (Lott and Bullock 2010). Should this look grim, imagine women in Africa. Dimandja (2004) grimly restates what the International Monetary Fund and the World Bank have stated: "the poorest person on earth lives somewhere in Sub-Saharan Africa and is probably a woman" (1). According to Ademiluyi and Adedamola (2010) and Zaman (2006), political participation is one of the main ways for women to have passage to power, and thus control over issues that are vital to their well-being in society. Without empowerment women are relegated to more common female roles of having children, staying at home, nurturing the family, molding character, imparting life-long skills on children, and being wives, in some instances, having no say in any decision making; and in other aspects, they become partners in decision-making. Amenga-Etego (2013), writing about Ghanaian society, explains that until this day in time Ghanaian women are socialized to be subordinate to men and because the country for the most part is patrilineal, men dominate decision-making.

Writing on sex and gender, Marini (1990) explains disparities in social roles. While acknowledging that social roles across genders have from time immemorial been different in every society, she also maintains that men's roles have better positioned men to attain control of resources that place them in more powerful stance. In part as Marini explains, men and women tend to agree that there are certain traits as for example, "instrumental" traits that are linked to men, and "expressive" traits that are associated with women, and that, regardless of age, race, social standing, religion, or other factors, this belief is shared by most, and thus perpetuates a stereotype.

SOCIAL LEARNING APPROACH/LEARNED HELPLESSNESS

In the context of criminology, social learning theory applies to the process of learning criminal behavior from those with whom one associates. While several versions of the theory exist (see Sutherland 1934; Bandura 1977; Akers 1998; Andrews and Bonta 1998), Akers has expanded the theory to include four concepts:

1. "Differential Association" relates to the process of placing oneself in a position where one receives cues from others that are favorable or not favorable to conforming behavior or to illegal behavior.
2. "Definitions" relates to how one construes or assesses a behavior or situation, that is, whether one thinks something is right or wrong.
3. "Differential Reinforcement" relates to the likelihood of an act being committed or repeated giving the reactions that others have for the behavior.

4. "Imitation" refers to the probability that one will emulate a particular behavior based upon the response that was given to that behavior.

These aspects of learning theory relate to victimizers, but then following Akers' elaboration of his theory to include social structure as well, he makes clear how variations in rates of criminal behavior rest on the extent to which tradition, norms, and other forms of social control, influence conforming behavior. When the norms of a society endorse or promote behavior that is conducive to female marginalization, the society in essence acquiesces or approves the values placed on women. We learn behavior as Sutherland (1934) states from those we associate with the most. We also learn rationalizations or attitudes that favor those behaviors from those persons. This is true as it relates to criminal or conformist behavior.

Earlier studies on sex role learning put forth three theories to explain differences between the sexes (Maccoby and Jacklin 1974). These categories are: (1) those that emphasize imitation, (2) those that focus on self-socialization, and (3) those that highlight reinforcement. In a simple style, Maccoby and Jacklin explain that imitation relates to children emulating parents or others of the same gender, and by so doing, children start playing the roles society ascribes to that gender. Self-socialization, as Maccoby and Jacklin explain relates to the role a child grows to associate with. In essence, through role-playing, what society expects of those of the child's gender, becomes the role the child adopts. Reinforcement relates to the reactions toward the child from parents and others who can influence the child's behavior. Reinforcements can be done by providing rewards, and may also take the form of negative comments or punishments to let the child know that behavior that is contrary to what is expected of a particular gender is unacceptable.

Marini (1990) discusses facts that reveal the association between social learning and gender roles. She concludes, "The development of visual-spatial abilities, for example, has been demonstrated to be associated with practice" (1990, 102). In supporting her conclusion, she discusses studies by Connor et al. (1978), in which first grade boys scored higher than girls on tests related to "visual-spatial ability," but with practice, girls were able to make quite noticeable improvements, but improvements of boys were minuscule. This finding, as Marini concludes, demonstrates that boys did not need any further improvement of skills they had already developed, but that with practice, girls did just as well as boys.

According to Bargai et al. (2007), "learned helplessness is a psychological trait, which, theoretically, results from repeated exposure to uncontrollable and aversive events" (268). Li et al. (2012), provide a simpler definition: "learned helplessness is . . . the inability to take control over one's life due to a previous lack of control in important life outcomes" (500). In essence, a woman feels doomed in whatever aversive circumstance she is in, and thus accepts her plight as is, and keeps on enduring it. As Walker (1979), Doener and Lab (1998), explain, "learned helplessness" entails three aspects: (1) information of foreboding, (2) knowledge of the inevitable (sees recurring themes of her life or absence of them), and (3) reaction to what transpires. Reaction varies upon how entrenched the woman's perception of the situation is. If she feels that she has no capability of controlling the situation, she gives up and resigns her fate to all that happens next. This especially is the case of an abused or battered woman. Even when there is a reprieve in abuse, she feels doom lurking the horizon, and therefore succumbs to a state of hopelessness and helplessness.

Findings from a study in India by Li et al. (2012) show that women with higher education who are employed are less likely to succumb to learned helplessness, more so than their counterparts with no formal education who are housewives. Having some fulfillment at work may lessen any stress experienced at home. Further, as Li et al. (2012) suggest, since employed women have other avenues of socializing, and engage in activities that sharpen their intellect as well, they have healthier coping mechanisms than uneducated women who maintain routine duties at home, without control of many aspects of their lives. Indian culture is similar to that of many African countries with regard to gender roles. Consequently, it is easy to see how Li's et al. (2012) study can be replicated in many African countries with likely similar results.

In a more current study on learned helplessness, Odabassi (2013) explains a model of the subject produced by Peterson et al. (1993). The model contains three deficient behaviors that one who is afflicted with learned helplessness exhibits: motivational, mental, and emotional. With regard to lack in motivation, a person gives up trying to effect a change in circumstance. As it concerns the mental/cognitive deficiency, a person is incapable of making decisions or solving problems. A person lacks the ability to logically think over things and make rational decisions. With regard to emotional deficiency, regardless of the situation, a person exhibits high uncontrollable levels of anxiety. As a result of low self-esteem, there is also an increased likelihood of depressive tendencies. The concept of learned helplessness handicaps one from moving beyond one's situation in life. The belief that one has no control over one's situation, reinforced over time either by others or by failed attempts to effect a change, determines one's reactions to future situations (Seligman 1972).

Part II

Issues Affecting African Women

Chapter Two

Poverty

The World Bank Organization defines poverty thus:

> Poverty is hunger. Poverty is lack of shelter. Poverty is being sick and not being able to see a doctor. Poverty is not having access to school and not knowing how to read. Poverty is not having a job, is fear for the future, living one day at a time.
>
> Poverty has many faces, changing from place to place and across time, and has been described in many ways. Most often, poverty is a situation people want to escape. So poverty is a call to action—for the poor and the wealthy alike—a call to change the world so that many more may have enough to eat, adequate shelter, access to education and health, protection from violence, and a voice in what happens in their communities. (www2.gnb.ca, 2008–2009)

In a 2014 study conducted by this researcher in the South West Province/Region of Cameroon, women were asked to explain what poverty meant to them, and if they considered themselves and others affiliated to them poor. Not surprising, what being poor was explained similarly by each woman with just nuances in choice of words. There was a one-on-one interview session with 18 women, and three focus group interviews with four women in each.

In one of the focus group interviews, a woman in her thirties explained that poverty meant "staying home as a child of school age to work in the farm, and to do petty trade just to get a few francs, while your friends go to school." A woman in her sixties explained that being poor means "watching your children starve because there is no money to buy food, seeing their friends attain an education while your children stay at home; seeing your children fall ill, and you have no money to buy medicine." A woman in her forties immediately interjected, "that's right, and worse, nothing changes, they live in that condition for all of their lives. What they call home is a hut whose roof leaks when it rains, and they sleep day in and day out on mats on a hard floor." Yet, a woman in her mid-forties explained that "poor" means, "struggling every day to live, wondering where your next meal will come from, constantly remaining in debt, and not being able to smile, or to laugh even when something is funny because you only think of your problems."

When asked if they or others they were close to were poor, 9 out of the 12 (75 percent) in the focus group said they were poor. Of the 18 participants in the one-on-one interviews, 14 (78 percent) said they were poor. All participants acknowledged having family members, friends, neighbors who were destitute, and some even characterized some of the people they knew as "very poor." Those who alluded to some they knew as "very poor" were asked to explain. One woman said, "You have to see them to get a sense of what 'very poor' means." Another woman described being very poor as "when the family does not even have a hut to call home, or a mat to sleep on, and nothing to eat, even roasted cocoyam."

Participants in the study were asked to explain what they thought the causes of poverty in their society were. Responses to this question encompassed several issues including lack of formal education, parents choosing boys over girls to get an education, laws that stall women's access to real estate, lack of agricultural equipment, poor roads, and lack of trading acumen, among others.

To delve more into the study, participants were asked what they considered to be the reason for poverty. Responses to this question for the most part centered on lack of education, although a few participants added other reasons. This question brought out very emotional responses from many of the participants. For example, a single lady in her 30s who does petty trading for a living, with a quivering voice said:

> See where I am today. It is not because I am not clever. I am poor because I lack education. I did not go to secondary school. I am an orphan and have been an orphan since I was a young girl. I have no family support. I have younger sisters to take care of, so the little money I make when I sell some of the things I trade in, I have to take care of my sisters. It is worse for orphans, and for children who have poor parents; even when they have rich relatives, the rich relatives abandon the poor ones. How can you have an education when you have no one to pay your school fees? How can you ever get out of poverty when from childhood you have no one to help you?

Another woman explained that she and other family members are poor because they never obtained any formal education. They had no one to pay their tuition, so all they did was to become farmers, and since they did not have money to buy a big parcel of land, they only grew crops for subsistence, and for petty trading. She further explained that when she was growing up not much premium was placed on female education because the expectation was that girls would get married, and move away from their families. This lady went on to state, “early marriages, rape, early pregnancies are also setbacks in women’s educational pursuits, and without education, you remain poor.” A widow in her 70s in the one-on-one interview expressed disgust at practices that still allow girls as young as 12 to be sent off for marriage. She explained with exasperation that the girl is almost doomed for life since before long she would bear children, and thus must spend all of her time taking care of the children. She acknowledged that such practices persist because families are destitute, but expressed no sympathy toward parents who use their daughters to bail out of dire financial difficulties because as she said “under no circumstance should a parent sacrifice a child for their needs.”

A lawyer in her late forties explained that while all the reasons given by the women are correct, not to be ignored are legal and customary practices that restrict women’s rights to property, time poverty, and how the economy in general is managed. When asked to elaborate on her response, she explained that an easy way of getting rich is to have real estate, and other property that one can sell to make a decent amount of money, but as she explained, while the law gives women rights to land ownership, the reality is that men exercise control and dominion of such land and property. She further explained that while customary practices are to blame, the law too plays a role. She cited Articles 1421 and 1428 of the Cameroonian Civil Code that regulate spousal rights to communal property. Such rights as she explained invariably gives the man rights to mortgage or sell such communal property even without the wife’s consent. As she further explained customary practices and “custodians of customs”—that is, men who act as traditional counselors and judges, perpetuate such unfair practices. The lawyer went further to explain that besides issues relating to property, the law also restricts women’s chances of upward mobility through Article 74 of the 1981 Civil Status Registration Ordinance. She explained that while Article 74 (1) gives women the right to pursue any profession they wish, Article 74 (2) in essence restricts such right by letting men “object to the exercise of such trade in the interest of the marriage and children.” So, if a woman has a well-paying job, or a job through which she can rise up the corporate ladder, her husband can by law have her give up such a job if he thinks she ought to devote more of her time to being a housewife. She went on to explain that with regard to time poverty, many women spend most of their time doing household chores, working in a small farm for subsistence, and engaging in petty trade. Such activities, as valuable as they are, do nothing to lift women from poverty, the lawyer explained. The lawyer also explained that the country’s economy is lopsided. Just a small portion of the population is affluent. Without addressing reasons why money stays in the hands of just a few, most people, and especially women are likely to remain poor, she concluded. The researcher asked why there is such a huge gap between the rich and the poor, to which the lawyer simply said, "I wish I were a politician and not a lawyer; I don't have an answer to your question."

A woman in her sixties who had worked with the Agency for Community Development had several explanations to give. She explained that women had limited land rights, and many women depend on agriculture. "How can you get rich when you have no land?" she rhetorically asked. Then she elaborated on her response:

> Many women rent land, and some own it. You pay rent for the land first, and then plant crops, so if the crops don't do well, it is your loss. Boys get preference for land, but now things are changing. People now see that in many families it is the girls that end up helping their father and mother, so especially for girls who do not get married, some families prefer to give them title to land.

She also went on to explain that some women are timid to apply for loans that could help them get started with a small business. Further, she noted that many women are not exposed to more modern ways of farm work. "They till the same soil year after year, and expect to get the same amount of harvest. They don't know that the soil gets old and tired, and after a while crops don't produce as they used to." She went on to explain that because many parents are poor, they are unable to provide even basic necessities for their daughters. That makes girls vulnerable; "the girls thus sleep with anyone who can give them basic necessities like soap, oil, or money to buy those things, and before long they are pregnant and have to drop out of school," the lady explained. A woman in her 40s added that, "the environment where the person is from matters. Villagers prefer to send boys to school than women, and for others it is poverty. Some families have to rely on cocoa sales and if that is not enough, they prefer to send their boys to school."

Another woman in the focus group explained that in the South West province (which is where this research was conducted)

> Farm work is still labor intensive, so women bind in groups of about 50 and till soil for one woman, and then they rotate. Even small machines that can be used to grate cassava we don't have. Also, trade practices like custom duties and tariffs make some of us not even want to have large farms because we cannot travel to sell the produce. We also have very bad roads, and this is a big problem. We cannot take our produce to big markets because it is hard to transport them. Much of the produce eventually get bad because we don't even have ways of preserving them. We dry some produce in the sun, but sometimes birds, insects, and animals eat them, and the produce do not taste as good as before.

A grade one teacher, who has traveled to Europe and to the United States, had a different take to the issue of poverty. She explained that investment opportunities are sparse or non-existent, and even banking money to get interest is something that many women do not do. When asked why women do not save money in banks she gave two reasons. First, she explained that many women are not informed about the benefits of saving money in banks. Second, as she explained, people do not have confidence in banks. They worry about embezzlements and mismanagement of money by those who work in banks. She furthered the discussion by explaining how there had been periods of time when people could not even withdraw the full amount of money that they had in banks because the banks just did not have the money. She explained that even though the problem stemmed from government rationing salaries, there was a corresponding mistrust of banks. As well, as she ultimately admitted, because the banking system is not refined as those in the western world, the interest that one gets for saving money in banks is quite minute. Consequently, there is no incentive to save in banks; instead, women bind in groups, contribute an agreed upon amount of money and each month one woman is given all the contributions. This goes on all year until each woman gets her turn. Locally, this process is called *njangi*. Other women find safe places in the house to hoard or hide money.

While the women agreed that these problems are evident throughout the country, they were quick to explain that they are more noticeable in Anglophone Cameroon; the impact is more felt there, and any remedies even minimal are implemented last there.

This study in Cameroon sets the stage for other scholarships that explain causes of women's marginalized stances in Africa.

TIME POVERTY

McFerson (2010) discusses the fact that African women remain economically deprived because all of their time and energy is expended on labor that does not fetch much in markets. As well, domestic and subsidiary functions deprive them of opportunities to participate in more robust and more beneficial markets. One of the early writers on "time poverty," Clair Vickery (1977), used the United States to explain the dynamics between households with limited leisure time and low standard of living with those with more money and more leisure time. In this regard, she explained that households with little money and little leisure time are indeed poor. The converse is true in the sense that households with more money and more leisure time are relatively well off, unless by choice and not by need, some work more and indulge in pleasantries less. Bardasi and Wodon (2010) define people who are time poor as "individuals who have no choice but to work long hours because they are already poor or would become poor if they worked less than the time poverty level" (70). The International Labor Organization (ILO) in 1919 visited the issue of work time and drew the conclusion that too much work with little rest and leisure time poses health problems and is destructive to family solidarity. The International Labor Organization has since then periodically offered guidelines on appropriate or satisfactory work standards that take in to consideration work place safety and overall health of workers. The International Labor Organization's effort is directed at "promoting opportunities for women and men to obtain decent and productive work in conditions of freedom, equity, security, and human dignity" (ILO 1999). Whether or not this has been realized in the context of African societies is debatable. Bardasi and Wodon (2010) are of the opinion that the ILO's goal, which more realistically speaks to work time in money-generating labor work as opposed to domestic work, is not quite applicable to the African economic reality.

Pandolfelli et al. (2007; 2008), Blackden and Wodon (2006) have written about the time poverty phenomenon that inevitably consumes much of African women's time and thus inhibits them from either attaining education or focusing their time and effort in more lucrative and competitive ventures. Abdourahman (2010) bluntly states that in African societies, women who devote the bulk of their time doing household chores, subsistence farming and sales, and community service are "considered as not working" (17). After all, the Human Development Report of 1995 reveals "much of women's work remains unrecognized and unvalued. This has an impact on the status of women in society, their opportunities in public life and the gender blindness of development policy" (UNDP 1995). Focusing on informal labor markets and cultural standards that relate to African women in ten Sub-Saharan countries, Herrera and Torelli (2010) surmise that women perform over 80 percent of household work, while also engaging in about 43 percent of "market-based work" which, when combined, constitutes a "double day."

Discussing the plight of Malian women, Bardasi and Wodon (2010) explain that time poverty is even more entrenched in rural areas than previous research reveals. They allege that when time poverty is viewed in conjunction with variables such as consumption, households that are consumption poor fare worse. They lay the blame for this on two main reasons: (1) Women more than men spend much of their time on necessities, engaging in house work, or collecting firewood or looking for water for household usage. (2) Those factors aside, even when women engage in paid jobs, the income they make is minute and the meager resource gets them little to nothing besides the barest minimum of needs. In essence, besides being time poor, they are also consumption poor.

Most African countries lack the requisite technology and methodological skills to collect data regarding time use. Abdourahman (2010) contends that such data collection is necessary for scrutinizing the connection between market and non-market work, logging this information into a larger system such as the Social Accounting Matrices (SAM) to enable the addition of non-market work to the national accounting system.

The World Bank explains work in two ways. The first explanation projects work as "formal and informal market work and non-market subsistence work for production of goods, and is the basis for calculating the Gross Domestic Product (GDP)" (Kes and Swaminathan 2006, 14). This first definition is also counted in the System of National Accounts (SNA). The second explanation is "formal and informal employment." As well, "subsistence production, reproductive work, and volunteer work" are included (Kes and Swaminathan 2006, 14). What functions are ascribed to men and to women are sometimes determined by cultural norms. Most, if not all, African countries designate "reproductive and volunteer work" to women, while "formal work," that is, work that generates income, is assigned to men. Kes and Swaminathan (2006) further explain that the composition of children in a family, that is, whether they are older, and whether they are boys or girls, may also determine how much time a woman spends in "reproductive work." Time poverty increases income poverty in many ways as Kes and Swaminathan (2006) explain:

1. Low-productivity in many non-market tasks renders them time and labor intensive, thus reducing the availability of time to participate in more economically productive activities.
2. Due to the gendered division of labor that causes poor substitutability of labor allocation in non-market work, individuals, particularly women, are unable to take full advantage of economic opportunities and participate in income-generating activities.
3. Time poverty also impedes individuals' ability to expand capabilities through education and skills development, thereby enhancing economic returns in the market place. (17)

According to Abdourahman (2010),

> In South Africa, women's contribution in non-market production to the national economy was found to be almost double that of men. Consequently, women there had 30–40 percent less time for personal care and leisure than men at the household level. According to the South African 2000 time-use survey, males between the ages of 15 and 65 years spend on average only 84 minutes per day on unpaid work, while for females, this increases to 215 minutes. (19)

Charmes (2006) provides the following data to explain how women are more "time poor" than men based on market System of National Accounts (SNA) and household non-SNA functions.

Kes and Swaminathan (2006) explain that women in Sub-Saharan countries face even more challenges because of poor water supply, substandard energy plants, poor transportation, and lack of access to technological gadgets and equipments that may enhance their needs and lessen their work burdens. Researchers have found that improved transportation alone will drastically cut down on time women spend to fetch water, firewood, or other necessities that consume so much of their time, and access to technology and more market services will yield higher productivity (Bardasi and Wodon 2010).

A study conducted in Mbale, Eastern Uganda, and Kasama, Zambia, illustrates the time-saving effects of better infrastructure: If woodlots were within 30 minutes of the homestead and if the water source were within 400 meters, Mbale households, specifically women and girls, would save more than 900 hours/year around 240 hours in firewood collection and 660 hours in water collection. Similarly, in Kasama, Zambia they would save 125 to 664 hours a year in water collection and 119 to 610 hours a year in firewood collection. Further discussion by Kes and Swaminathan (2006) reveal that the responsibility of fulfilling domestic needs rests on women, and to this end, they spend at least 70 percent of their time, and 80 percent of hard work. Having lived in Cameroon, and made frequent visits there as recent as 2014, I can attest that this conclusion is valid. In the city of Kumba, South West Province of Cameroon, for over half a year in 2013, there was no running water in most parts of the city because of problems with defective pipes and problems from the main source of water supply. When the problems were

Table 2.1. Time Devoted to Economic Activity and to Work, by Gender in Benin (1998), South Africa (2000), Madagascar (2001), Mauritius (2003) (Minutes per Day)

	Benin		South Africa		Madagascar		Mauritius	
	Women	Men	Women	Men	Women	Men	Women	Men
SNA Production	235	235	115	190	175	290	116	296
Non-SNA-Production care and domestic activities	208	67	228	75	221	47	277	73
Total Work	443	302	343	265	286	337	393	369
% SNA in total work	53%	77.8%	33.5%	71.7%	44.2%	86.1%	29.5%	80.2%

The data here is from Kes & Swaminathan (2006, 17). Gender and Time Poverty in Sub-Saharan Africa. World Bank Working Paper.

*Data: Courtesy of The World Bank. World Bank Working Paper no. 73 Gender and Time Use Patterns in Sub-Saharan Africa. World Bank. CC BY 3.0 IGO License.

corrected, and water supply restored, the water was brownish in color for several months. During that time, many families relied on water from wells or springs. In an earlier study by Malmberg-Calvo (1994) in Ghana, Tanzania, and Zambia, similar findings were made. She concluded that in these countries, women spend about 71 percent to 96 percent of their time in travels that are directly connected to domestic needs. Men's travel activities that include crops entail weeding and transportation of crops (activities that women are heavily involved in). Kes and Swaminathan (2006) suggest that in order to maximize women's efficiency while saving time, they need alternative energy sources and access to liquefied petroleum gas. These energy-saving options will, as Kes and Swaminathan explain save women time, and the time saved can be channeled toward other means of generating income, participating in community activities, bonding more with their children, or simply relaxing.

Even though women's farm work is intended more for subsistence, Charmes (2006) makes an accurate assessment that some of the harvest is sold, and the proceeds usually go to purchase supplies for the household; but such contributions are usually not reflected in data collections, nor are women given much credit for such contributions. Further, as Charmes (2006) notes, more women than men are engaged in several jobs and statistical measurements for multiple jobs have not been fully developed; consequently, the Gross Domestic Product (GDP) does not reflect the secondary jobs that women do. It follows that if a woman's primary activity is agricultural, any secondary ones as, for example, manufacturing will not be included in the GDP.

Besides the non-recognition of the significant contribution of women in agriculture, trade, and manufacturing, their remuneration is significantly low. Further, as volunteer workers, they take care of neighbors, in-laws, and other extended family members. They entertain guests, and even when men are breadwinners, the welfare of the family rests on women. Personal observation based on the years I lived in Cameroon confirms this. Kes and Swaminathan (2006) conclude:

> What the time data show is that there are important differences in gender roles, which constitute a major obstacle to development and poverty reduction in Sub-Saharan Africa. Women's significant, though understated, roles in economic production (agriculture and the informal sector, predominantly) and their pivotal position in household management and welfare (food preparation, health and hygiene, childcare, and education) are central to sub-Saharan Africa's economic development and social survival. Time use data confirm the evidence available in the agricultural sector showing that women are indeed the continent's principal food producers and have primary responsibility for assuring food availability in the family: they are therefore central to the attainment of Sub-Saharan Africa's food security goals and to meeting family nutri-

Table 2.2. Time Spent per Day on SNA Non-Market Activities in Three Countries (in hours and minutes)

	Benin (1998)		South Africa (2000)		Madagascar (2001)	
	Women	Men	Women	Men	Women	Men
Crop farming	11	29	5	4	20	29
Tending animals, Fish farming		13	1	10	9	37
Hunting, gathering	4	11		1	5	5
Digging, stone cutting, and caving				1		
Fetching water	45	12	8	3	27	9
Collecting firewood	16	4	6	3	7	13
Food processing & preservation	26	8			20	3
Preparing/selling food & beverages			2	1		
Making/selling textiles/crafts	2	2	3	1	16	
Building and extension of dwelling			1	3	6	1
Total	1h 44	1h 19	24	27	1hr 50	1h 37

*Source: Charmes, Jacques (2005, 49). Gender, Time Use, and Poverty in Sub-Saharan Africa. World Bank Working Paper, No. 73. CC BY 3 0 IGO License.

> tional needs. Women are the principal gatherers and users of wood for fuel and water for washing and cooking: how they do this critically affects the pace and extent of environmental degradation and the fertility of the soil. Women have primary responsibility for child rearing and family health: on this the future productivity of the country's human resource base depends. (26–27)

Olorunsanya and Omotesho (2014) contend that because poverty is by and large a result of low productivity of crops or of fluctuating productivity especially for those dependent on agrarian livelihood, women are likely to be most affected.

As Bardasi and Wodon (2010) observe, the educational qualifications of either gender, more so women in urban areas, strongly correlates to time poverty in that the more educated a woman is the less likely she will be time poor. This unfortunately is not the case with women in rural areas whose educational level seldom exceeds primary education.

As reckoned, Islam is prevalent throughout Africa. While it is noted that Islam does not discourage education of women (Virani 2007), the Organization of Islamic Cooperation in 2013 revealed that education of girls is still restricted in many Islamic nations (Ufuk 2013). UNICEF (2007) documented that in a sample of twenty-four countries that had enrollment rates of lower than 60 percent, seventeen were Islamic countries. It is clear that lack of education goes hand in hand with poverty. The World Economic Forum 2012 report on gender gap among one hundred and thirty-five countries noted that of the eighteen worst performing nations, seventeen were Islamic countries, and of these were several African countries including, Algeria, Egypt, Mali, Morocco, Cote d'Ivoire, and Chad (World Economic Forum, 2013). More on education is discussed in chapter 3.

Clearly, time poverty is an impediment to women's upward mobility in Africa. Women work extremely long hours every day and seldom find free hours for relaxation. Nonetheless, they remain poor, indeed, extremely poor, because they lack opportunities for education, and necessities such as water and electricity. They thus have to spend a good deal of their lives doing chores that could have been facilitated had they had access to water and electricity, and to technology that could speed up, and make less tedious the chores they do at home, and the hard work they put into their farms. Compounding on the time African women spend on home chores is the wrath HIV/AIDS has meted on them as victims and caregivers, and in more recent times, the wrath of Ebola.

RESTRICTED PROPERTY RIGHTS

Following revelations from The International Monetary Fund and The World Bank, the poorest person in the world is a woman and she most certainly lives in Africa (Dimandja 2004). Other reports indicate that half of the world's population comprises women, but grimly approximately 70 percent of the poor are women (McFerson 2010; Moghadam 2005). As it relates to human rights, poverty is the deprivation of capabilities (McFerson 2010); and McFerson explains this as "the absence of agency, options and opportunities" (McFerson 2010, 52). Lack of opportunities has been explained by some as inadequate representation in the global economy (McFerson 2010; Moghadam 2005). Globalization brings the world closer and opens up a variety of opportunities in different spheres. In the economic domain, the influences of those who control the economy count significantly. If those controlling the economic sector are disproportionately male, women may be adversely affected. This may be a reasonable inference in Africa giving established prevalence of male subjugation of women. Rather than explain female subjugation as an issue with globalization, the explanation fits better with prevailing attitudes and customs in Africa. McFerson (2010) is quick to point out that "the roots of the special poverty problems of African women are to be found not in globalization but in restricted property rights, weak governance and frequency of civil conflict" (52) (see also Collier 2007; Cornwall 2005; Gordon 1996).

According to Article 17 (1) of the Universal Declaration of Human Rights, "everyone has the right to own property alone as well as in association with others." Further, Article 16 (h) of the 1982 Convention on the Elimination of All Forms of Discrimination against Women calls for egalitarian rights to property between men and women be it at time of acquisition or with regard to management or ownership. Following the Human Rights Based Approach (HRBA) to promote equity, as vital assets land and other natural resources are to be owned and enjoyed equally by all. As such, the following initiatives are proposed:

- promote fairer and more equitable distribution of natural resources in order to facilitate civil order, peace, and economic growth
- redress the history of racial, ethnic, social, and gendered inequality in ownership and access to land
- promote more productive uses of land through instituting and clarifying rights to land through formalization
- decentralize government functions to lower levels. (Ikdahl et al. 2005, 1)

These provisions, however, clash with prevailing cultural practices. Take Cameroon, for instance, where laws and cultural practices that have endured over time stall women's rights to land. According to secretariat.thecommonwealth.org (2013), in Cameroon, men own 86.6 percent of land while women own just 9.6 percent. Cultural practices in most of Africa have always defined gender roles making men breadwinners and women solely responsible for taking care of children, doing farm work for subsistence, fetching wood, cooking, doing laundry, cleaning the house, and performing a slew of other duties. Further, laws that relate to property rights do not factor in customary roadblocks on women's rights to land.

As an example, Fon and Edokat (2012) explain that in Cameroon, Zimbabwe, and Burkina Faso, the law grants women rights to own land and trees, but the reality is that men are in control of almost all property. More telling is what the Cameroonian Civil Code states about land ownership "the husband has the right to administer communal marital property, thereby giving him the right to sell or mortgage the couple's property without his wife's consent" (Art. 1421 and 1428). Even when laws seem to give women certain rights, accompanying subsections water down the rights. Article 74 (1) of the 1981 Civil Status Registration Ordinance, for instance, gives a woman freedom to engage in any profession she chooses, but Article 74 (2) gives a man the right "to object to the exercise of such trade in the interest of the marriage and children."

The UN Human Rights Committee (2012) reports:

> Notwithstanding the prohibition of discrimination enshrined in the Constitution of Cameroon, the committee is concerned that women are discriminated against under articles 1421 and 1428 of the Civil Code concerning the right of spouses to administer communal property, article 229 of the Civil Code regulating divorce, and article 361 of the Penal Code that defines the crime of adultery in terms more favorable to men than women. (paragraph 8)

In Rwanda as well, even though formal laws stipulate that women and men have equal rights to land, women who are married to men following traditional or religious rites are exempt from benefiting through the law. Incidentally, a good proportion of women there are not in civil unions; they invariably go along with traditional and religious marriage ceremonies.

As seen so far, customary law mediates the marginal thriving of African women to a large extent. To another extent, deprivation, particularly when it relates to land, may be brought about by governmental practices of displacing whole communities for the purpose of development or conservation. While such practices affect men as well, women bear the brunt of the hardship. Traditional African female roles require that women handle all household chores, including cooking, subsistence farming, fetching water and wood, laundry, and a variety of other functions. As Scalise (2012) reports when the Batwa community of Uganda was displaced by governmental order to create a national park, other problems ensued. Getting access to water in their new community now meant sharing water holes with their Bakiga community. With persistent conflict over water holes, Batwa women had to trek for over half a mile to fetch water in uncontested water sources. This time used in trekking could have been used to do something more productive to lift the women's positions in society.

Even when communities have vested rights to land, women's rights are at best tenuous. Based on customary practices of the people, and how much if any land will be allocated to women vary. Following customs and traditions in many African societies, land ownership tethers to family relationships and inheritance rights. Consequently, while boys in succession order from oldest to youngest are more likely to inherit land and other property, women are often left out since the expectation is that the woman will marry and move away to the husband's; and, since they are considered to be the husband's "property" they are to own nothing since "property can't own property" as the Acholi men of Uganda say (Scalise 2012, 53).

Even when there is flexibility among men to have their wives have access to land, upon the men's death relatives may disinherit their widows. Further complications arise in polygamous families. Even if the women had access to land, upon their husbands' death, they are stripped of such privileges, as the sons of the oldest wives have more rights to it. This point was brought up during a focus group interview in Cameroon by this researcher in 2014. While one woman thought that polygamy had no bearing on how property is distributed if the man of the family clearly explained what belonged to whom, a woman in her 70s strenuously objected, stating that there always are problems, especially if some of the wives were younger than the male sons of the older wives. The older sons, as the woman explained, claim ownership of all their fathers' property and much of the time, the younger wives and their children are stripped of any property they claim.

Acholi women who complete all traditional marriage rites may have supervisory powers over land, and can assign or turn over land to adult sons upon the husband's death, but this is not the case for women who did not fulfill all requirements of traditional marriage. Such women have no *de facto* rights to land. This confirms what Benschop (2002) has expressed:

> Even if national legislation will fully recognize women's equal rights to own, co-own, access, control and inherit land, housing and other property, existing practices will not automatically be changed; *wider changes in social cultural attitudes* are necessary for this legislation to reach all women. Only then would women be able to enjoy *substantive* equal and independent rights, which entails the enjoyment of access to rights in and control over land and housing. Obstacles to equal substantive rights like continued application of customs, difficulties in paying court fees, violence against women and lack of sufficient economic resources still exist. Shifts in social and power relations may still take several generations. (180)

In the case of Ghanaian women, those in the northern part of the country are quite poor and do most of the subsistence farming, yet they are precluded from sitting in and from participating in any decisions made on land and any natural resources (see Scalise 2012). Customary law regulates eighty percent of land in the country. Ghanaian law grants women rights to inherit land, but the country's constitution recognizes customary law as well as formal law. Under customary law, however, gender and family lineage play an integral role in who gets land. Despite these, women have to work harder, and pay additional customary taxes, in order to get some rights accorded to them. Being saddled by work on their husbands' family land, women are left with little or no time to work on other land to which they potentially could be allotted portions.

In Tanzania, a Land Policy enacted in 1995 was the subject of much debate among scholars, NGOs, and civil society with a focus on the provisions as they relate to rights, particularly women's property rights (Tsikata 2003). In 2001, the president of Tanzania signed a Land Act that had been enacted by Parliament in 1999. This Land Act extended ownership rights to both gender, demarcated village land, and extended rights of village authorities to supervise such land. The 1999 Parliamentary enactment as well as the 2001 Presidential Act expressly harped on issues of discrimination. Section 3(2) in both the Parliamentary enactment and the 2001 Presidential Act state: "The right of every woman to acquire, hold, use, and deal with, land shall be to the same extent and subject to the same restrictions as a right of any man." Further, laws such as the Law of Marriage Act 1971 stipulate that there must be an agreement by both spouses before any matrimonial property can be sold or discarded.

Tanzania distinguishes discriminatory customary inheritance law from the principle of non-discrimination. Using the case of *Ephraim v. Pastory and another*, High Court (PC) Civil Application No. 70/89 (unreported) delivered on February 22, 1990, the High Court reiterated the principle of non-discrimination enshrined in the Constitution, CEDAW, and the African Charter on Human and Peoples' Rights. In that case, a woman who sold land that had been bequeathed to her by her father in his will, was challenged by a nephew who claimed that the sale was illegal pursuant to Local Customary Law Order. His contention in essence was that women could only have "user" rights to land that gave them no rights to sell land, and that only men had legitimate rights to do so. The High Court upheld the District Court's ruling that the woman had the right to sell land. The Court made it clear that both statutory and customary laws were to be applied in ways that did not promote discrimination.

Property rights of a woman after the death of her husband or a divorce remain an ongoing problem in Tanzania. Indeed, the country acknowledges that one of the primary contested issues brought to court by women is property adjustment upon the death of the husband or upon a divorce (Ikdahl et al. 2005). Even though the law requires that rights of everyone be respected, the law also requires that customs of the parties be respected. This is where the problem lies, as customs usually are discriminatory against not only Tanzanian women, but also African women in general. After vigorously fighting to promote women's rights, lobbyists were successful in having Paragraph 4.2.6 in the National Land Policy modified. The paragraph initially read:

> In order to enhance and guarantee women's access to land and security of tenure, women will be entitled to acquire land in their own right not only through purchase but also through allocation. However inheritance of clan and family land will continue to be governed by custom and tradition. (Ikdahl et al. 2005, 41)

The current modified version of the policy reflects the following wording: "however, inheritance of clan and family land will continue to be governed by custom and tradition *provided they are not contrary to the constitution and principle of natural justice*' (Ikdahl et al. 2005, 41).

Besides limited rights to land it is contended that limited rights to own livestock and any assets in general are factors that account for gender wealth gap. In addition, the inability of women to get loans and credit also disproportionately affects them. In a workshop the following list of complaints were brought up as summary of what had been aired at other workshops:

> Slightly over one-half of groups at the workshops mentioned that cultural customs and traditions were an obstacle to poverty reduction. A related issue that was cited by about one sixth of the groups was gender discrimination, especially in regard to customary ownership of property; participation in wage employments; and decision-making at the national and household level. A breakdown, by gender, of the concerns of the workshop participants revealed that (1) rural women were proportionately more concerned about the role of cultural customs and traditions than rural men; (2) women raised the issue of gender discrimination more frequently than men; and (3) about one quarter of the women expressed concern about laziness and drunkenness among men. (URT 2000, 13–4, quoted in Ikdahl et al. 2005, 43)

Mozambique was colonized by Portugal and when colonization ended, some vestiges of Portuguese laws remained applicable in Mozambique. Today, what obtains in the country are a mixture of Portuguese laws, and Mozambique formal and customary laws—a combination that at times prompts contradictions. One way of controlling Africans was by the Portuguese introducing the *prazo* system that involved land contracted out by the Portuguese to Africans. Women who married Portuguese men usually were awarded *prazos*, and such land could be inherited matrilineally. The period in history from the 1890s referred to as the "scramble for Africa" was marked by colonialists and their companies acquiring the most fertile land in colonized Africa (see Ikdahl et al. 2005). Article 46 of the 1990 Constitution of Mozambique declared that land was the property of the state and could not be sold or mortgaged. After much back and forth tinkering with the law, the 1997 Land Law authorized private persons and corporations to purchase land. The process of acquiring land takes three months. Requests for more privatization of land became a new spin on land debate; and as Ikdahl et al. (2005) explain, those persons who were interviewed for their study were unanimous in their viewpoint that women would be negatively impacted if land were privatized. The authors also conceded that the issue was not even in the forefront of national debate.

Even though the government of South Africa is committed to parity in land distribution, policies that are in place seem to address racial ownership of land instead, and these policies are less gender-based. Efforts at creating an egalitarian land rights reform have been piecemeal. The Department of

Land Affairs approved a Land Reform Gender Policy in 1997. This legislation was intended to facilitate women's access, usage, ownership, and management of land. The government also advocates the inclusion of a "gender perspective" in all its programs and policies. However, as Cross and Hornby (2002), Walker (2003), and Ikdahl et al. (2005) note, these legislations and programs are at best perfunctory.

The 1996 Constitution of South Africa as relates to land reform advocates programs that relate to redistribution, tenure, and restitution. With regard to redistribution, the program's goal is for government to by 2015 transfer 30 percent of land owned by Whites to people who were disenfranchised during apartheid. As well, a Land Distribution for Agricultural Development (LRAD) program was introduced to provide grants for projects such as "food-safety-net projects, equity schemes and support for agriculture in communal areas" (Ikdahl et al. 2005, 62). Very early on, Cross and Hornby (2002) expressed skepticism regarding the efficacy of the program especially as it relates to the very poor who are widowed, husbandless, or who do not have anyone in a position to advocate their rights. They explain that because of traditional gender roles, limited information, and limited access to legal avenues, women are less likely to benefit from LRAD (Cross and Hornby 2002).

With regard to Land Tenure Reform, the purpose was to upgrade the rights of work tenants, farm workers, and those who did not have vested rights to land. While the intent was good, how to go about implementing the reform was another issue. In 2003, the responsibility of administering land was vested on traditional councils, in essence, shifting back powers to those who controlled land during the era of apartheid. This basically was another blow to women who had long suffered from privations, exclusions, and marginalization based on customary laws.

Regarding Land Restitution, the government's objective is to give back land to persons who were ripped off their property because of the racist practices in South Africa. While the process of restitution is ongoing, studies have not delineated how restitution has lifted women's well-being in that society.

Following customary practices in the majority of countries in Africa, the oldest male in the family is first in line to inherit family property. This is the case in South Africa, and while the passage of time, and modern ways are gradually eroding this practice, many are still unaware of their rights, and the fact that such customary practices could be challenged. In South Africa, the case of *Bhe v. Magistrate, Khayelitsha and others* (2004) (Constitutional Court Case CCT49/03) shed light on more acceptable rights of inheritance. The ruling in that case watered down male primogeniture. In the case, plaintiffs a nine-year-old girl and her two-year-old sister, with the assistance of The Women's Legal Center in Cape town, brought action since they were denied inheritance to their deceased father's estate. Following customary law the oldest male descendant of their father was to inherit their father's estate, or the father of the deceased if that father was still alive. In this case, it meant their grandfather who was still alive, and who was intent on selling the estate. The court's ruling in favor of the girls provides impetus for others in similar predicaments to use the law to get what is rightly theirs.

A pervasive, yet vexing way of viewing women in South Africa commercial farm areas is to see them as "subjects" while men are seen as "citizens" (Ikdahl et al. 2005). Their tenancy and even that of black men on the white owner's land is based on the discretion of the white owner. Despite the Extension of Security of Tenure Act (ESTA) of 1997, which is intended to shield workers from arbitrary eviction, whites still evict black workers and tenants at will. This practice in essence makes the ESTA a lame legislation. White owners of land decide when to replace workers. When such replacements are done unceremoniously women and children are disproportionately affected. Loss of the husband's job means leaving the farm, and without any source of income, children's educations are frequently interrupted, and mothers have to come up with creative ways of sustaining the family. Divorce, separation, and death may also lead to women's eviction from the farm. For the most part, women are hired for temporary positions, and are perceived as "convenient, cheap, flexible and easily available seasonal labor force that can be employed and dismissed according to needs" (Ikdahl et al. 2005, 67). Without job security any chance of a decent life is tenuous.

As in many other African societies women's progress (with regard to optimally attaining set goals in all works of life) in South Africa is stifled by male-dominated governments, male-dominated rural social movements, and male-dominated programs that foster men's rights. Laws reforming land ownership in South Africa tend to address racial inequities, and that invariably eclipses the need to improve women's rights to land and other property.

Unless one reads the internal laws of Kenya, one at first glance may assume that because the country is a signatory to just about all international conventions and charters that advocate the rights of women, Kenyan women are in excellent stance in their society. Kenya is a signatory to the International Covenant on Economic, Social and Cultural Rights; the Convention on the Political Rights of Women; the Convention on the Elimination of all Forms of Discrimination against Women; the International Covenant on Civil and Political Rights; the United Nations Charter; and the Universal Declaration of Human Rights. It is also a member of the United Nations. To effectuate legislations that promote women's rights in Kenya, legislators have to enact laws that make it mandatory for these international conventions and charters to be respected in their entirety, and to set in place mechanisms to address rights violations. Courts are usually not fully committed to break away from the status quo in favor of international commitments. Article 70 of Kenya's Constitution speaks to the need to observe the rights and freedoms of everyone, while Section 82 bans several forms of discrimination. Worthy of note is the fact that Section 82 (4) makes exceptions to bans on discrimination. Among some of the issues to which Section 82 does not apply are laws that relate to foreign nationals, adoption laws, matrimonial issues, and transference of property upon death laws, private law issues, laws that govern tribal or racial issues. As Ikdahl et al. (2005) note, these laws for the most part disproportionately affect women.

Ownership of land following customary practices was replaced by the Torrens title system that requires registration and marked boundaries of each person's parcel of land (Okoth-Ogendo 1989; Ikdahl et al. 2005). Land tenure, which is a process of rights to a parcel of land, does not give a person absolute rights to the land. The government has to inform on how land can be used. More current legislation that governs individual ownership to land in Kenya is The Land Registration Act of 2012. Section 4 of the Act requires Registration of interests in all public, private, and community land. The Act provides that tenants in common as, for instance, spouses cannot be left "homeless" or without some land even when the other party contests a partition.

With regard to property rights in general, since 1971, the legal system of Kenya makes it clear that rights to property belong to spouses equally (Ikdahl et al. 2005). In reiterating that marital property is equally owned, the Kenyan Court in the case of *I v. I* (1971) applied the provisions of the English Married Women's Property Act of 1882. The Act (Section 1, 1) which in a nutshell advances women's property rights by providing that a married woman just like a single woman can purchase, own, and dispose of property, is still used in the country to address spousal disputes as they relate to property. Regardless of what system of law a marriage was contracted under, customary or civil, this ancient Act is invoked to control the court's decision. Even though this act promotes equality, it does not advise on how property should be divided upon the dissolution of a marriage when such property was registered in the name of just one spouse; or even when registered in both names, it does not help the parties determine how much each contributed to the property. Stay-at-home mothers whose contributions relate to running the home and doing subsistence farming, may be disadvantaged especially since the discussion on time poverty shows domestic work does not count in a country's GDP.

Why women have limited rights to property has been summarized in three categories: "gender-biased legislation" that conflicts with standards set by international law, "flawed litigation and enforcement mechanisms" that comprise limited access to judicial forums that promote justice, and "lack of awareness" of rights, especially women's rights brought about by customary and social practices (see Strickland 2004).

POOR HEALTH CARE

In developed countries, it is possible to purchase health insurance policies personally, or to get health coverage through a job. At worst, even without health insurance policy, a sick person who checks into an emergency care facility will receive medical attention. Such is not the case in most Sub-Saharan African countries. In Cameroon for instance, in order to receive medical attention, a patient has to pay cash up front, and have cash to buy all prescribed medications. This was observed in at least three hospitals in the country in 2014, by this researcher. It follows that persons with no money received no help, and those who could not buy medications died needless deaths. Many of the illnesses are simple illnesses that are treated in outpatient doctors' offices for only patient co-pay in countries like the United States. It was surprising to hear that patients in some hospitals in Cameroon who could not pay their bill for their hospitalization had to do some type of work for the hospital to pay off their debt before they could be discharged from the hospital. As well, even though this was not personally observed, there were stories of corpses not released to families until hospital debts were cleared. There is a direct correlation between poverty and access to health care and premature deaths. Peters et al. (2008) explain that poverty leads to poor health, and poor health gives rise to poverty. Poverty brings with it malnutrition, and malnourishment causes health issues, and without the requisite funds for health care, quality of life is severely impacted.

At their current levels of development most Sub-Saharan African countries provide no public funded health care nor are there private insurance companies that provide such services. To compound this, hospitals do not provide patient care. In the event that a patient is hospitalized, friends or family have the responsibility of providing personal and hygiene care to the patient (*garde medicin*). They sleep on mats in the hospital, or they stay in private rented lodging nearby. This also means additional expenses for meals and boarding. The use of credit cards is sparse in Cameroon, and no hospital in the country takes checks or credit cards. All transactions are in cash. For poor people who fall ill, many resort to native doctors for traditional medicines, and those who venture to hospitals sometimes do have to sell some of the few belongings they have, or borrow money to pay for their health care. Peters et al. (2008) refer to the sale of personal items to generate money for health care as "distress spending" and using up huge portions of the household budget for medical care as "catastrophic spending."

Besides the thwarted strivings of the African people, at times hospital beds, doctors, and nurses are scarce. Peters et al. (2008) indicate that in 2007, there was approximately less than one bed for 10,000 people, 0.21 doctors for 1000 people, and 0.93 nurses for every 1000 people in Africa. As well, distance to hospitals is a problem for many. Take the case of Cameroon, for instance; people in villages have no hospitals nearby. They have to travel for hours if not days to get to a hospital. There are few if any ambulances, no emergency services, and the most they can find along the way are local dispensaries that are ill equipped, and staffed with no doctors.

As for prenatal care, Galarpe (2013) reports that almost half of pregnant women in developing countries do not get prenatal care. Further, Galarpe's report states that approximately 3 million babies die within their first month of birth, and most of them die at time of birth, in developing countries. Tawiah (2007) explains that 1 in every 16 women in sub-Saharan Africa dies during child delivery as opposed to 1 in 2,800 in developed countries. Most women fail to receive even the required minimum of 4 prenatal visits to check on the pregnancy. Basing his studies on Ghana, Kenya, Nigeria, Uganda, and Zambia, Tawiah discloses that only 41.9 percent of Ugandan women get at least 4 prenatal visits to a clinic. He also states that 47.4 percent of Nigerian women, 66.7 percent of Kenyan women, 69.4 of Ghanaian women, and 71.6 percent of Zambian women make at least 4 prenatal visits to a clinic. Tawiah's study also finds that most women in the rural parts of these countries give birth at home. He attributes this to the level of education of the woman, where the woman resides, and the occupation of the woman and her spouse. Uncontrolled childbearing is another problem that many African women experience (Tawiah 2007). The lack of use of contraception is a huge problem as he explains. Many women do not use contraception so they bear too many children. For families already suffering from privations, adding numerous children makes things worse financially. Certainly, couples have the right to determine how many children they want to have, and when to have them. Indeed they have the right to control their fertility. This is a right recognized at the Fourth World Conference on Women 1995, the International Conference on Population and Development 1994, and the World Summit for Children 1990.

CIA World Factbook reveals the following statistics regarding maternal mortality rate in 2015. Among 103 countries, the top 20 countries with the highest maternal mortality rates are in Africa. Table 2.3 shows the top 20 countries with highest maternal mortality rate based on deaths per 100,000 births.

This report is consistent with other reports that place Sub-Saharan Africa as the most risky part of the world where a woman is most likely to die from complications of pregnancy and childbirth (see ibitimes.co.uk). Indeed, following a 2013 report by ibitimes.co.uk, in 2013, there were approximately 289,000 maternal deaths worldwide, and of this number 62 percent that is, about 179,000 were from Sub-Saharan Africa. A 2013 data from The World Bank shows slightly lower numbers than the above numbers in these countries (World Bank, Maternal Mortality Ratio, 2013). It follows that maternal mortality rates are increasing instead of declining.

Table 2.3. Top 20 Countries With Highest Mortality Rate

South Sudan	2,054
Chad	1,100
Somalia	1,000
Sierra Leone	890
Central African Rep.	890
Burundi	800
Guinea Bissau	790
Liberia	770
Sudan	730
Cameroon	690
Nigeria	630
Lesotho	620
Guinea	610
Niger	590
Zimbabwe	570
Rep. of Congo	560
Dem. of Congo	540
Mali	540
Mauritania	510
Mozambique	490

Maternal mortality rate by country: *Source of Data: CIA World Factbook, 2015.

While there is access to contraception, where the woman resides, level of education of the woman, how independent the woman is in making decisions about her health, are the determining factors as to whether she will use contraception. These factors as reflected in Tawiah's (2007) study are indeed crucial as results indicate women who live in rural communities are less likely to use contraceptives—less than 1 percent of such women in Ghana, Nigeria, and Kenya, and 3.4 percent in Zambia.

With regard to the woman being able to take charge of decisions relating to her health, Tawiah's (2007) study shows that how empowered a woman is determines if the woman or her husband makes decision about her health. Tawiah's (2007) study reveals the following statistics: 12.8 percent women in Nigeria, 33.1 percent women in Zambia, 36.7 percent in Ghana, 38.8 percent in Kenya, and 45.3 percent of women in Uganda, make decisions about their health.

The level of a woman's education is directly correlated with her ability to make decisions about her health. The more educated a woman, the more likely she is to take control of her life. Tawiah (2007) reports that that for the most part is the case. In his sample of 5 countries, 4 confirmed that hypothesis except for Nigeria where 23.4 percent of women with higher education had their partners make decisions.

Joint decisions between spouses about health care were significantly low among couples in Tawiah's (2007) study. It was determined in his study that among Nigerian couples 8.3 percent, Zambian women 9.2 percent, Kenyan women, 13.1 percent, Ugandan women 16.2 percent, and Ghanaian women 19.4 percent joint decisions on health care were made. Religious affiliation also had a role to play in a woman's control of her health care. According to Tawiah (2007) 85.1 percent of Muslim women in Nigeria, 52.8 percent of Muslim women in Uganda left their health care decisions to their husbands.

Voanews.com (2010) reports that because of the tediousness of trekking for miles to get to a health care center, most Ethiopian women do not get prenatal care, and this is the situation the majority of African women who live in villages far remote from the big towns and cities experience. The consequences of no prenatal care range from difficult pregnancies and deliveries to deaths. For women who survive, further physical complications such as fistula may arise. Voanews.com (2010) outlines challenges that make opening health care facilities in Ethiopian rural areas important. There are difficulties in constructing roads linking big towns to rural areas, providing education in rural areas, and getting health care professionals to live and work in rural settings. These challenges are not endemic to Ethiopia; they are challenges faced in just about every African country. Further, the African Diaspora has left many African countries short of educated professionals. Tawiah (2007) states that the biggest impediment to getting health care is lack of money, and then distance to the nearest health care center, and then lack of means of transportation. This assessment is based on experiences and observations during years of living in Cameroon, and from experiences in subsequent visits.

Besides the lack of prenatal care, receiving antenatal care is also a severe problem. According to Kinney et al. (2010) "every year 4.4 million children—including 1.2 million newborns—and 265,000 mothers die in Sub-Saharan Africa. This amounts to 13,000 deaths per day or almost nine deaths every minute. Sub-Saharan Africa has half of the world's maternal, newborn and child deaths" (1). This is the state of things in Sub-Saharan Africa despite the Millennium Development Goals (MDGs) for maternal and child health before 2015. Countries in west and central Africa, with Nigeria at the top, as Kinney et al. (2010) explain have the highest rates of both maternal and children below 5 years of age mortality. Causes for these deaths have been attributed to complications during pregnancy and childbirth, illnesses among newborns, infections, malnutrition, and HIV/AIDS. Childinfo.org (2012) lists hemorrhage, hypertension, eclampsia, sepsis, embolism, and complications from crude abortion methods, as leading causes of maternal deaths. Kinney et al. (2010) state:

> According to the most recent World Health Organization (WHO) analysis, most maternal deaths in Africa are related to direct obstetric complications that occur around the time of childbirth—mainly hemorrhage, hypertension, sepsis, and obstructed labor, which combined account for 64 percent of all maternal deaths (figure 4). Non-pregnancy related infections, such as HIV/AIDS and pneumonia, account for 23 percent of the deaths and unsafe abortion accounts for 4 percent of maternal deaths in Africa. More than half of maternal deaths take place within one day of birth. Malnutrition, including maternal anemia, iodine deficiency, and poor quality diet, also contribute to maternal mortality and the high incidence of stillbirths and congenital abnormalities. HIV-infected mothers' risk of dying is ten times higher than that of HIV-negative mothers. (3)

While there is progress in that some countries are working toward reducing maternal mortality, whether this trend will continue, and the pace at which it will continue, are not readily known. According to Reliefweb.int and Childinfo.org, maternal death lifetime risk was 1 in 39 for Sub-Saharan African women in 2010. As explained by these organizations, lifetime risks of maternal deaths constitute complications from pregnancy and childbirth over a woman's childbearing age, in addition to the fertility rate of the woman and the maternal mortality ratio. Reliefweb.int has the following data for 2010 lifetime risk of maternal death globally.

Even though there are reportedly 880,000 stillbirths every year in sub-Sahara African countries, not much attention is placed on this phenomenon. Many of these deaths as is reported should not have occurred if there was just basic medical intervention (Kinney et al. 2010). According to Kinney et al. (2010), besides medical complications and diseases that are instrumental to maternal deaths, poverty is a huge contributor to deaths, as well as female repressiveness, marginal or low levels of education, and inability to make decisions on their health and that of their children. In a nutshell, these factors boil down to dependence on men due to women's meager financial circumstances.

Approximately half of the world's population resides in rural areas. This population has just about one quarter of the world's doctors (Buchan et al. 2013). This shortage of physicians stalls the equitable access to, and benefits of, health services. There is high mortality in these areas; residents of rural areas have to seek medical attention in urban areas, thus leading to a clogging of medical case files, and increased medical fees. A different response may also be observed, that is, when overstaffed personnel in urban areas lead to

Table 2.4. Lifetime Risk of Maternal Death, 2010

Region based	Lifetime risk of maternal death On 1 in.
Sub-Saharan Africa	39
Middle East and North Africa	190
South Asia	150
Latin America and the Caribbean	520
Industrialized Countries	4,700
Developing Countries	150
Least Developed Countries	52
World	180

*Source: Trends in maternal mortality: 1990 to 2010, WHO, UNICEF, UNFPA and the World Bank (Reliefweb.int, 2012, 55).

limited use of their services, and thus the urge to relocate (Buchan et al. 2013).

FAMINE, WARS, VIOLENCE, AND DISEASE

Time poverty, restricted property rights, poor health care systems apart, Africa unfortunately is notorious for famine, floods, drought, and pests—insects that ravage crops. Ethiopia, for instance, remains one of the poorest countries in the world because of many of these reasons (Danchurchaid.org 2007). The rainy season is at times brief, while the dry season is prolonged; at other times when it rains it is torrential with floods that destroy homes, roads, and crops. Take the 2007 floods in Amhara and Gambella, for instance, over 60,000 people were severely impacted, over 1,107 quintals of grains were destroyed, and over 5,576 hectares of farmland were swept off in the Amhara region. In Gambella, about 46,667 people were affected, and over 37,997 had crops and food supplies damaged (Danchurchaid.org).

According to Oxfam.com "famine is the 'triple failure' of (1) food production, (2) people's ability to access food and, finally and most crucially (3) in the political response by governments and international donors. Crop failure and poverty leave people vulnerable to starvation." Further, as Oxfam.org explains, "Stage 5 'famine/humanitarian catastrophe'—requires that more than two people per 10,000 die each day, acute malnutrition rates are above 30 percent." The United Nations disclosed that about 260,000 people, half of whom were children died in Somalia from 2010–2012 due to famine—a stage 5 catastrophe.

The famine in Somalia was created or exacerbated by conflict and violence in the country. As victims of famine themselves, women are left in more precarious situations as the burden of saving their starving children falls in a large part on them even if that means trekking miles with babies on their backs to find relief for their children. Bachelet (2011, in un.org) explains that besides malnutrition, starvation, disease, and all the other hardships Somali women are exposed to other forms of victimization including sexual violence. Such violence occurs as they trek to relief centers, or in relief camps due to lapses in security.

Desertification has been pinpointed as an additional threat to the development of Africa (Dietz 2004; Naisse et al. 2004). Soil deterioration in Africa has been blamed on man-made activities that comprise deforestation, excessive grazing and cultivation, improper irrigation methods, population surge, climate variations that include drought and loss of moisture, and a variety of other problems. Much of Africa relies on arable land especially for farm products as well as to trap carbon that increases climate change. However, because of desertification, soil erosion is rampant, crop yields have dropped, and water is rare to come by in some places.

According to the United Nations Food and Agriculture Organization (FAO), Africa is likely to lose about two thirds of its fertile land by 2030 if desertification is not contained (Africa Renewal 2012). Desertification makes it difficult for land to support humans, wildlife, as well as domestic animals, and crops. It is reported that in South Africa about 300–400 million tons of topsoil is lost every year (Botany.uwc.ac.za). With soil not being soaked by water, and with shortages of plant nutrients, plants are bound to wither and die off. Desertification is responsible for about 12 million hectares of land getting barren annually. Put in context, it translates to "10 percent of the total area of South Africa or 87 percent of the area of cultivated lands" in South Africa (Botany.uwc.ac.za). The rapid deterioration of arable land is reported throughout the countries of Southern Africa.

The Convention to Combat Desertification (UNCCD.int) explains that because of desertification, poverty and depressed socio-economic conditions are rife. To begin with, 2/3 of Africa is arid/desert land and of the remainder of the land, 3/4 of it has deteriorated greatly in some areas. These conditions have led to entrenched poverty. Poverty is brought about when production drops, supply becomes limited, and hunger and malnutrition set in. Problems of desertification are not only experienced at the personal level, nationally the effects are felt as crop sales decline and the Gross National Product drops.

Water scarcity is a problem in Africa. Such scarcity is brought about by lack of physical water, or because of human waste. The majority of farmers particularly in Africa rely on rain and the season for rain is limited to about four months a year, and in arid areas rain seldom falls. Scarcity of water does not only affect farmers, it affects everyone. Population surge and lifestyle have increased the need for useable water. In some societies modern methods of irrigation are used, but such techniques are sparsely used in Africa. In arid areas, there is insufficient water and even with modern methods of extracting water from the ground, it is likely that there may not be sufficient to sustain a growing population, their farms, and other needs for an infinite period of time. Some facts are worth noting in Africa: After Australia, it is the next driest continent in the world; 66 percent of the continent is extremely dry, or quasi-arid; approximately 115 people living in Africa die every hour from diseases associated with poor sanitation, substandard hygiene, and contaminated water, and more than 1/4 of the inhabitants spend to and fro about 1.5 hours fetching water (UNDESA 2012).

According to the International Food Policy Research Institute (IFPRI 2013), much of Africa's scarcity of water is not a result of the absence of water rather it suffers from "economic water scarcity." IFPRI (2013) explains "economic water scarcity" as the failure to invest in resources (which include financial, human capital, and equipment) that may help in drilling the soil to extract water so as to limit water scarcity—a point UNDESA (2012) concurs with. Many African countries do not allocate sufficient funds for water and sanitation projects in part because they are more invested in other public projects, or do not have the funds, or do not see such projects as worthy of any more attention than what is already given to them. Further problems such as poorly crafted policies and goals and poor coordination among staff hamper any progress towards attaining the Millennium Development Goal of clean water in 2015. Natural factors also stand in the way of progress in getting clean water to the population and to significantly solve the problem of economic water scarcity. The climate of Africa fluctuates, and at times the continent experiences extreme weather patterns. Countries around the equator experience extreme dry temperatures, the northern countries experience arid temperatures, while some of the countries in the middle parts of the continent experience semi-arid temperatures. There is plenty of rainfall in Sub-Sahara Africa, during the months of June—September and that sometimes results in flooding. Flooding destroys farms, livestock, and homes, and for many inhabitants such destruction sweeps away their entire livelihood.

Drought too is another natural disaster that plagues some African countries. Record high temperatures in the horn of Africa particularly in Kenya, Somalia, and Ethiopia, and absence of rains threatens these countries. The United Nations reports that starvation is entrenched throughout the horn of Africa. Starvation in this part of Africa is caused by a combination of conflict, increases in food prices, and drought (Africa Renewal Online 2014). Somalia in particular has been reported by Africa Renewal to be experiencing the worst drought in a century. It is reported that over 11 million people are in dire need for food. The United Nations estimates that as measured by the median global acute malnutrition (GAM) Somalia's rate of mal nutrition linked to drought increased from 16.4 percent to 36.4 percent in the southern and central parts of the country in 2011. The threat of drought also threatens the Turkana region of Kenya. Here, over 1 million people are desperate for food and other humanitarian aid. This region under different circumstances should not be affected by drought since as is reported by BBC News the area is above a water reservoir that has the capacity of supplying water to all of Kenya for 70 years.

The United Nations Department of Economic and Social Affairs (UNDESA, 2012) states that almost 1.2 billion people, approximately 1/5 of the world's population, live in areas where there is scarcity of water, and about 500 million more people are at risk of facing water scarcity (see also, Water for Life Decade 2014). Further, 1.6 billion people which is roughly 1/4 of the world's population are at risk of facing economic water scarcity (Water for

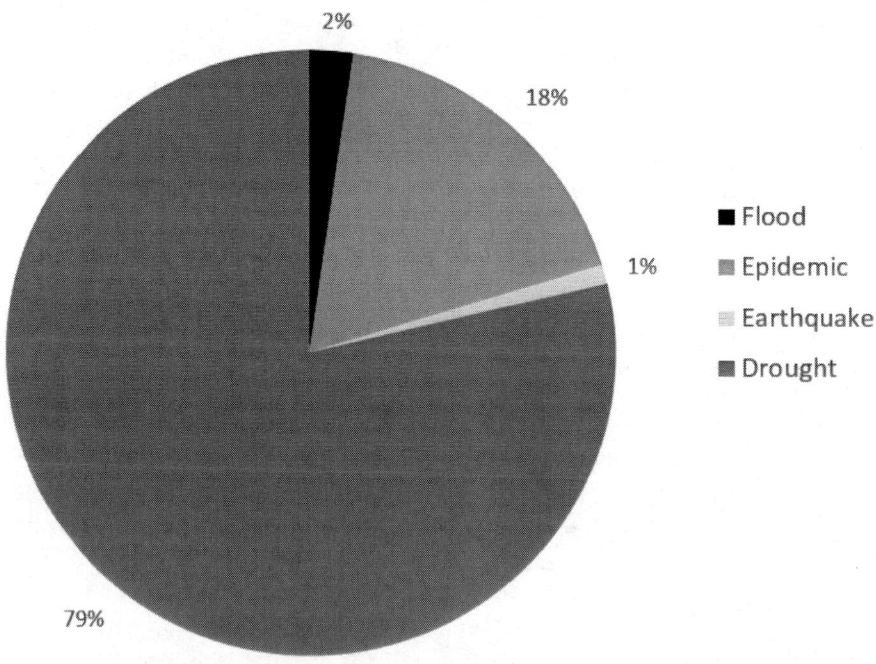

Figure 2.1. Statistics by Disasters Type. Percentage of people reported killed by disaster type. Region profile for Natural Disasters from 1980–2008. *D. Guha-Sapir, R. Below, Ph. Hoyois "EM-DAT: The OFDA/CRED International Disaster Database—www.emdat_be—Universite Catholique de Louvain-Brussels, Belgium. http://www.emdat.be/database.*

Life Decade 2014). By 2025, it is projected that 1.8 billion people will inhabit regions with outright scarcity of water, while 2/3 of the global population will be living under the threat of impending water shortage (UN Water Factsheet on Water Scarcity 2013). With climate change, it is projected that by 2030, about 1/2 of the population of the world will live in countries where there will be a high possibility of water scarcity. Those likely to find themselves in these countries are between 75 million to 250 million in Africa (UNDESA 2012). In the arid areas and quasi-arid areas between 24 million to 700 million people will be displaced. With Sub-Sahara Africa having the most number of countries that are in danger of water scarcity, it is inevitable that water scarcity will exacerbate poverty in the continent.

Poverties.Org (2013) explains that climate change is responsible for some of the conflict in Africa. According to the organization, with the Indian Ocean warming, there is a corresponding decline in rainfall in the eastern parts of Africa. This decrease, which is approximately 15 percent, coincidentally happens during the planting season, and thus makes land arid. With groups struggling to occupy what fertile land there is, tension erupts. While it may appear that irrigating land may be remedial for groups fighting for fertile patches of land, problems with irrigation have been detected.

Researchers for IFPRI discuss four types of irrigation technologies that can be used in Africa: motor pumps, treadle pumps, communal river dimension, and small reservoirs. However, as the researchers concede, the use of motor and treadle pumps also come with their own problems. Since these methods of irrigation rely on pumping water from the ground, the risk of depleting the water is high. To avoid this, there have to be regulations in place as to how water is used; and mechanisms of monitoring the system and use of it have to be implemented. Others contend that when water is pumped from the ground, there is severe indentation of the land, and this causes the sea level to rise, spreading saline (Nhanenge 2014).

The International Strategy for Disaster Reduction (ISDR 2007) explains that 70 percent of earth is water, and provides 97 percent of total water supply globally. The problem is that except for 2.5 percent of water that is fresh water, the rest is salt water. With rising population and demands for water, Sub-Sahara Africa faces shortages in fresh water. As the world's poorest region, and admittedly most underdeveloped region in the world, providing fresh and clean water to the masses, has been an Achilles heel for most of the countries in the region. Coupled with that is the inability to provide proper sanitation services in the region. Improper sanitation further degrades the quality of water in the area. With statistics that show that countries across Sub-Sahara possess the largest numbers of urban slums, and the numbers will rise to about 400 million by 2020, it is estimated that some of the population will live in areas prone to floods, landslides, and earthquakes.

These combined with water scarcity is likely to impact the continent drastically (UNDESA 2012).

Progress in accomplishing the Millennium Development Goal to clean water, 2015, has been slow in many sub-Saharan countries. Northern Africa has made great strides in meeting the 2015 goal on water. Indeed, it is reported that it is on schedule to meet its 94 percent development goal on water by 2015. Unfortunately, Sub-Saharan Africa is less likely to meet its 75 percent target by 2015 (UNDESA 2012). The use of fresh water varies on income levels in Africa. Data from 35 countries in Sub-Sahara Africa reveals vast disparity between the richest and poorest in society. More than 90 percent of the richest quintile in towns and cities use clean water, and over 60 percent of them have such clean water piped into their homes. On the contrary, less than half of the population has access to any type of enhanced water source, while for the poorest 40 percent clean water is non-existent (UNDESA 2012).

Shortage of water makes sanitation problems worse. A vast majority of houses do not have water system toilets, and very few public places have them. It is not uncommon to have people defecate anywhere; waste is disposed everywhere and used water is disposed anywhere. The percentage of people with upgraded sanitary facilities in their homes is quite low. Only about 40 percent of people in 2010 had access to improved sanitary facilities, a meager 5 percent increase from 1990. This is even worse when a comparison is made between urban and rural residents when urbanites experienced a 54 percent improvement in sanitary conditions as oppose to 31 percent experienced by rural residents (UNDESA 2012). These practices have been linked to the transfer of bacteria and water-borne diseases like cholera (UNDESA 2012). Infants in West and Central Africa are disproportionately affected by contaminated water supply and poor sanitation. It is reported that these regions have the highest mortality rate of children under five years old with 191 child deaths for every 1000 births (UNDESA 2012). Overall in sub-Saharan Africa, the campaign for clean water and proper sanitation and hygiene has not yielded many positive results. Instead, poor water and sanitation continue to generate water-borne diseases.

Climate change too poses a problem to food supply, health, and livestock. While crop adjustments can always be made to adjust to climate patterns, such adjustments are likely to be slow in Africa giving the slow pace at which it catches on to any advancements whether to technology or to socio-economic realities. Climate change is also going to change the vegetation in lots of places, and streams and rivers may significantly dry up. Without prompt adjustments to such changing conditions, food shortages are likely, food prices are thus likely to rise, and hunger is likely to become pervasive. Lifestock and aquatic life will significantly be depleted, and the impact on the livelihood of those who depend on hunting or fishing will be greatly impacted.

United Nations Secretary-General, Ban Ki-moon summarizes the predicament of water scarcity thus:

> All are places where shortages of water contribute to poverty. They cause social hardship and impede development. They create tensions in conflict-prone regions. Too often, where we need water we find guns. . . . There is still enough water for all of us but only so long as we keep it clean, use it more wisely, and share it fairly. (UNDESA 2012)

Researchers have also suggested the likely nexus between climate change and civil conflicts (Barnett and Adger 2007; Sarsons 2011) even though others like Nodas and Gleditsch (2007) caution against such early conclusions. This connection between climate change and conflicts is speculated based on poverty that may arise following drastic declining marine life, livestock, crops, and other resources. Further, as it is speculated, climate change is likely to increase environmental pollution, and with financial institutions and governments stretched to the limits with other internal issues, social and political tensions are likely to ensue. Such precarious conditions have the potential of breeding terrorism and other kinds of violence (McGarrity 2014). It is reported that a UN agency cautions that controversies in the Sahel region of the northwestern part of Africa arise because of climate change that causes crop and food shortages (McGarrity 2014).

Certainly, these natural disasters affect everyone regardless of gender or age, but the effects are particularly poignant and long-lasting for women. While there is a dearth in specific longitudinal studies on the effects of famine on women affected by famine in Africa, research by Roseboom et al. (2006) in The Netherlands may shed light. Using a sample of 2414 people born sometime during and shortly after the Dutch famine (1943–1947), Roseboom et al. (2006) discuss issues associated with maternal malnutrition. Findings from the study confirm a link between maternal health and fetal health among women exposed to famine during different stages of pregnancy. Among the illnesses and problems they determined from the sample are: glucose intolerance, coronary heart disease, atherogenic lip profile, blood coagulation, increased risk of breast cancer, micro albuminuria, blocked airways disease, high levels of stress responsiveness, and others (Roseboom et al. 2006, 485).

According to Roseboom et al. (2006, 485), "Coronary heart disease remains a major burden on public health in the western world, and is taking on epidemic proportions in developing countries." Their study provides insight as to how maternal undernourishment during different stages of gestation may be instrumental to several diseases to mother and fetus.

Besides the problems listed in the table, Roseboom et al. (2006) further discuss that based on the finding of their research women become less fertile during famine, and chronic diseases that fetuses inherit emanate from the womb due to the malnutrition of the mother. Further as the researchers contend, the stage of pregnancy at which the mother was when famine set in also determines the effects on the fetus/baby. Roseboom et al. (2006) surmise that:

> Maternal malnutrition during gestation may permanently affect adult health without affecting the size of the baby at birth. This gives the fetal origins hypothesis a new dimension. This may imply that adaptations that enable the fetus to continue to grow may nevertheless have adverse consequences for health in later life. Coronary heart disease may be viewed as the price paid for adaptations made to an adverse intrauterine environment. (489)

Thompson (2011) explains attacks both sexual and physical perpetrated on Somali women who have to trek sometimes for over 200 kilometers to fetch firewood to patch their dilapidated tents and for cooking. Such attacks are easy to carry out because more than 90 percent of the women are unaccompanied by their husbands, and because some have over four children to cater for, they are left vulnerable. Even when these women eventually make it to refugee camps like the Dadaab, safety is not guaranteed. Both the camps and makeshift tents on campgrounds are subject to random attacks on women either to rape them, or to rob them of any few possessions they may have.

On April 14, 2014, Islamic extremists of the Boko Haram group in Nigeria, stormed a school in Chibok, in the northeastern part of Nigeria and kidnapped 270–300 schoolgirls. While the girls have not been rescued as of

Table 2.5. Long-term consequences of Exposure to Famine According to Timing During Gestation

	Exposure to famine	
In late gestation	In mid-gestation	In early gestation
Glucose Intolerance	Glucose Intolerance	Glucose Intolerance
	Micro albuminuria	Atherogenic lipid profile
	Obstructive airways disease	Altered blood coagulation
		Obesity (women only)
		Stress Sensitivity
		Coronary heart disease
		Breast Cancer

*Source: Roseboom, T., De Rooji, S. & Painter, R. (2006, 488). Elsevier.com.

June 2016, and the cause of the kidnapping remains speculative, it is clear as reports indicate that school attendance for girls is more a privilege in the northern parts of Nigeria than in other areas of the country (see independent.co.uk 2014). Reports indicate that of the 57 million children worldwide who do not go to school, 10.5 million are in Nigeria, and of this number approximately 6 million are Nigerian girls. Some are the 6 million girls who at some point enrolled in school of whom less than two-thirds of them completed primary school (independent.co.uk 2014).

While the fate of the girls kidnapped by Boko Haram is not known as of June 2016, some reports contend some of these girls who are between the ages of 15–18 have been forced into marriages, or even transported across borders, and a few are reported to have escaped their captors. Even though the abduction itself is an act of violence perpetrated by an extremist group, the contention is that the abduction is predicated on the limited value placed on girls' education. This is a problem in many parts of Africa, and in parts of Nigeria, especially in the north where sending girls to school is considered an expensive and wasteful undertaking. It is noteworthy that the country has legislation that advocates free universal education at least to a certain level, yet many girls are restricted from benefiting from it. Despite the legislation, criticisms are levied against the government for not allocating more resources for education. Not withstanding the global recommendation that 6 percent of the Gross Domestic Product (GPD) of a country should be allocated for education, Nigeria spends just about 1.5 percent of its GPD (independent.co.uk 2014).

If or when the missing Nigerian girls will be found is uncertain. The psychological effects of their captivity is likely to have far-reaching consequences, some of which may include paranoia, trauma from sexual and physical violence, inability to concentrate and focus on educational aspirations, and fear of venturing out of their homes, among other effects. These experiences may impede the girls' pursuit of a stable and productive life if proper counseling and other remedial measures are not put in place.

Actionaid.org (2013) reports that violence against girls in many African countries remains quite prevalent. According to the report, 83 percent of girls in Ghana, 90 percent of girls in Kenya, and 80 percent of girls in Mozambique in the time frame of 2012–2013 experienced some type of violence. In Mozambique, because of the influx of migrant workers to urban areas, sexual violence against girls is on the rise. Actionaid.org also acknowledges that droughts, floods, and conflict, particularly in the case of Kenya, as well as family crises, personal issues, bereavements, impact on girls' motivation to pursue education. Violence in general is high in South Africa, and sexual violence is even more alarming. It is reported that there were 66,387 rapes and other sexual acts in March 2013 (Africa Check 2013; Nhanenge 2014). Further acknowledgement of the problem is by South African police officers who report that every 36 seconds a woman is raped. While many rapes go unreported, it is also believed that rapes perpetrated on young girls and children are quite high in Africa (Nhanenge 2014).

UNICEF.org (n.d.) explains that the effects of war are far more ravaging than the toll of death in the sense that suffering as a result of war persists in different ways even long after the war ends as the following discussion indicate. UNICEF.org explains that there is a nexus between war and dropout rates, and declining enrollments of girls in schools. In Somalia, for instance, as the organization explains because of safety issues, as for instance being waylaid en route to school, girls drop out of school. Further, because of the non-presence of men, either because they fell victim to war, or had to take their cattle miles away to graze, girls and women had to make sacrifices including dropping out of school to assume breadwinner roles that hitherto were for men. At times girls and women simply resort to early marriages. According to the World Bank, the most vital contributor to a country's economic growth is education (UNICEF.org). "Girls and women who are educated will have fewer children and those they have are more likely to survive and thrive" (UNICEF.org). In essence, the level of education of a country's citizens determines the growth of the country's economy; and if a significant segment of the population (girls and women) are not receiving any kind of education, that significantly impacts the economy.

Caryl Stern, president and chief executive officer of U.S. Fund for UNICEF poignantly reveals the predicament of mothers:

> Pregnant and breastfeeding women often can't get the nutrition and health care they need, and women in general shoulder an especially high burden in the care of their families, sometimes at the expense of their own wellbeing. . . . Half a million children are at imminent risk of death and require immediate lifesaving attention to survive. That's half a million children whose mothers, famished themselves, are now watching their children suffer, wither, and beg for food that is not there. (Huffingtonpost.com 2011)

Marshall (2004) discusses the impact of war on society, and in particular of women and children. She indicates that "women always become the spoils of war; their deaths are considered collateral damage and their bodies are frequently used as battlegrounds and as commodities that can be traded" (Marshall 2004). At wartime, women fall victims in all ways including: rapes, brutalization, unwanted pregnancies, sexual slavery, sex trafficking, forced labor, and disease infections such as HIV/AIDS. According to Marshall (2004) 80 percent of the world's casualties of war and conflict are women and children, and of the 40 million refugees in the world, 80 percent are women and children. Another dimension of the effects of war that is not frequently discussed as it affects humans, and women in particular, are toxins from military equipment that are improperly disposed. Marshall (2004) reports that such toxins sip into groundwater, and pollute drinking water and food and also "the breast milk of nursing mothers. It is also likely that perchlorate impacts reproductive health." United Nations Population Fund (UNPFA 2001) describes things this way:

> The impact of conflicts on women and girls' reproductive and sexual health can never be underestimated. Their psychological, reproductive and overall well-being is often severely compromised in times of conflict. Conflicts tend to increase the incidence of sexual violence; rape; sexually transmitted infections (STIs), including HIV/AIDS; and unwanted pregnancies. In addition, essential social services, such as medical facilities, on which women heavily depend for their well-being, are greatly disrupted by armed conflicts. (III)

In 2012, Sudan was hit quite hard by floods, flies, fever, and famine (allafrica.com). Reports from the Zamzam camp in Darfur portray very grim pictures of declining health, spread of disease, displacement, lack of food among children, pregnant women, and the elderly. Similar reports came out of Nyala and Zalingei camps where diarrhea, malaria, and other diseases killed children, pregnant women, and the elderly in shocking numbers.

Following violence in Darfur, Sudan, over 200,000 refugees most of them women and children fled to Chad (Ezard et al. 2005). These refugees faced the same fate their compatriots in camps in Darfur faced: outbreak of malaria, lack of medications, or severe shortages of medications and insecticides to help treat or prevent the illness. The majority of these vulnerable persons were women and children. These reports were consistent with reports from Tanzania, Ethiopia, and other African countries that harbored displaced people.

Allafrica.com reports that recent fighting and violence in Central African Republic displaced approximately 210,000 people; the report also notes that the United Nations suggests that over 710,000 people have been displaced and 75,000 have been forced into exile. Reports indicate that France's United Nations Ambassador stated in December 2013 that the country of Central African Republic "has collapsed, and this country is now simply plundered, looted, the women are raped, people are killed by thugs" (news.yahoo.com 2013).

UNICEF.org (n.d.), lists the following as gender-based factors that contribute to higher levels of deaths and illnesses among women at war time:

- Violence against girls and women, including rape and sexual slavery;
- Hunger and exploitation in camps for refugees and internally displaced persons, when men take control of food distribution;
- Malnutrition, when food aid neglects women's and children's special nutritional requirements; and

- Culturally inappropriate and/or inadequate access to health services, including mental and reproductive health services.

Further as UNICEF.org (n.d.) notes "Health services for women, girls and the children in their charge break down in wartime, just when they need them most." Worldrevolution.org like other organizations impresses the point that regardless of the venue be it at home, or in camps, women and girls are quite susceptible to "sexual violence, trafficking and mutilation." As well, the organization indicates that women suffer further violence, rejection, sexual humiliation, and other atrocities long after war is over.

Rackley (2005) explains that an insurgence of violent crimes such as rapes and robberies erupted during time of conflict in Burundi. Unfortunately, most rape victims failed to report their victimizations making data collection difficult. As well, failure to report victimization also gave rise to problems of accounting for infections of sexually transmitted diseases such as HIV/AIDS. Rape victims faced double jeopardy in that being victims of such a horrendous crime also resulted in victims being ostracized, rejected, and abandoned by their husbands and families. Even though these victims were usually attacked by armed men who exerted force or threat of violence, the women seldom filed complaints for fear of reprisals. Further, unexpected pregnancies from rapes frequently led to women using crude methods of abortion that occasionally led to deaths. At times, babies born alive were abandoned. As Rackley (2005) points out, women in some parts of the country contended that perpetrators of these acts of violence on them were not usually soldiers, or former rebels; they were locals.

Rackley (2005) adds that sexual attacks on women get unchecked in part because of cultural reasoning that make women less inclined to challenge a rapist since women traditionally assume subordinate roles. Rackley confirms this premise by introducing statements from counselors who deal with trauma victims in several parts of Burundi such as Ruyigi and Gitega that suggest that women would rather let peace be than fuel any conflict or expose men who abuse them. One of the counselors explains that keeping up appearances rather than facing realties is more important to Burundians based on culture (Rackley 2005). Some of the women maintained that rape of women has been a way of life even prior to the war, but that with intervention from Non-Governmental Organizations, women's and youth's groups, victims are beginning to come forward.

Rackley (2005) explains widowhood and prostitution as other problems that stem from war. Some of the women explained away why they had to resort to prostitution or to being mistresses, or second or third wives as a way of achieving security. Being alone with no man to count on for support or protection was perceived by the women as placing them in worse circumstances than if they were prostitutes or widows going through life alone.

With regard to widows in Burundi, Rackley (2005) explains:

> Widows suffer particular discrimination under Burundian law, as they cannot inherit property from their dead husbands. With no inheritance rights, widows lose all belongings and property to their late husband's family. Poverty and desperation are the direct result of widowhood. Under the weight of shame and destitution, widows flee with their children and turn to prostitution for survival. This descent is accelerated when the threat of armed attack and rape keeps rural women from working in their fields. . . . The daughters of widowed women tend to drop out of school or do not attend school at all. They marry prematurely, often as a second or third wife because there is too much poverty at home. (35)

The war in the Democratic Republic of Congo has been characterized by USA TODAY as "Africa's deadliest war." It has claimed millions of lives, and "tens of thousands of women, men, girls and boys" have been raped (usatoday.com 2013). In a peculiar twist, everyone in the country is vulnerable to sexual violence, and the violence includes gang rapes, insertion of objects, and other crude and despicable acts. As stoprapeinconflict.org notes: "More than 400,000 women ages 15 to 49 experienced rape between 2006 and 2007 in the Democratic Republic of Congo. That is the equivalent of 1,152 women raped every day, 48 women raped every hour, or four women raped every five minutes." The incidences of rape are so widespread throughout the country, and since offenders are not brought to justice, impunity persists. Troops, former troops, police officers, men of power, and the list goes on, are not immune from being victimizers. As worldwithoutgenocide.org states, the number of rapes and other sexual violence in the country surpass any numbers reported anywhere else in the world and with this comes the spread of HIV/AIDS and other sexually transmitted diseases.

By and large, since men, and worse armed men, have the power to plunder with impunity, defenseless women and children bear the brunt of suffering, through loss of life, the ease of moving around without fear, separation of families, diseases, and the extra burden of taking care of extended family members. On a broader scope, the whole society suffers. Conflict, no matter what, ends in a no-win situation for all parties involved. Each party would have lost something, the everyday enjoyment of a peaceful well-being, loss of family members, a community that has been ravaged by war, and a sense of insecurity. The most lasting effects continue to be poverty, diseases present, unknown, and those that set in later in life. The consequences of poverty are far reaching—pregnant mothers are likely to have miscarriages, underweight children, stillbirths, and other complications primarily from malnourishment, and no prenatal care. Children born into poverty and those who grow in poverty are more susceptible to illnesses, dropping out from school, or not attending school at all.

Domestic abuse and violence escalate during times of suffering; and even when there is no armed conflict studies show that under normal circumstances, men become abusive when their wives become pregnant, or if the abuse had started prior to that, it becomes more rampant and more severe (Marquis and Butler 2001).

An outbreak of contagious disease usually slows the economy because out of panic people tend to stay at home and limit any daily interactions with others. This translates to a disruption of businesses for the individual, the private sector, and for the government. The outbreak of Ebola, 2014, in Guinea, Sierra Leone, and Liberia already is projected to lead to a slower growth of the economy of Liberia in 2014 as the country's Finance Minister explains. Indeed in an interview on April 11, 2014, the finance minister with pessimism stated that the Gross Domestic Product of the country would drop from an 8.7 percent growth in 2013, to a 6.8 percent in 2014. He blames the Ebola disease for the slow growth of his country's economy, the reduction in trade across borders, investments, and custom revenues (Bloomberg Report 2014).

Discussing infectious diseases, and their connection to social inequalities, Farmer (1996) states "In fact, many "tropical" diseases predominantly affect the poor; the groups at risk for diseases are often bound more by socioeconomic status than by latitude" (260–61). This is the fear with the 2014 outbreak of Ebola in Africa. Ebola is not the only disease to ravage Africa—malaria, cholera, typhoid, HIV, and others have taken a toll in that continent at one point or the other. Everyone is susceptible to illness or disease, but the reality is that the poor disproportionately are infected and affected. While preventative measures and medicines at times are available, developing countries, and especially the poor in such countries are the last to have access to such preventative or curative measures. The current Ebola alarm in Guinea, Sierra Leone, and Liberia, 2014, exposes the vulnerability of the poor, disenfranchised, and the divide among nations in regard to their level of development, and knowledge of science. Farmer (1996) all so well explains "We live in a world where infections pass easily across borders—social and geographic—while resources, including cumulative scientific knowledge, are blocked at customs" (265). He further explains that as we extend our studies across borders we will run into inquiries about social inequalities. In this regard he alludes to the inaccessibility of curative measures to those in disenfranchised, or bluntly stated, poor countries. We see this in the current Ebola outbreak in Guinea, Sierra Leone, and Liberia. American doctors and caregivers infected with the disease are flown back to the United States to receive treatment, even if experimental (Huffington Post 2014), while such experimental treatment is not available to those infected in Africa. With the virus spreading, the World Health organization determined that it was alright for the United States to send the experimental drugs to patients stricken by Ebola in Africa; that is after the death toll topped 1,000 (Cable Network News [CNN] on August 12, 2014). Farmer (1996) states "The study of borders qua borders means, increasingly, the study of social inequalities. Many political borders serve as semi permeable membranes, often quite open to diseases and yet closed to the free movement of cures" (266). Independent.co.uk (2014) echoes similar sentiments. That news medium reports that a top public health physician in Britain believes that a vaccine for Ebola has not been found because the disease is confined only to Africa—a "moral bankruptcy" as he calls the failure. The British physician, Professor John Ashton equates the slow reaction to Ebola to the HIV breakout. He states:

> In both cases [AIDS and Ebola], it seems that the involvement of powerless minority groups has contributed to a tardiness of response and a failure to mobilize an adequately resourced international medical response. In the case of AIDS, it took years for proper research funding to be put in place and it was only when so-called 'innocent' groups were involved (women and children, hemophiliac patients and straight men) that the media, politicians, scientific community and funding bodies stood up and took notice. (Independent.co.uk 2014)

Africa, the poorest continent continues to be afflicted by wars, poverty, and disease. The impact of the Ebola disease affects tourism, travel, trade, farming, gaming, and other agencies. This is the response whenever there is an epidemic. For a continent that is already so backward when compared to others, this is another unneeded setback in its development and progress. That the continent is once more helpless is evident in Professor John Ashton's words. He says: "The real spotlight needs to be on the poverty and environmental squalor in which epidemics thrive and the failure of political leadership and public health systems to respond effectively. The international community has to be shamed into real commitment . . . if the root causes of diseases like Ebola are to be addressed" (Independent.co.uk 2014).

It is reported that about 75 percent of tuberculosis and HIV infected people live in Africa (UNAIDS 2013). While the HIV epidemic is a chronic disease now because of antiretroviral treatments, there were still 1.6 million new infected people and 1.2 million AIDS related deaths in Africa in 2012. Effects of the HIV virus have been especially devastating on women and children. At its apex in the decade 1990–2000, the average life expectancy of most people in Africa was 49.5 years. This was to a large extent the result of infant mortality caused by HIV transmission to babies by their mothers during pregnancy. In 2011, it was reported that there were 17.3 million children orphaned because of AIDS, and of this number, 88 percent were in Africa (see AVERT.org 2013). Life expectancy in many African countries remains low with just 48.9 in Swaziland, the country with the highest number of HIV infected people globally, and 48.7 in Lesotho (AVERT.org 2013).

Other key facts about HIV in Africa as it relates to women:

- HIV disproportionately impacts women.
- The vulnerability of women and girls to HIV remains particularly high in sub-Saharan Africa; about 76 percent of all HIV-positive women in the world live in this region.
- In nearly all countries in sub-Saharan Africa, the majority of people living with HIV are women, especially girls and women aged 15–24. In South Africa, HIV prevalence among women aged 20–24 is approximately 21 percent compared to about 7 percent among men in the same age range.
- In Lesotho, nearly 8 percent of young girls aged 15–19 are living with HIV, compared to about 3 percent of their male counterparts.
- The most recent prevalence data show that 13 women in sub-Saharan Africa become infected with HIV for every 10 men. (UNAIDS Global Report Fact Sheet, sub-Saharan Africa, 2010).

AIDS has disrupted the education of youths, and has deep-seated effects on labor and productivity in general. The impact is even worse at the family level since adults generally are breadwinners, but most die, or remain sick—some helplessly sick. Teenage children assume roles of breadwinners, or are sent to live with relatives. Many families are thrust further into poverty because family funds are depleted due to health care expenses. Some surviving women are driven in to the sex industry as a means to generate income for the family. The sex industry has also been blamed for the spread of HIV. It is estimated that 32 percent of people newly infected with HIV in Ghana, and in Kenya 14 percent, and 10 percent in Uganda, is as a result of sex work (UNAIDS Global Report Fact Sheet, sub-Saharan Africa 2010). Women, as reported, are timid to request condom use of their partners, and are more likely to be coerced into non-consensual sex (see Avert.org, n.d.).

GOVERNMENT FAILURE

In a blog posted in 2008 titled "Ending poverty in Africa and elsewhere," Shanta Devarajan asserts that the solution is to "overcome government failure." He went on to elaborate his response by first drawing a parallel between government failure and "market failure." In that regard he explained that "failure" is not suggestive of "evil governments" or "incompetent or ill-intentioned" governments. He simply is insinuating that failure reflects circumstances where government intervention translates to a worse outcome than what was anticipated. To substantiate his point further, Devarajan (2008) points out that African governments do finance primary education in order for poor children to attain education. However, as he notes, if teachers' salaries are guaranteed even when they do take extended leave of absence from work to engage in activities that have no relevance to education, as for instance, campaigning for a politician, the outcome is the perpetuation of illiteracy—having children who cannot read or write—a reverse outcome. This, as Devarajan (2011) contends, also plays out in "health care, water supply, sanitation" and other government programs. That governments allocate money for education, health, and other programs that help alleviate poverty in Africa has really not been the issue; what has been at issue as Devarajan states "is that much of the money spent on these sectors is captured by powerful elites before it reaches the poor" (2012). He goes on to assert that this is what happens in Chad where as he notes just 1 percent of government funds for health care get to the clinics. He also explains that to have spending distributed to various programs and sectors in African societies that help the disadvantaged, government failure must first be addressed.

Kurfi (2009) asserts that the leadership style of a head of state dictates the success of a country. Weak leadership as Gatut (2013) states is the precursor of a country's economic woes. He contends that an egoistic leader who also adds corruption to his repertoire is most likely to tank the country's economy, and generate economic misery among his people. Further, he contends that such leaders are usually puppets of foreign governments and design trade laws and policies to accommodate such foreign interests, even when such policies disenfranchise their people and sink their countries' economy even more. As long as the leader and his clique are financially secure and viable the leader remains unperturbed by what goes on in his country. Gatut (2013) goes on to draw analogy between such weak and corrupt government with the plight of the people of the Republic of Congo who have been embroiled in war for years unending, and who with all the diamonds in the country, remain very poor. Further, he notes that between 2004 and 2005, Nigeria was the 6th largest producer and exporter of oil, but then it fell to the 12th position by 2006—a decline which he attributes to "poor leadership and management" (Gatut 2013, 13).

Corruption and cronyism remain the biggest culprits of Africa's demise (Okoro 2009). As well, ethnic discord and rivalries that persist in Africa, and uneven distribution of wealth and economic opportunities, account for wealth huddled in a small segment of people (see Asante and Gyimah-Boadi 2004). Indeed, Gatut (2013) relying on Asante's and Gyimah-Boadi's (2004) study, posits that Rawling's government in Ghana exemplified a society where corruption, ethnic rivalry, and political dissension were rife and instrumental in thrusting Ghana into an economic abyss.

Many have chimed in to express dismay at unaccounted aid money sent to African countries, and the corrupt practices of many of the continent's leaders (BBC News/Africa/Cameroon 2007; Erero and Oladoyin 2000; Otu 2012). Gupta et al. (2002) and Negin et al. (2010) find a causal link between corruption and poverty, and Yusuf et al. (2014) find a nexus among corruption, poverty, and economic growth. As Yusuf et al. (2014) explain corruption severely negatively affects poverty by initially influencing economic growth, while variables that influence economic growth are also instrumental to poverty. While debates are raised about what influences poverty, a consensus approach is that corruption stifles economic growth by restricting investments and this invariably leads to poverty. More specifically, corruption reduces the quality of goods and infrastructure, quality of talent, and manpower needed for the production of goods, and corruption brings about evaluators endorsing sub-par products. Following a co-integration base error-correction methodology Yusuf et al. (2014), conclude that corruption and economic growth cause poverty in Nigeria. Importantly, economic growth causes corruption in the short run, but then reduces corruption and poverty eventually. They surmise that good governance that emphasizes economic growth is more likely to suppress corruption and poverty in Nigeria. Otu (2012) chronicles how corruption limits development in Africa:

1. Corruption stifles and kills skills, it undermines quality, and it reduces productivity. Corruption promotes incompetence as unsuitable and wrong persons are often put in undeserved positions to perform important tasks.
2. Corruption affects the investment level and the overall socioeconomic development of a country. The dominance of corruption means that nothing works unless the palm is greased. It increases bureaucratic bottlenecks and redtapeism, which are obstacles to innovation and due process.
3. Corruption has the capacity to cause political instability, leading to social revolution and eventual military incursions into the body polity.
4. Corruption can exacerbate inequality and poverty in society. This is the leading argument regarding the negative consequences of corruption. Again, in most poor nations of the world, the major cause of the pervasive poverty has been identified as the high rate of corruption in these countries.
5. Corruption and the efforts to control it also waste resources and further limit the capacity of government to render the needed services to the citizens.
6. Corruption dents the image of a country and its citizens. Corruption demeans their dignity and social standing, at home and abroad.
7. Corruption brings about ineffective government policies; corruption breeds nepotism and favoritism. (427–29)

Besides corruption being an indicator of poor governance, poor economic planning is also associated to it (Gatut 2013). Poor investments, investments that disproportionately benefit foreign governments and foreign investors and that have marginal or no effects on the populace stagnates the economic and financial well-being of the populace. Compounding on this is the compilation of foreign debt. A country (and the majority of African countries are guilty of this) that has accumulated excessive foreign debts is less apt to cater to its citizenry, and with these other social problems such as unemployment, prostitution, higher crime rates, emerge.

Whenever the issue of poor governance is brought up, African states for the most part become the focus of the discussion. Many of the countries including Cameroon, Nigeria, Democratic Republic of Congo, Burundi, Zimbabwe, Eritrea, Equatorial Guinea, Chad, Guinea Bissau, Libya, South Sudan, Sudan, Somalia, have been listed by Transparency International as the most corrupt countries in the world at one point or the other.

With corruption always at the forefront of public discussion on Africa's economic state of affairs, several have advised that unless corruption can be contained, Africa's economy is likely to stagnate if not degenerate. President Barack Obama of the United States in 2009 succinctly stated in a speech in Ghana:

> No country is going to create wealth if its leaders exploit the economy to enrich themselves, or police can be bought off by drug traffickers. No business wants to invest in a place where the government skims 20 percent off the top, or the head of the Port Authority is corrupt. No person wants to live in a society where the rule of law gives way to the rule of brutality and bribery. That is not democracy, it is tyranny, and now is the time for it to end. (Huffingtonpost.com 2009)

In Cameroon, the scale of corruption in government and parastatal agencies is macabre. Those agencies are plagued by graft, mismanagement, and fraud. Approximately 500 employees in the Ministry of Finance in Cameroon were in 2005, accused by the prime minister of the country of fraud and mismanagement of funds. These employees over a period of time engaged in paying themselves extra money or putting in their accounts salaries for ghost workers—that is non-existent workers (see BBC.co.uk 2005). Reports alleging fraud, bribery, and mismanagement of funds are fertile in the literature on corruption in Cameroon.

As Time (2012) states:

> The aggregate impact of corruption and mismanagement of resources in Cameroon quite substantially exceeds that of street crimes. This assertion is not limited to the economic cost of crimes; rather, it encompasses deaths resulting from sub-standard medical care because of inadequate funding to hospitals, deaths resulting from profound suffering caused by unemployment, low wages, preventable diseases, and other hardships, which are a direct result of mismanagement of funds, graft, and apathy for the masses. (161)

In an article titled "Cameroon Corruption Hinders AIDS Fight," the BBC expressed skepticism regarding use of funds allocated for HIV/AIDS testing and treatment in Cameroon. The BBC was apprehensive as to whether the $133m (68m pounds) allocated to fight HIV/AIDS in Cameroon would be applied to its intended use. Pursuant to investigations that revealed gross mismanagement and misappropriation of the funds, BBC concluded that: "Tackling AIDS cannot happen until a cure is found for Cameroon's second deadly virus—corruption" (BBC. News/Africa/Cameroon corruption hinders AIDS fight). This goes to show the level of corruption and mismanagement of funds in that country.

As others have surmised (Debatewise.org 2014), when a country relies on aid money from other countries for health care of its citizenry, it hardly can improve the economic growth of its people. In the case of Nigeria, the Order of Truth (2014), a think tank organization reports that the continuous pouring of huge sums of aid money from Britain to Nigeria only goes to fill the pockets and coffers of corrupt government officials. The estimated aid funding from Britain to Nigeria in 2014–2015 is 305 million pounds a substantial difference from 141 million pounds in 2011. The think tank group claims that with base annual salaries of 122,000 pounds, Nigerian Legislators are on top of the salary bracket of any legislators anywhere in the world. Meanwhile, 70 percent of Nigerians wallow in poverty below a meager 1.29 pounds a day. Despite its crude oil reserves of approximately 35 billion barrels, plus over 100 trillion feet of natural gas, shockingly, there is a constant shortage of fuel, just as the masses remain poor.

Order of Truth (2013) reports that an estimated $380 billion (245 billion pounds) of government funds have been stolen in Nigeria since 1960, the year it became independent from British rule. Alarmed at the continuous aid money from Britain which mostly goes unaccounted for, and the wasteful spending by the Nigerian government on space programs and missions which the think tank group alludes to as a "fantasy," the think tank group concludes that "the delusional belief that increasing foreign aid without efficient controls in place will make any difference is ridiculous in the extreme" (Order of Truth 2013).

The Democratic Republic of Congo has for decades been marred by severe regional and internal conflicts, and if that is not bad enough, it has suffered and still suffers from "weak governance, mismanagement of natural resources and entrenched corruption" (Transparency International 2014, 2). This country, along with Niger, as Transparency International explains, has "the lowest human development score in UNDP's 2013 Human Development Index (UNDP 2013)" as a consequence of entrenched mismanagement and misallocation of funds. Poor governance in the country is evident in just about every agency including, mining and oil, forestry, budget and finance; and when not corrupt, some like the judiciary, media, are constrained in what they can do. When the government restricts information that can be made available to the public, be it budgetary/ revenue, or just state of the well-being of the nation, the impression it projects is that leadership is either dictatorial or rife with corruption.

Speaking of Africa's poor governance, Philip Booth, Editorial and Program Director at the Institute of Economic Affairs and Professor of Insurance and Risk Management at Cass Business School, London declared:

> In Africa, aid is a side-show at best and damaging at worst. Poverty is falling in the region due to a reduction in conflict and the emergence—in some parts of the continent—of more stable democracies. The rapid reduction in poverty experienced in both India and China demonstrates that it is not development aid and international action but homegrown policies to promote economic liberalism which succeed.
>
> The role for international action is limited. A self-appointed political elite is clearly not best placed to dictate development priorities to other countries. Rather than providing foreign aid, we should be gently encouraging and assisting poor countries to develop the basic economic, legal and institutional frameworks to allow business and enterprise to flourish. (Order of Truth 2013)

Chapter Three

Problems and Weaknesses in Educational Systems

Philosophers such as Aristotle and Plato had lauded the benefits of education especially as a tool that enriches the mind and the general health of a society. Contemporary researchers concur with this as they highlight facts that educated people are more likely to be healthier, happier, wealthier, more engaging in civic duties, and more likely to make better choices in life (Baum and Payea 2004; Baum et al. 2013; Behrman et al.1997; Riddell 2004). In 1970, Julius Nyerere (1970) proclaimed that education "has to prepare our young people to play a dynamic and constructive part in the development of society in which all members share fairly in the good or bad fortune of the group and in which progress is measured in terms of human wellbeing"(239). His ideas about education were not limited to formal school training; he extended that to any mental development that promotes a "sense of commitment" toward civil society. That many leaders in Africa are aware of the benefits of education is evident in their pledges to rid their various countries of gender biases and disparities in obtaining education by 2005 (Johannes 2010). Of course, it is now 2016, and issues about gender disparities and biases in education in Africa still fill discussions.

The leitmotivs that are discussed as impediments to girls' education include costs of education, customary practices that promote boys' education over that of girls, child marriages, distances to schools, and other auxiliary factors.

As a means to a better end, education is vital. Riddell (2004) distinguishes between two types of returns of education: the private and the social. As Riddell (2004) explains, the private benefit is exclusively that of the person who attains the education, and the benefits that ensue from these include a stable source of income based on higher possibilities of employment, job satisfaction, increased length of years, and an overall joie de vivre. Social benefits of education on the other hand, as Riddell explains, may constitute both positive and negative benefits that were not fathomed at the time when educational pursuits were on-going, and which may affect everyone who is involved in making decisions about the educational pursuits of a person. So, if others have to be disadvantaged by spending much of what they have, they may be less inclined in investing toward the education of that person, especially when there is no government assistance. This, in some measure explains what happens with many in African societies and especially to women. Investing in the education of one is likely to generate the urge to educate others, and this inevitably leads to the betterment of life among those in the society. By investing in the education of others, one spreads wealth to others, opens up opportunities for others, and on the whole, the Gross Domestic Product (GPD).

Statistics from The Organization for Economic Cooperation and Development (OECD) countries confirm that education creates lots of advantages. Of those 15 OECD countries that have data on the topic, men in their 30s who have tertiary education are likely to live 8 years longer than those who do not attain that level of education. There is a dramatic difference in life expectancy among men in Central Europe based on their level of education. Take the Czech Republic, for instance: a 30-year-old man who obtains tertiary education is expected to have an increased lifespan of 17 years over that of his compatriot who does not get beyond secondary education (see oecd.org, 2013). The data however reveal that women with tertiary education have a likely lifespan of 4 years more than that of women without such education. This revelation for women does not eclipse the other benefits of higher education because the study goes on to suggest that people with higher education are happier, more likely to do volunteering and social activities, develop interpersonal and institutional trust, and a keener political interest (oecd.org 2013).

Based on entrenched cultural practices in Africa that place more of a premium on male education many families of less affluence sacrifice a girl's education, and at times, even have the girl work to earn money toward her brother's education, or she marries early so that her dowry could be allocated for her brother's education. According to achieveinafrica (2009), 33 million children in Africa of primary school age do not go to school, and of this number 18 million are girls. Further, only 2 out of 3 of children who attend primary school eventually graduate. While achieveinafrica.wordpress.com acknowledges that literacy rates have improved in the continent, the site also acknowledges that 50 percent of women above the age of 25 are illiterate and overall 40 percent of Africans above 15 years of age are illiterate.

Watkins (2013) also portrays a pessimistic picture of education in Africa. Dropping from school as Watkins (2013) contends is on the rise in Africa, and because of wars in Somalia, The Democratic Republic of Congo, Sudan, children in these countries are even more disadvantaged. While Watkins (2013) applauds educational strides made in Ethiopia, Kenya, Tanzania, Zambia, Mozambique, and Senegal, it nonetheless reveals a grim picture in that Africa failed to meet the Millennium Development Goal target of attaining universal primary education by 2015. There is more likelihood that there may instead be a rise in dropout rates.

Far different from the assessment of achieveinafrica (2009), Watkins (2013), a survey that assessed the state of learning in Africa, approximates one out of two of the 61 million children in the primary school age range will not be able to read, write, or do elementary arithmetic when they reach their adolescent years. In utter frustration, Watkins (2013), states that based on how things are, these children are heading to a life of destitution and unemployment, and this stalls any future economic growth in the most backward continent of the world.

With regard to secondary education, Watkins (2013) states that Africa's record is the worst in the world. Only 28 percent of secondary age youths are enrolled in school; tuition, books, and miscellaneous expenses increase at this level, and without government assistance, 90 million children have to look for whatever type of work they can find. While the problem is grim for every child, females are disproportionately affected. According to Watkins (2013), 80 percent of children in member countries of the Organization for Economic Cooperation and Development (OECD) will likely get some tertiary education, but then only 6 percent of children in Sub-Saharan countries will get the same. As the organization contends, this picture is even worse for the poor African female "being poor, rural, and female carries a triple handicap." Girls become the sacrificial lamb in that "gender roles can mean that young girls are removed from school to collect water or care for their siblings." Compounding on this as UNESCO (uis.unesco.org 2012) surmises are other societal constraints such as religious constraints, sexual harassment in schools, and exposure to AIDS and HIV. School policies and practices that are sensitive toward the needs of girls, and that are empowering as for example, course work, or other curricula, are missing in many African countries as UNESCO puts forth. Further, parity in gaining access to education does not necessarily translate to egalitarian benefits of education.

While education may express an individual's achievements, it also reflects a society's health and growth. That education is reflective of a society's prosperity also suggests that society should invest in the education of its citizens, and this is a more compelling suggestion to African countries. Cunningham (2006) states:

> Many studies underestimate the benefits of higher education because they do not include the social benefits. In fact, analysts estimate that the standard rate-

> of-return projections used to measure the benefits of increased learning may capture only three-fifths of the full value of education. Even if some portion of the societal benefits can be attributed to characteristics of the people who tend to enroll in postsecondary institutions in the first place, higher education produces impacts beyond those that would be predicted. (1)

Parents with higher education are more likely to provide a better livelihood for their children, as well as a better education for their children. While some social programs such as health insurance and retirement benefit unemployment compensation, food programs have not been introduced in many African countries. Cunningham (2006), notes that in the United States, persons with higher education are more likely to have jobs that provide health insurance and retirement benefits, and less likely to rely on government for unemployment compensation, food programs, and other social programs. Further, the higher educated one gets, the lower the incarceration rates relative to those whose highest level of education is high school.

The challenges facing most African countries that stall proper and adequate education for women are: insufficient funding toward education and the less enthusiasm and regard for female education. In the case of inadequate funding, there appears to be discord with regard to management. Which sector of government federal, state, or local, has jurisdiction to direct education is at times not obvious. Take Nigeria, for example: Madori (2013) reports that each sector of government has partial control of primary education, a situation that makes it difficult to have a robust and efficacious primary educational system. The central problem is that there is no sector in definite control thus making it less tenable for funding and management. Compounding the problem is the fact that the national budget allocated for education is below that recommended globally. The global recommendation of a country's GPD according to Actionaid is 6 percent, but Nigeria allocates approximately 1.5 percent (statement by Mr. Archer of Actionaid in plight of missing Nigerian schoolgirls . . . in independent.co.uk 2014).

Foreign aid to Liberia has been consistent over the years. Since 2010 the amounts have significantly increased with development aid at times exceeding $765 million (The Spectator 2014). However, in 2013 all 25,000 students who applied for admissions into the University of Liberia failed the entrance examination (The Spectator 2014). As the Spectator (2014) pithily surmised "All of the aid is still failing to provide a decent education to Liberians." Liberia has experienced its own share of political instability; that aside, it is clear that all the aid money poured to the country has not provided a promising change of course to the country.

In Cameroon, two main problems are reported as challenges to the educational system. They are poor management of the educational system and absence of accountability of funds and other resources allocated toward education (siteresources.worldbank.org 2013). Budget allocation among the ten regions of the country, and even within each region also account for disparities in educational opportunities for students. The central government is responsible for budget allocation, and as siteresources.worlbank.org, 2013, reports, the central government transfers allocated funds to lower levels of government including the divisions and inspectorates, but then fails to channel such funds through the level directly next to it which is the regional government. As a consequence of a vital sector of government being omitted in the link, accountability with regard to the use of funds is compromised. "Financial management and accounting is very weak across the divisions and control missions from the central government are too infrequent to adequately monitor budget and expenditure accounts" (siteresources.worldbank.org 2013). Other problems envisaged in this include the fact that funds from the central government to schools are not on a needs base, and do not reflect budget proposals nor population size. Budget proposals themselves sometimes do not reflect needs; costs of programs and projects are inflated, and it is not uncommon to have shady deals between government officials and contractors that provide services of some kind to schools.

Research reveals that school enrollments in the Northwest and Littoral provinces of the country are significantly higher than in the Far North region, and this is the case regardless of the financial standing of the parents of children in both the Northwest and Littoral regions; but in the Far North region, attending primary and secondary school at times depends on the viability of the family. Siteresources.worldbank.org, 2013, reports that about 250,000 children of primary school ages are either not enrolled in school, or have dropped out. Children in urban areas and from affluent families are more likely to attend school, while those in rural areas and from poor homes are five times less likely to enroll in school. To compound the problem, completion rates in primary schools for girls in the Far North region is 36 percent, while in the Littoral region it is 88 percent.

Further, retention of qualified teachers poses enormous problems. Limited budgets for schools also impacts the salaries of teachers, as well as teaching tools such as computers and internet services. There are far too many students for the few teachers. Disgruntlement and frustration lead some to change careers, and many to not venture into the profession. In Cameroon for instance, siteresources.worldbank.org, 2013 notes that funds allocations do not take in to consideration numbers as they relate to ratios of students and teachers. As well, funds are allocated for new schools in areas where it is not practical to have new schools either because of demographics or because the area is unsafe for a school. Salaries for teachers are unattractive, student teacher ratios are outrageously high, and interventions from parents by way of financial contributions and hiring of teachers have not been the needed panacea. Parent Teachers Association hires more teachers for secondary schools in the Far North region than the government does, and this is at their own expense (see siteresources.worldbank.org). Nationally, as this organization reveals, the ratio of pupil to teacher was 52 to 1 in 2010, but in the Far North region, it was 72 to 1, and that included teachers paid by parents. Without teachers hired and paid by parents, the pupil teacher ratio skyrocketed to 104 to 1 in the Far North region, as opposed to 41 to 1 in the Littoral region.

Getting schools to account for funds and services is almost impossible since there is no standard for data collection and inspections are quite sporadic. Scarcity of personnel, means of transportation to rural areas is difficult, and that makes inspections quite infrequent.

In South Africa, reports indicate that there is a shortage of teachers, especially qualified ones, as well as a shortage of resources and infrastructure (Cepd.org.za 2009). On the part of government, weaknesses stem from poor inspections of schools and of curricula. Further, South Africa also experiences structural issues as those experienced in Nigeria and Cameroon as they relate to education. Cepd.org.za (2009) reports that policies that apply to education are enacted at the national level without consultation or in concert with the provincial levels, yet the provincial levels are required to comply. The report indicates that those policies are not adhered to, and for the most part are considered to be "irrelevant." A 2014 book on the educational system in South Africa pretty much portrays an on-going problem (Legotlo 2014). The book discusses the sub-standard learning conditions, especially lack of books and other resources necessary to facilitate education, as well as poor infrastructure, meager salaries for teachers, unqualified teachers, lack of motivation on the part of teachers in part because of low salaries, and other unfavorable teaching conditions.

It is easy to tell that the educational system in much of Africa is in shambles, and any attempts for improvement have been hollow. Reasons for the suffusion of subpar educational systems in Africa are connected with the absence of robust governments that pay attention to education. A female student in Liberia is reported to have made the following comments:

> At school, I have problem with how our teachers' salaries are not paid on time. Whenever their salaries are delayed, they stay away from classes; sometimes for months or weeks until they are paid. As a result of this, I have to remain at home until the teachers are paid and ready to come back to teach us. (Plan International.Org 2012, 35)

Senegal reports similar problems. Clasby (2013) observes that enrollment in primary schools in Senegal is low, drop-out rates of students is high, teacher quality is below standard, and funding for educational programs and teacher salaries are below acceptable standards especially when compared to Mali, Benin, Ghana, Gambia, and Guinea (Clasby 2013).

Female teachers, particularly in secondary schools are few, and as Plan International. Org (2012) asserts:

> There is widespread evidence of the positive influence that female teachers can have on girls' enrollment, retention and learning outcomes. Well trained, supported and motivated female teachers can act as effective professional role models for girls, offering an alternative to the traditional roles of women in the community. The presence of female teachers in schools can also help to create a more 'girl friendly' learning environment in which girls' needs and perspectives are more likely to be understood and addressed. (35–36)

It is reported that across the continent, at the primary school level, 43 percent of teachers are female while at the secondary school level the percentage drops to 29 percent. These numbers dwindle even further in some countries like Togo with just 7 percent, and a dismal 4 percent in Liberia. Security concerns and commuting difficulties are explained as some other reasons why there is paucity in the numbers of female teachers particularly in some communities. That female teachers and women in general can play a vital role in the educational and public sectors is being giving close recognition by the Kenyan government which has legislated that at least 30 percent of women be given leadership roles in these sectors. The presence of female teachers in schools mitigates the stereotypical notion that boys are smarter than girls and as such more premiums should be placed on boys' education. Having female teachers also allows for different perspectives on issues, and opens up school curricula. As Plan International.Org informs, The Forum for African Women Educationalists' (FAWE) Gender Responsive Pedagogy has developed models on gender sensitivity training, so as to make school experience likeable by all students.

Further impediments to the educational system in most African countries are the absence of technology, and technological gadgets in classrooms and libraries. Many students have not touched a computer, or even done any type of research via the internet. Most schools do not have any computers at all or if they do, they are very few making it impossible for students to have any access to it. Even when there are computers, internet services are unavailable. In Cameroon for instance, recent visits to the country in 2013, and 2014, revealed to this researcher the difficulties students have in gaining access to internet services and this is true of the public in general. Electrical power appears to be rationed without warning, there is blackout at different parts of the city, and this could be for days. The city of Kumba is notorious for blackouts, and this issue obtains even in Yaoundé, the capital of the country. Reports of this nature are also common in other countries including Nigeria. It appears that many African countries are unprepared to cope with the rapid surge in population, environmental changes such as global warming, scientific and technological advancements, and all advancements associated with globalization.

The aforementioned problems impact the education of both boys and girls, but then other issues disproportionately impede female education. Of particular relevance is the limited value placed on female education. Girls in many parts of Africa are still commoditized, and are pushed off for early marriages in order to relieve parents from financial constraints in raising the girls and paying for their tuition in school. Such early marriages also bring in dowries that can be used to sponsor their brothers in school, as well as help their parents pay off debts, or just get a break from their thwarted financial circumstances. These points were also brought up during a focus group interview of women in Cameroon. When asked by this researcher why women were relatively poorer than men, a woman in her thirties explained that one of the reasons was because some families prefer to send boys to schools than girls because girls are expected to go off and marry to generate dowry for the family, and to shift the burden of raising the girl to the husband. Many other women in the group concurred, and one added that since many families rely on sales of crops especially cocoa, if the yield is not much, then they would rather send boys to school than girls. A woman in her forties explained that because of parental neglect girls as young as 12 years old get involved with men to get things that their friends have, and in the process get pregnant. That completely frustrates any prospects of an education. A professional woman in her sixties who had worked in community development explained that because of family hardships, some parents force their daughters to get married early because they become a source of income. She further explained that customary practices require girls to help take care of their parents and the home. Saddled with too many responsibilities, girls drop out of school.

Lambert et al. (2012) explain that in the predominantly Islamic northern parts of Ghana, female education is not valued much. In these areas women are seen as second-class citizens if not subservient. Compounding on this is the prevalence of HIV/AIDS, early marriages, and teenage pregnancies. With arranged marriages so prevalent from when the girl is still an infant, it is inevitable that the girl will get married young, and start having children thereby foregoing an education. Further, with use of contraceptives so sparing in the country, 20 percent as Lambert et al. (2012) state drawing from UNICEF data, and AIDS education not prevalent, many girls get pregnant and some infected with HIV, thereby stalling prospects for education. With sexual harassment as another impediment in schools, girls are leery to go to school especially since they cannot confront their teachers or any others involved in the harassment. Of all the impediments listed by Lambert et al. as reasons why girls' attendance in schools in Ghana is low, poverty is the key factor. Following their study just about all students claimed that some financial impediment precluded them from getting an education. The study comprised 195 primary school children, 128 being girls, and 130 junior high school students, 69 of them females. Eighty four percent (85.4 percent) of junior high school students indicated that inability to afford school supplies including uniforms was a huge problem for them. Moreover, 25 percent of the 325 students indicated that they frequently went to school with empty stomachs. Even though education is free at these levels in Ghana, families are responsible for providing school supplies, uniforms, and transportation money, and these for many families is still burdensome. Students confirmed that prevailing attitudes of some parents made it difficult for them to be enrolled in school, or to stay enrolled in school. Of the 130 junior high school students, 39.2 percent revealed that as a matter of practicality their parents would rather they work and earn money than go to school; while 16.9 percent of the students indicated that their parents' preference was for them to stay at home and take care of their younger siblings or the parents.

Even with efforts to make education free and mandatory up until junior high school, Lambert et al. report that in some parts of Ghana this opportunity is not utilized. There are approximately 120,000 children of school age in the Abura-Asebu-Kwamankesie region of Ghana, but only 30,000 attend school. The rest of the children either stay at home as care givers, or become street vendors, or vagrants. This problem is even worse as the children get to high school. Dropout levels increase because students have to pay tuition, purchase supplies and uniforms, and for the most part pay for room and board since many of the high schools are away from home. Even though the aggregate amount of these expenses was the approximation of $1,027 per academic year in 2012, the average Ghanaian as Lambert et al. (2012) report makes significantly less than that amount a year. It thus explains why several children are not enrolled in school. Scholarships that are awarded to deserving students do not offset the financial need that most of them have.

Plan International.Org (2012) explains that children especially girls in Africa who are enrolled in Early Childhood Care and Education (ECCE) programs are more likely to continue on to primary school and to stay in school because of the preparation and lessons they learn from those programs. Despite the benefits of these programs which have led to increased enrollments of primary school-aged children to schools in Sub-Sahara Africa in the last decade, Plan International.Org explains that the enrollment level is the lowest globally at 17 percent. President Sirleaf of Liberia also made this point. In a 2014 interview by Cable News Network, U.S.A. (CNN), President Sirleaf indicated, "the highest rate of girls not in school is across the African continent" (Sirleaf 2014). Poverty and the limited number of ECCE programs account for this statistics.

The Millennium Development Goals (MDGs) set by the United Nations is intended to foster gender equality in part by emphasizing the education of girls. The intent is to ensure that both boys and girls complete primary and secondary school education in order to ensure parity by 2005, with further plans of ensuring higher education for both genders by 2015. Plan International.Org explains that even though many countries in Africa no longer require students in primary schools to pay tuition, meeting the objectives of the MDGs in 2015 is unlikely. President Sirleaf expressed similar concerns, as she stated that as of 2014 just a year before the deadline of the MDGs, 30 million girls in Africa were still unable to attain basic education. Admittedly, there has been a rise in primary school enrollments in Sub-Saharan Africa with 42 million enrollments from 1999–2007, reflecting an enrollment hike of girls from 53 percent to 71 percent (One.Org 2010). Muabu and Ackerman (2013) place percentage increase of primary school enrollments within the last decade from 59 percent to 77 percent in sub-Sahara Africa. Results on the 2015 MDGs had not been published as of June 2016.

Some countries like Ethiopia have seen a remarkable increase in primary school enrollments from 30 percent to 75 percent within ten years; on the contrary, Niger and Eritrea have witnessed enrollments that have leveled and remained below 60 percent (PlanInternational.Org 2012). Regardless of what data reveal on aggregate levels, local realities show that "factors of poverty, location, ethnicity, disability, and social and political unrest combine with gender discrimination to make education a remote possibility for many girls. Unless these intersecting issues are identified and tackled directly, further progress will not be possible" (PlanInternational.org 2012, 21).

As PlanInternational.org (2012) explains, 7 out of 10 children will enroll in primary school in Sub-Saharan Africa, and of that number 59 percent of girls in Ethiopia and 57 percent in Liberia are likely to drop out. As a result of free education in primary schools, several students enroll, but then this surge comes with unpreparedness of schools. Classrooms are jam-packed; there are insufficient teachers, and even when there are teachers, at times many of them lack the requisite qualifications to teach. These factors and the constant demands of families to have their female children attend to home and family issues make continued school enrollment untenable.

With regard to secondary education, it is noted by PlanInternational.Org (2012) that 62 percent of girls transition from primary to secondary school in Sub Saharan Africa, but transitional rates vary among countries. Some countries like Tanzania have just a 32 percent transitional rate. While countries like Uganda have made education free even at secondary school level, most countries have not done that. Without free access to secondary education, less than one quarter of girls enroll in school in Sub-Saharan Africa, and enrollment levels tank in countries undergoing conflicts. In times of conflict, those less likely to enroll in school are girls. While there is no comprehensive data on completion rates for girls in secondary school in the various countries in Sub-Saharan Africa, the few countries that have data portray a grim picture: 3 percent in Niger, 17 percent in Malawi, 25 percent in Ethiopia, 29 percent in Uganda.

It is worthy of note that the age at which girls transition from primary to secondary school coincides with the age of puberty 12–17. This provides a myriad of problems; they are old enough to take care of younger siblings and parents, and they are at the age when they could be forced to marry early so as to generate money for their families. Their chances of furthering their educational pursuits is thereby rendered slim.

Achieving high enrollments for students is one thing; giving them quality education is another issue. As a consequence of free public education in primary schools, resources have been exhausted, and staffing has been sub-par. The result has been a decline in the quality of education, and this is evident from what students who eventually drop out learned, and from grades of those who stayed enrolled in school. As PlanInternational.Org (2012) reveals 20 percent of students who leave primary school cannot read a sentence, and in Uganda the rate exceeds 25 percent. In Mali, as the organization states, 90 percent of second grade students cannot read a "word of connected text." It is reported that inferior quality of education takes a bigger toll on girls than on boys. This is evident by national examinations results. The following support this assertion: In Kenya only 29 percent of girls and 50 percent of boys passed the national primary school leaving examination. In Rwanda, only 38 percent of girls passed the exam, and in Tanzania, 43 percent of girls passed as opposed to 56 percent of boys. Certainly, the blame cannot be placed on the school per se, other issues factor in. If girls have to spend much of their time nurturing siblings and attending to parents, it leaves little room for them to study. The consequence of failing exams means either dropping out or enrolling in that class all over. For many destitute families, the choice is clear—drop out and help take care of the family. This is demonstrative of the need to intervene in children's education in Africa, and that of girls in particular. Be that as it may, any investments to improve the quality of education will almost be tantamount to putting a golden ring on a pig's nose if the predicate causes of why girls lag in school are not addressed.

Abdourahman (2010) explains that because of limited education and job opportunities experienced by Sub-Saharan Africans in the years 1960–1992, per capita growth for women dropped by 0.8 percent. The opposite effect could have been realized if both genders were equally educated and occupied in jobs that promote economic growth. The 0.8 percent drop would have resulted in a 0.8 percent spike in growth in 30 years. As Abdourahman (2010) suggests, the 15–20 percent growth difference between Africa and East Asia can be explained by gender inequality. Abdourahman concludes that one top reason for Africa's lag in growth may be blamed on the vast disparity in educational and employment level. He goes on to explain that customary practices of having girls drop out of school to help with family chores and maintenance expose gender disparities in education and employment and thus account for limited economic growth in many Sub-Saharan African countries (Ellis et al. 2006).

PlanInternational.org (2012) has tried to figure out why girls lag in education in Africa. The organization concludes that:

> Constraints of poverty, location, gender stereotypes, social norms, customs and harmful practices all form a shifting and interconnected web through which girls, their families and their communities have to navigate on a daily basis. In particular, students, teachers and parents highlighted the way in which poverty lies at the heart of many of the challenges that hinder girls' access to, and experience of, education. The pressures of poverty mean that parents must constantly make decisions about how to utilize extremely limited resources and how best to provide a secure future for their family. In the context of the range of factors explored below, the choices made often mean that girls' opportunities and life chances are severely constrained. (25)

A survey of parents reveals that parents still prefer their sons to be educated over girls. In Mali for instance, 48 percent of parents stated that they would rather have their sons stay in school than daughters, and if compelled to make a choice, only 28 percent of the parents elected to have their daughters stay in school. This statistic spiked in the Ashanti district of Ghana where 50 percent of parents in the survey voted to have their sons in school as opposed to 10 percent in favor of that choice. When such surveys are made, parents look more at the immediate usefulness of girls than in the future utilitarian values of their daughters. Auxiliary factors such as traditional roles of girls as caregivers, and patriarchic views of girls play heavily on whether parents will have their daughters enroll and stay in school. Parents in Ethiopia, Kenya, Senegal, and Mali revealed that men who were not as educated as girls were less likely to marry educated girls. Parents were conflicted about the value of education for girls since they eventually marry and start a life with some man, but boys always retain the family genealogy and thus remain heads of family. What is more telling is how girls viewed themselves. In Mali as reported, girls conceded that boys were more apt to succeed because they were smarter than girls (see PlanInternational.org 2012). The combination of parents' reluctance to send their daughters to school and the girls' self-doubt about their intellectual capabilities at times bears on decisions if the girl will enroll in school, and if she will stay on to graduate. A father in Uganda made a very poignant statement—"My preference goes to boys, because there is no benefit of sending girls to school. Most of them did not succeed. They did not go beyond primary grade 4. This is a waste of time and money for us" (PlanInternational.org 2012, 27).

The cost has been marked as the biggest impediment to a vast number of children obtaining an education. Article 11 of The African Charter on the

Rights and Welfare of the Child holds that "States . . . shall in particular (a) provide free and compulsory basic education; (b) encourage the development of secondary education . . . to progressively make it free and accessible to all." PlanInternational.org (2012) explains that even though many countries respect the Charter in that they are make education free in the primary school level, schools still have hidden costs which require a huge chunk of money out of parents' pockets. Such costs include: registration fees, examination fees, uniforms, books, transportation, supplies, and many others. According to PlanInternational.org (2012), a survey of parents in Liberia showed that 58 percent of them pinpointed costs of education as the main reason for not sending their children to school. Not surprisingly, 36 percent of parents and 38 percent of children explained that school fees and costs of uniforms were indeed reasons for low enrollments in schools. In Guinea-Bissau, costs of education have been on the rise, with 89 percent of parents stating that fees for examinations, had vastly increased since 2007, and 87 percent of the parents pointed at rising costs of school supplies.

These financial burdens become worse when the child completes primary school and has to head on to secondary school. The odds of girls continuing with their education beyond the primary school level diminish for several reasons: cultural practices not to sponsor girls' education beyond that level, cost of secondary education, and girls being at "marriage age" (see archive.unu.edu).

Transactional sex is another issue that stalls girls' retention in schools. While numbers/data are not available, transactional sex is on the rise as this is the last chance for girls to get items that their families are not otherwise able to provide. This involves the exchange of sex for money or gifts; it is prostitution in essence. It is reported that even though a small fraction of boys engage in it, primarily it is a way by which girls ward off poverty. PlanInternational.org (2012) reports that 70 percent of Ugandan girls, and 33 percent of boys stated they had been involved in the exchange of sex for gifts transaction. In Mali 78 percent of girls and 64 percent of boys had been involved in transactional sex. Girls and boys who engage in transactional sex say they do it to get basic hygiene items like soap, and for food and clothes. Indeed, 91 percent of girls in Ghana and 74 percent of those in Liberia said they engaged in transactional sex to get just basic necessities, and it was not uncommon for some to cite goods of ostentation like cellular phones as reasons for engaging in such sexual activities (PlanInternational.org 2012; see also Archive.unu.edu). Further, 41 percent of children in Guinea Bissau, 50 percent in Senegal, and 24 percent in Uganda, cited need for tuition money and other school requirements as reasons to engage in transactional sex. While some girls find transactional sex as a way out of poverty, teachers and school administrators think differently. In Kenya and Malawi as teachers and administrators report, transactional sex is a distraction that negatively impacts girls' education. 47 percent of parents in Liberia attribute transactional sex to girls' drop out from schools. It is easy for some of the girls to justify why they had to engage in transactional sex. A girl in Ghana is reported to have said:

> Since nobody was taking care of me I received money and gifts from men; in order to please them I have to have sex with them. That is how I become pregnant in school … at first I wanted to abort the pregnancy but in the process I almost lost my life… with the man responsible he does not take care of me he only gives me money for my hospital bill. Because I am not schooling I feel very sad when I see my friends dressed in their uniforms, sometimes I cry. I dropped out of school due to the pregnancy and life is so unbearable. (PlanInternational.org 2012, 29)

Transactional sex comes with other problems, sexually transmitted diseases and unwanted pregnancies. Sexually transmitted diseases especially HIV is debilitating and saps energy that the girl could be channeling toward her studies. Besides this, the costs of seeking medical attention for HIV and for other sexually transmitted diseases are overwhelming. Coupling such expenses with those entailed in sending children to school most parents end up withdrawing their children from school.

Early pregnancies drastically limit a girl's chances of continuing with school. Many factors account for early pregnancies: child neglect, forced marriages, rapes, transactional sex, and lack of sex education. PlanInternational.org (2012) states that over 50 percent of girls get pregnant in Sub-Saharan Africa before they get to be 20 years old. Being pregnant inevitably results in school drop out for the vast majority of girls. In Uganda, 57 percent of students pointed at pregnancy as a primary cause of girls' drop-out; while in Liberia 61 percent of students stated that they knew at least a girl who had been pregnant, and of that number, very few had re-enrolled in school as 5 percent of the students reported. School policies that prohibit pregnant girls from enrolling in schools, forced marriages, cultural approval of early pregnancies, bullying from schoolmates are deterrents to a pregnant girl returning to school.

Even though Article 11 of the African Charter on the Rights and Welfare of the Child requires that "States . . . shall have all appropriate measures to ensure that children who become pregnant before completing their education shall have an opportunity to continue with their education on the basis of their individual ability," PlanInternational.org (2012) reports that schools seldom comply. Many of the pregnant girls are forced to marry their baby's father, and that at times is the case even when the girl was raped.

In many instances, the baby's father is a student, and at times, a teacher; that is why some parents are wary to send their daughters to school. According to PlanInternational.org (2012), 84 percent of parents in Ghana, and 91 percent in Uganda perceived pregnancy as a deterrent to girls' education. PlanInternational.org (2012) reports that 17 percent of teachers in Togo, 16 percent in Mali, and 15 percent in Uganda were responsible for the pregnancies of their students.

Attending school and excelling is frequently difficult for many students as they have to work at home, or for others, at times, tediously even at such tender ages. With girls burdened with home chores and care taking of young, elderly, or infirm family members, they are left with little time to concentrate on schoolwork. This is evident from testimonies of schoolgirls in Guinea-Bissau. Over 40 percent of school girls surveyed in that country revealed that they spent at least five hours working at home and that took time away from their studies, or even school attendance. Teachers confirmed this, and also agreed that such demands on girls' time were instrumental to them eventually dropping out from school (see PlanInternational.org 2012). For girls orphaned because of the scourge of AIDS, they have to work to sustain themselves and their siblings. Most drop out from school because taking on parental roles and attending school is too overwhelming. It is not unusual for girls to migrate to bigger cities or to destinations beyond country borders, or even out of the continent in search of jobs. Certainly, such moves end their educational aspirations, and with many finding themselves working in the sex industry, the possibility for exploitation increases, as well as exposure to sexually transmitted diseases including HIV.

The commute to school is also a severe hardship to students in Africa especially as most have to trek. This hardship in some way accounts for poor attendance, tardiness, and dropouts. Statistics by PlanInternational.org (2012) show that 22 percent of girls in Togo, 21 percent in Uganda, and 26 percent in Guinea-Bissau picked out distance to school as the vital reason for not going to school. Of more concern though are issues of safety and security. As discussed in the chapter on trafficking, Agnew (2005) explains how in South Africa, girls are kidnapped on their way to school by men who think that having sex with virgins will cure them of HIV. PlanInternational.Org also discusses how parents in Ethiopia terrified of their daughters being kidnapped en route to school prefer not to have the girls go to school at all. A way out of such worries is to have secondary school-aged students attend boarding schools, but that too comes at a cost that many parents cannot afford. Even having girls rent rooms close to campus generates issues of costs, as well as safety of the girls living alone. Building more schools as an option may only be feasible if there are sufficient numbers of students or potential students in a particular jurisdiction, and if government budget can be stretched that far. President Sirleaf of Liberia commented that in order to provide access to education for African children, and to improve the quality of education, more money needs to be directed toward such goal, and that can be done with sound decisions made with the help of reliable data (Sirleaf

2014). Sirleaf also indicated that 4 out of 5 girls in rural parts of Africa do not complete primary education, and that 30 million girls in Africa are thereby stripped of their human rights to an education (Sirleaf 2014). She noted "some countries lose more than $1 billion a year by failing to educate girls to the same level as boys" (Sirleaf 2014).

Violence in schools also plays a significant role in girls' education, and at times is a determining factor if girls will stay enrolled in school. Four types of violence are prevalent in schools: verbal abuse, sexual assault, physical abuse, and corporal punishment. Neither gender is immune from violence, but girls overwhelmingly are victims of sexual abuse. PlanInternational.Org reports that survey results in the Democratic Republic of Congo reveal that 46 percent of girls have experienced violence and sexual harassment at school. Eighty eight percent (88 percent) of teachers in Niger acknowledged the prevalence of teacher-student sexual relations. In Uganda as data from PlanInternational.Org reveals both boys and girls suffered severely from verbal and corporal abuse, with girls being verbally abused more than boys, while boys received more corporal punishment than girls. With regard to physical violence, boys were subjected to it slightly more than girls, while girls alone experienced sexual violence. Boys and teachers perpetrate sexual abuse in schools. Students in several countries including Mali, Ghana, Guinea-Bissau, Senegal, Liberia, and Uganda revealed to PlanInternational.org (2012) that it was not uncommon for teachers to coerce girls into sexual relations in exchange for passing grades. Such dealings have led students to coin the expression "*moyennes sexuellement transmissibles*" translated as "sexually transmitted grades." Even though violence, exploitation, and abuse of all types are prohibited, the absence of sound enforcement allows for the persistence of impunity.

In summary, several issues stand as roadblocks to education in Africa, especially that of females. They include poverty, cultural norms that denigrate female education, violence in schools, poor quality of teachers, lack of resources and equipment, transactional sex, and a host of other problems.

Chapter Four

The Impact of the Economy on Women

An anemic economy disproportionately affects women. Many African countries are chronically poor, the economy persistently remains stagnant, employment is constantly low, unemployment is high, and while earnings for both men and women drop, women are more impacted since they are usually paid lower than men. Influence over the economy is primarily that of men in most countries following the underrepresentation of women in economic decision- making. The economic impact on women is even more debilitating during economic upheavals. This has been proven true by the 2008 economic crisis dubbed the worst since the great depression of the 1930s (see UNAIDS.org 2012).

The fact that women earn less than men, are more likely to lose their jobs, are more likely to be discriminated against, has been documented (see UNAIDS.org 2012). According to UNAIDS.org (2012):

> Women globally have lower wages than men, with a 22 percent pay gap, and are often the first to lose their jobs. Women also face discrimination in education, with 96 girls for every 100 boys enrolled in primary school in developing regions in 2011. Lower levels of education mean that women are more likely than men to be involved in lower-paying jobs or low-skilled labour and are therefore more susceptible to financial crises. Since women are often responsible for the unpaid care of children and sick family members, their choices of what paid work they are able to take on and their bargaining power within these paid positions are often compromised. The International Labour Organization reports that across sub-Saharan Africa, the female working poverty rate exceeds 22 of 27 countries based on the available data. (3)

Reports also indicate that girls in countries that have low school registration and attendance records, as well as high child mortality rates are of greater risk of having their education cut short in response to unfavorable economic and political climate. Girls in the following countries are deemed to be most vulnerable: Democratic Republic of the Congo, Ethiopia, Mozambique, Nigeria, United Republic of Tanzania, Zambia, Burkina Faso, Chad, Gambia, Ghana, Kenya, Mali, Niger, Sierra Leone, Sudan, and Togo.

Many studies have shown that there is an indisputable link between knowledge and the promotion of economic growth and better standard of living (Barro 2001; Riddell 2004). Riddell puts in perspective the relevance of the "new growth theory" a theory that highlights the role of knowledge in fostering robust standards of living over time. According to the theory, even when growth is not rapid, as long as it is steady, even those with middling circumstances will experience significant changes in their lifestyle. Of significance to the new growth theory is the assumption that public policy can influence the creation of knowledge and economic incentives. The drift here is that creative ideas promoted by universities can help bolster the economy. Focus should thus be placed in understanding and promoting dynamics responsible for long-term growth. In advancing the importance of long-term growth to the economy Lipsey (1996) makes the following pronouncement:

> All the other concerns of economic policy—full employment, efficiency in resource use, and income redistribution—pale into significance when set against growth. . . . All citizens, both rich and poor, are massively better off materially than were their ancestors of a hundred years ago who were in the same relative position in the same income scale. That improvement has come to pass not because unemployment or economic efficiency or income distribution is massively different from what it was a century ago but because economic growth has increased the average national incomes of the industrialized countries about tenfold over the period. (4)

Projections of The World Bank (2013) were that the Gross Domestic Product (GDP) of Sub-Saharan Africa will increase to 4.9 percent in 2013, and that number will rise to 2014 and to 5.5 in 2015. An increase of domestic demand and higher productions in sectors like mining, agriculture, and service will remain evident as the Bank projects. While war torn areas like Sudan have not seen growth in the economy, other countries like Niger and Sierra Leone have prospered since 2012 according to the World Bank. Other countries that have seen a reasonable spike in growth for over ten years as the World Bank reports are Ethiopia, Mozambique, and Rwanda. South Africa has not fared well because its trading partners in Europe have also experienced a sluggish economy.

Overall, poverty is still profound and pervasive in Africa, and this is the case even though many African countries are endowed with bountiful human and natural resources. Time poverty, crude and inefficient methods of tapping resources stagnate fiscal and developmental growth. Even though many governments have increased investments toward infrastructure (see Ghana,

Nigeria, Niger, Ethiopia, Tanzania, South Africa, and Zambia) including deals in international markets that net millions to billions of dollars to those countries, the overall gross debt-to-GDP ratio is on the rise. In 2008, the debt-to-GDP ratio was 29 percent, but this increased in 2012 to 33 percent (see Worldbank.org 2013). The World Bank also notes that some African countries like Cape Verde and Eritrea have debt-to-GDP ratios higher than 83 percent.

Even though production of commodities is at a rise, prices are on a decline. In 2013, the World Bank reported that index prices of agricultural goods, metals and minerals, and oil declined by 9.0 percent, 8.8 percent, and 5.6 percent, respectively. This tank in prices certainly affected the economies of sub-Saharan countries, particularly those that rely heavily on these exports. Even with the reported resurgent demand of oil and continuous demand for it, and the ascent of revenues from a 4.9 percent close in 2013 to a hike of 5.3 percent in 2014, and to 5.5 percent in 2015, the economy of sub-

Table 4.1. IMF Numbers of Government Debt in Selected African Countries

Government (G'mt) % debt as of GDP

Increase in debt between 2012–2014

	Total Gross G'mt debt as % GDP	Net G'mt debt as % of GDP
Cape Verde	112.199	107.691
The Gambia	77.179	77.179
Sao Tome & Principe	75.503	
Ghana	56.526	53.125
Malawi	54.903	51.15
Mauritius	50.29	50.29
Kenya	48.185	43.167
Mozambique	46.628	
Senegal	45.002	
Sierra Leone	44.471	0
South Africa	42.282	35.561
Tanzania	41.391	
Madagascar	38.309	
Uganda	34.532	
Chad	24.983	

*Source: Government gross and net debt 2014. See IMF.org. International Monetary Fund (IMF) World Economic Outlook Database (WEOD), April 2015.

Saharan countries as well as that globally remains frail (Worldbank.org 2013).

United Nations World Tourism Organization (UNWTO) (see Worldbank.org 2013), states that there has been noticeable growth in tourism in countries like Cape Verde, Kenya, Mauritius, Seychelles, and Rwanda. This growth however is not sufficient to offset the deprivations suffered by much of the population. While tourism plays an integral part in the economies of these countries, it is not sufficient to offset the needs of the people. Many Sub-Saharan countries are dependent on food commodities not only for subsistence but for import as well. Unfortunately, projections from the World Bank are not promising. Prices for maize, sorghum, rice, and wheat as the World Bank reports declined in 2013, with sporadic increases in May and June of that year, but then the decline remained evident thereafter.

Low prices of food commodities notwithstanding, many African countries continuously base their economies on producing and exporting raw materials. Either through lack of know-how or through the absence of initiative to turn unfinished products into finished products, many of these countries run into financial problems because market prices for raw materials fall, or because of over production of raw materials. As well, advanced technology in developed countries make these materials obsolete. Reliance on just raw materials or specific products without diversification has not served many African countries well (see what happened in Libya, Gabon, Uganda, and the Democratic Republic of Congo/Zaire). Libya, for instance, witnessed a tank in its GDP in the 1980s when dependence on oil sales became unsustainable due to global oil recession and sanctions imposed on the country. Gabon experienced a crisis in its economy when reliance was placed primarily on oil exports in the 1980s, and oil prices dropped. Kentor (2001) bluntly notes that Africa's way out of economic slumber is through a revitalized economy, sound domestic investments, which promote social programs like health care, improved infrastructure, and other programs that enhance the well-being of the masses. The problem is that in order to diversify production or to introduce advanced technology to assist in producing materials, many African countries rely on foreign assistance either by way of aid or loan. For the most part, the money is obtained by way of loans—loans that become an albatross, a further hindrance to accomplishing anything else. George (1990) explains that debt is convenient since the lender has immediate access to the debtor's raw material and infrastructure, and other assets at significantly less than the actual cost. Further, since many similarly impoverished countries must compete in the same market, such saturation diminishes incomes of borrowers while fattening the coffers of the lenders. George further suggests that to be of any help to developing countries, the IMF must understand that for a country to bolster its economy, the right path to take is to invest in the health and education of its people.

Even with intermittent growth of the economy of Africa, poverty remains entrenched. Indeed, the World Bank (Worldbank.org 2013) states "poverty in Africa remains unacceptably high, and the pace of reduction unacceptably slow." The World Bank projects that even with optimistic projections, the poorest people in the world in 2030 will be living somewhere in Africa. This is likely to be the case especially since there is an anticipated spike in the population in Sub-Sahara Africa of about half a billion people by 2030, with further projections of a total of more than two billion people by 2050 (Worldbank.org 2013). In order to offset poverty in this region, the World Bank suggests that it will require:

1. Resilience to external shocks
2. Improvements in agricultural productivity
3. Productive nonagricultural jobs in both rural and urban areas, and
4. Better safety net programs, particularly in countries benefiting from large economic rents from natural resources (Worldbank.org 2013).

Besides backlash in prices of food commodities, there was a corresponding drop in oil prices. This caused "a budget deficit of -7 percent of GDP in 2009 against a surplus of +7 percent of GDP in 2008 and 3.8 percent of GDP in 2007" (ACON Chief Economist's Office 2009, iii). Asifatu (2012) also explains that insufficient investment in social welfare services and education has resulted in increased child mortality and degradation in natural resources, and an overall stagnation in economic development.

Political instability, graft, and ineffective private sectors all add to the economic decline of Africa. As noted by Winnie Byanyima, a blogger for Allafrica.com, Africa experiences more losses from unlawful, covert outflows than what it derives from aid and investments. This is a result of corrupt officials acting in connivance with heads of mining and oil companies that engage in tax evasions and other corrupt practices (Allafrica.com 2013). Byanyima goes on to explain that the natural resources of Africa have the promise of lifting millions of Africans from their impoverished state, but clandestine capital flows and income disparities are robbing Africans of this promise. For decades, Susan George, an economist, has been writing about debts of third world countries. She explains how a small fraction of the population—elites in third world countries—plunder their countries by way of loans deceptively intended to improve their countries' economies. Not to be absolved from the plight of these countries are creditors of such loans. George (1992; 1993) explains how either purposefully or recklessly, creditors make debtors enthralled to their interests. Whether the debts are repaid or cancelled, George contends that creditors make huge profits regardless.

While Cameroon has been the archetype of graft (see Transparency International 2003; 2006; Corruption Surveys and Indexes), other African countries including Nigeria have received that notorious honor too. Ayodele et al. (2005) express with exasperation the abysmal failure of aid programs to Africa. According to Ayodele et al., between 1960 to 1997, Africa received more than $500 billion in foreign aid, yet there has hardly been anything to show for as development; instead, a culture of dependency on aid has been created, and the authors cited the budgets of Ghana and Uganda as exceeding 50 percent of aid dependence. Citing Percy Mistry of the Oxford International Group, Ayodele et al. reveal that stocks held by Africans in foreign countries may range from $700 to $800 billion. Further, they contend that Nigeria's military dictators embezzled about $500 billion in 2005 alone, an amount that exceeds aid given to Africa over a span of 40 years. While a tiny amount of the stolen money was recovered ($983 million), it does nothing to solve the country's malady—poverty.

Apparently, Africans themselves are aware of the fiasco of foreign aid. It is reported that a former Kenyan parliamentarian stated:

> Foreign aid has done more harm to Africa than we care to admit. It has led to a situation where Africa has failed to set its own pace and direction of development free of external interference. Today, Africa's development plans are drawn thousands of miles away in the corridors of the IMF and World Bank experts who draw these development plans are people completely out of touch with the local African reality. (Ayodele et al. 2005)

Aid from western countries or from the World Bank or the International Monetary Fund for the most part comes by way of loans. These loans, as is reported, are crafted in ways that borrowers cannot make sufficient money to repay, and to a large extent agents of the recipient country misappropriate them. Borrowers thus find it extremely difficult to repay, and at times, interests that accrue become too burdensome, and year after year, all the borrower is able to pay is the interest. Debts owed to the World Bank and to the International Monetary Fund are earmarked to be the most difficult to avoid repayments, yet on occasion, these institutions do forgive these loans. In 2006, for example, The World Bank did forgive Cameroon's debt (BBC.news 2007). How these funds were used has not been evident. Inability to repay the loan suggests that either the loan was used for investments that yielded no profits, or the money was not invested at all. Giving that Cameroon is notorious for mismanagement of funds, the latter explanation seems more plausible (BBC News/Africa/Cameroon corruption hinders AIDS fight (2007).

A culture of dependency on these institutions seems to permeate many African countries especially since these countries have to compete with one another to produce similar crops and commodities. A price war is thus generated, and this is how prices of commodities get compromised, thus giving lenders the upper hand in the market.

How helpful foreign aid has been to developing countries that rely on it has been discussed in some detail. Sachs and Collins (1989) expressed dismay with the economic utility of such aid because the returns from the loan are overshadowed by the interest rates. Clearly, foreign aid does not appear to be the relief from poverty in Africa. John Rwangombwa, governor of the Central Bank of Rwanda, not long ago opined that as a developmental plan for the long run foreign aid is not "sustainable" (BBC News 2013). Arnold (2001) foreshadowed the discussion of the viability of foreign aid to Africa. He explains:

> Two of the unfortunate consequences of these aid flows to Africa have been first, the creation of huge debts that can never be repaid but whose servicing cripples the recipient economies; and second, possibly even worse than the legacy of debt, the parallel creation of aid dependence on the part of the recipients, an expectation that aid will always be forthcoming, that the world owes Africa permanent economic assistance. (Arnold 2001, 121)

The stern and gloomy comments aside, it is not the aid that appears to be the problem; instead, it seems as though those who handle the aid/loan money are the problem. Goldsmith (2001), for instance, puts the issue in perspective. He explains that issues on this topic dwell on the following premises: foreign aid has adversely impacted Africa, and foreign aid has created a condition of dependence. In both areas, he fails to see a positive association. Brautigam and Knack (2004) explain the impact of aid funds, and then proceed to examine the impact of aid funds to Africa. First, they begin by defining what aid dependence is because it has been defined differently by scholars of the subject, and seems to be discussed in different ways. They define it as: "a situation in which a government is unable to perform many of the core functions of government, such as the maintenance of existing infrastructure or the delivery of basic public services, without foreign aid and funding and expertise (provided in the form of technical assistance or projects" (Brautigam and Knack 2004, 257).

Brautigam and Knack (2004) discuss a number of possibilities for Africa's dependence on aid, and why aid money hardly serves its functions. Among several factors they list, corruption is the main factor, then collateral problems such as "inadequate official information, weak mechanisms of accountability, poorly enforced rule of law, and bureaucracies that are ineffective and unresponsive" (259).

Liberated from colonial rule, African countries apparently were not ready for self-governance; as a result, a system of corrupt inefficient governance emerged in many of the independent nations. Ethnic divides, limited education—giving that the colonialists had established very few higher education institutions throughout Sub-Saharan Africa, war and political unrest all took a toll on the continent's ability to thrive; and that continues to be the case today in many parts of Africa. These factors cannot be divorced from poor governance and economic decline. Brautigam and Knack (2004) cite South Korea, Taiwan, and Botswana among the few countries that had clear understanding and objectives for foreign loans. Without proper objectives and set programs to which the loans will be applied and without mechanisms for monitoring, the potential for mismanagement is elevated. Good governance requires learning effective management skills, training relevant workers and supervisors of projects for which funds/loans are allocated. Given that studies (Arnold 2001; Ayodele 2005; Brautigam and Knack 2004) show that aid/loans if accounted for and applied well could lead to visible improvements, but if misused (as is so often the case in many African countries), and dependence is persistent these loans overtime can "weaken institutions."

Brautigam and Knack (2004) conclude:

1. There is a robust statistical relationship between high aid levels in Africa and deteriorations in governance, particularly when we correct for the tendency of donors to give more aid to African countries with improving, rather than deteriorating, governance;
2. There is a similarly strong relationship between higher aid levels and a lower tax share of GDP; and
3. Increases in GDP per capita tend to be associated with improvements in governance, while political violence is associated with declines in governance and in the tax share of GDP. Yet when we control for per capita GDP and violence, aid still has an independent, and negative, effect (276).

While a weak economy affects everyone, women are disproportionately affected in that they themselves are directly hit, and then as those who keep the household together, that extra burden weighs heavily on them. In times of economic upheaval, there is a lot of downsizing and women are more likely to be laid off before men. World Savvy (2009) outlined the following consequences of the economic crisis on women:

- With decreased demand for goods and services worldwide, unemployment is expected to hit men and women alike. Yet *women make up the majority of the flexible workforce* (relatively unskilled, hourly), and these jobs are usually the first to go.
- While men employed in traditionally male sectors (transport, communications, and mining) have been hit hard by job cuts in the early months of the recession, experts predict the next wave of cuts will likely come in the public sector, dominated by women.
- As tax revenues decline and governments fall on hard times, budget-cutting will affect fields like education, health care, and other public ser-

vices, creating a gap in societies that women will then likely fill through unpaid work. This will affect women in rich and poor countries alike.
- In many developing countries, *remittances* from migrant workers living abroad sustain entire families left behind. As workers all over the world lose jobs, remittances may dry up and plunge whole communities into extreme poverty. This will affect women as the primary providers and caretakers in families.

These points suggest that women like men suffer from a sluggish economy, if not more. During times of economic upheaval particularly in Africa, girls are likely to be withdrawn from school, families are likely to cut back on food rations, they are likely to bypass health care, and cut back on medical supplies and medications, and girls are more likely to resort to prostitution to help with family sustenance. In essence, a stride forward for women is so easily brought back due to an economic crisis.

UNAIDS.org (2012) points out that worldwide, there is a 22 percent pay difference between men and women, women frequently earn lower than men even in similar positions, and women are first to be stripped of their jobs, are less educated; as a consequence they engage in lower skilled and lower paid jobs, and are therefore more likely to suffer more from financial collapse. This is compounded by the fact that women invariably take care of their children and other family members whether they have funds to do so or not. Since women in 22 out of 27 Sub-Saharan countries are poorer than men (International Labour Organization 2011), a slump in the economy also disproportionately affects them. In times of economic crisis, women and girls are impacted most especially in the long run. These women experience increase in child and infant mortality, as well as a decline in school enrollments. Indeed the World Bank lists 15 countries as examples of where these factors are most evident: among them, the Democratic Republic of Congo, Ethiopia, Mozambique, Nigeria, Tanzania, and Zambia (UNAIDS.org 2012).

When demand for certain goods or commodities drop it puts a country that produces such goods in a volatile position. Inevitably, there are job cuts in countries that supply such goods or commodities. UNAIDS.org (2012) explains that since women in poor countries constitute between 60–80 percent of manufacturers in trade commodities, they more likely are going to be affected by fluctuations in trade patterns. Women in eastern and southern parts of Africa who work in export processing are reported to have been hit hard during the 2008 global economic crisis. Migrant workers regardless of industry easily lose their jobs in times of economic upheavals, as documented by UNAIDS.org (2012). Affluent families that have to cut back on expenses so frequently let go of their migrant domestic help. Entire families in home countries of the migrants are impacted by the loss of income of the primary breadwinner. These now unemployed migrant women resort to sex work. An increase in sex work was reported in eastern and southern Africa during the 2008 economic slump (USAID.org 2012). These women who hitherto were self-reliant, paid workers and now out of work and out of income, at times resort to street hawking and other forms of petty trading to help themselves and their families. These street jobs that UNAIDS.org refers to as "informal jobs" pose their own challenges. Following interviews in eleven cities in Africa, Asia, and Latin America, the researchers who themselves are women employed in informal jobs, found that 70 percent of the women interviewed reported that while they worked longer hours every week, weekly yields in income decreased, and that elevated their stress levels (UNAID.org 2012).

These problems notwithstanding, these African women suffer even more when the economy spirals down. With food and fuel prices at a rise, women have been placed in more precarious situations where they not only have to run the household; they have to take additional jobs to make ends meet. Samuels et al. (2011) report that in Nigeria, in March of 2009 unemployment rate went up to 19.7 percent an almost 5 percent increase from 2008. Among women, unemployment rose from 43.5 percent to 48.9 percent between 2007 and 2009. During such times, mothers tend to work longer hours to make additional income to take care of the family. The consequence of this is that quality time they should be spending with their children is compromised. "Parental time poverty," as this phenomenon is known, affects the bonding process between mother and her children. A squeeze in family income also means female children are likely to be pulled out of school to work in order to supplement family income.

Even though amenities to make school experiences excellent are sub-par, things were worse during the 2008 economic crisis. Providing school tuition and transportation to school became more daunting during the slump period. Samuels et al. (2011), as do other researchers (Sitesources.worldbank.org 2013; Watkins 2013), reveal that under normal circumstances a girl is likely to drop out of school to enable a brother or younger sibling to get an education. In Lagos, Nigeria, as Samuels et al. (2011) state, the likelihood of a girl as opposed to a boy being pulled out of school was 2 percent in 2006 and 2007, but by 2008 during the global recession, the odds skyrocketed to 10 percent. In essence, this reflects a retraction of the strides that are being made to achieve gender equality. The long-term effects are that the girl is deprived of a path toward alleviating herself from poverty; and for the country, it stalls the girl's role in promoting the country's development.

Even though accessibility to healthcare is a big problem in Africa, the problem is further exacerbated in times of a faltering economy. With hikes in food prices and that of other necessities, access to healthcare declines. Whatever money is left after food is bought is insufficient to pay for hospital/ doctors' visits, medications. Pregnant women skip prenatal care, and rely more on traditional births thus risking their lives and that of their babies (Samuels et al. 2011). Women are known to give up meals so others in the family can eat, mindless of their own health, and risks of what starvation can cause to pregnancy (Phillips 2009; UNAIDS.org 2012). This is more so because privations are felt at the very core of a woman's being.

USAID.org (2012) reports that austerity measures aimed at reducing spending on social and health services do affect women and girls first. As nurturers, women assume responsibility over their children and other family members including extended family. In essence, such cuts that are intended to regulate the economy thrust women into more precarious positions.

Samuels et al. (2011) indicate that malnutrition is a growing problem in many states in Nigeria, and in some malnutrition is extreme. In Lagos as Samuels et al. (2011) report, a spike in health problems was evident. The change showed a jump from 81 percent in 2008, and then to 88 percent in 2009, and then to 94 percent in 2010. They report too that this spike was compounded by a rise in food prices made worse by floods.

Times of suffering occasionally bring out the best in people, but then such help too can only endure if the giver remains viable. Informal networks of support and community solidarity and faith-based groups provide financial assistance and emotional support in order to promote community togetherness. Some churches in times of crisis even pay tuition for some poor but hardworking students, but such help too dwindles slightly during economic crisis. Such help as reported from support groups like NGOs and Faith Based Organizations (FBO) shrunk during the global recession, and some could not survive the economic climate. Drawing from their pool of resources without replenishing, and having debtors not able to pay back loans they got from these community network groups also are instrumental in bankrupting some of these networking groups. Women, mostly, rely on these networking groups for aid and little loans so when these groups become insolvent, women disproportionately suffer more. UNAID.org (2012) explains that women are perceived based on gender norms to be risky borrowers. That coupled with reductions in credit availability jeopardize women's chances of getting financial assistance. Further, women generally are paid less than men even for similar jobs. For those women who are engaged in part time jobs, they are in more untenable situations, and with the prevailing conception (or misconception) that men are invariable breadwinners, female workers are more likely to be fired or to get a pay cut when there is downsizing.

Privations at times breed abhorrent behavior particularly among those without healthy coping mechanisms. Times of financial crisis or want do generate anomie-induced strain that leads some to regress to crime commission or other deviant behavior. People who cannot mitigate their frustration may resort to violent tendencies or to crime. This is even more apparent when they are already predisposed to deviant behavior. In explaining General

Strain Theory, Agnew (2001) deciphered four characteristics of strain that are associated with crime: (1) when the strain is viewed as not just (2) when the gravity of the strain is high (3) when the strain is induced by low social control (4) when the strain generates an inducement to commit crime. Drug and alcohol consumption is also known to increase during times of strife (see World Health Organization 2011). Samuels et al. (2011) report that in their study in Nigeria, these responses to hard times were evident.

As well, family tensions heighten during times of a slow economy. During times of suffering people are either brought together, or they go asunder. Imbued with debts, and family responsibilities, domestic violence, spousal abuse, and child abuse become more prevalent. Fights over money and spending patterns become more rampant. Samuel et al. (2011) report that in their studies in parts of Nigeria, women told of increased levels of "depression, anxiety, frustration and general psychological ill being, which in many cases has been linked directly to food and fuel price shock" (8). Further, in times of a slump, and especially when they have no source of income, women tend to rely on men, such reliance may exacerbate domestic abuse, and in non-marital relations, lead to unsafe sex. UNAID.org (2012) reports that empirical studies in South Africa expose the reliance of women for survival on men, and how such reliance translates to unsafe sexual practices, and to the contribution of HIV infections. So, financial deprivations affect even those intimate levels of a woman's existence.

Chapter Five

Trafficking of Women

While UNICEF, and some NGOs and private organizations such as churches, are working to bring the issues of child trafficking to the forefront of human rights discussion, little is known about the realities of the problem as well as the subsequent impact it has on the victims. Not to be ignored as well is the trafficking of women. Much of the research on trafficking of children discusses the issue together with trafficking of women (Allais 2013; ILO 2012; Shelley 2010; UN.GIFT 2009). These sources also discuss that the absence of concrete data on the prevalence of women and children trafficked worldwide makes it difficult for comprehensive laws to be put in place and enforced. According to the International Labor Office (ILO), data collection on the prevalence on forced labor of children and adults is crucial. ILO, 2012, states:

> Reliable statistics are essential to understand the nature and extent of the problem, its causes and consequences, and to inform policy-makers and other stakeholders involved in action against forced labour. Regular data collection also enables the assessment of programs and impact of the implementation of policy, action plans and specific programs and projects to eradicate forced labour. (7)

Trafficking of children has especially been brought to light in the last several years after reports on smuggling of children and young girls for prostitution filled news programs in the United States and opened up a series of discussions at the United Nations. On March 28, 2000, Dateline NBC (a news and commentary program in the United States) aired a series on female slavery in Ukraine, Czech Republic, and Russia hosted by Maria Shriver, a journalist with the National Broadcasting Company (NBC). That year, a 14-year-old girl from Mexico was found in Florida working as a sex slave. The

Department of Justice Civil Rights Task Force put together by the then U. S. Attorney General Janet Reno made the bust. On June 9, 2009, Tom Brokaw, then NBC News Anchor discussed sex slavery in Kosovo. The United Nations Peace Force launched a rescue mission. On September 23, 2003, President George W. Bush of the United States addressed the United Nations regarding child sex trafficking. On October 17, 2004, Chris Hansen on MSNBC News aired a production that had been in the works from 2002–2003 on the Cambodian capital, Phnom Penh, where tourists go to get prostitutes. The Cambodian minister of Women's Affairs acknowledged that there were about 20,000 girls used as prostitutes. The International Justice Mission was reinvigorated to target human traffickers. Even before these episodes, *Migration News*, 1994, reported that based on data from Russian migration officers, there were approximately 2 million Asian and African illegal immigrants living in Russia. How these migrants got to Russia is suspect, but illegal migration due to economic crisis, political instability, other domestic issues at countries of origin, and human trafficking cannot be ruled out. These episodes just demonstrate how prolonged and entrenched the trafficking of humans has been in the last few decades.

The African Charter on the Rights and Welfare of the Child (1990) made strides in putting in place a foundational African initiative intended to curb trafficking. In a 2000 summit held in Cairo, Egypt, members present agreed to continue to take on issues relating to human rights and good governance. Members put together an action plan to counter human trafficking especially with regards to women and children. Sweden and Italy were the countries designated to monitor this project, and UNICEF Innocenti Research Center (IRC) was to provide logistics. A 2001 assembly of the Economic Community of West African States (ECOWAS) and the New Partnership for Africa's Development (NEPAD) put together ideas on combating trafficking. In a launching conference referred to as Africa-Europe Ministerial Conference, held in Brussels, Belgium, in October 2001, the problem of women and children trafficking was determined to be an urgent problem in Africa, for which a pledge to initiate an action plan to combat trafficking especially that of women and children was put in place. At the second World Congress Against Commercial Sexual Exploitation of Children, held in Yokohoma, Japan, in 2001, as well as at the United Nations Special Session on Children, further pledges to tackle trafficking of women and children were made. Hitherto, UNICEF Innocenti Research Center provided feedback on child trafficking in West Africa. It is also worthy of note that several international treaties and conventions such as the Convention on Rights of the Child and its Optional Protocols, the Palermo Protocol, the International Labor Organization (ILO), 182 on the Worst Forms of Child Labour, and other designated sessions on children, have made as a cardinal focus the welfare of children particularly against trafficking. These programs and action plans are not put in place only to signal child trafficking, but also to install preventative measures, laws, and procedures to bring to justice traffickers, and to find ways to reunite victims of trafficking to their families.

As much as the international community speaks about the issue, it is clear that not much is known about the realities of trafficking. In Africa especially because of a dearth in social science research on the issue, reliable data is absent (Sawadogo 2012). The void in scientific research makes it such that vital information necessary to alert communities and to educate community members on cautionary measures to avoid victimization is absent. Families are so easily duped to give up their children even when they should have known better; women so naively fall for scams that promise them a lucrative job in some foreign country; and so often the very systems put in place to protect victims fail to provide the necessary assistance victims should get. Due to the fact that these lapses exist, it is of utmost importance to review existing programs for more viable ways to combat the problem. In order to be effective in this regard, grass root efforts at understanding the problem have to be done.

The UN Protocol to Prevent, Suppress and Punish Trafficking in Persons, Especially Women and Children to the UN Convention against Transnational Organized Crime, known as the Palermo Protocol, defines trafficking as:

> Trafficking in persons shall mean the recruitment, transportation, transfer, harbouring or receipt of persons, by means of the threat or use of force or other forms of coercion, of abduction, of fraud, or deception, of the abuse of power or of a position of vulnerability or of the giving or receiving of payments or benefits to achieve the consent of a person having control over another person, for the purpose of exploitation. Exploitation shall include, at a minimum, the exploitation of the prostitution of others or other forms of sexual exploitation, forced labour or services, slavery or practices similar to slavery, servitude or the removal of organs.

Despite the seemingly detailed definition of human trafficking by the Palermo Protocol, some like Lee (2007) find problems with the definition. According to Lee, the definition is not conclusive. He contends that the following conceptualizations or notations should have been made along with the definition of human trafficking:

- Slavery, whereby human trafficking is viewed as a contemporary form of slavery characterized by temporary ownership, debt bondage, forced labour and hyper-exploitative contractual arrangements in the global economy as opposed to the legal ownership of one human being by another or long-term enslavement;

- Prostitution—where definitions of human trafficking have centered around contested positions on issues of prostitution, individual agency, and consent;
- Organized crime—human trafficking has been conceptualized within the framework of organized crime. The role of criminally sophisticated, transnational crime groups as a driving force behind the highly profitable trade of smuggling and trafficking unauthorized migrants or asylum seekers has been commented upon widely
- Migration-trafficking has been understood within the context of broader migration patterns, policies, and politics of migration control, and
- Human rights-trafficking has been conceptualized from a human rights perspective. The consolidation of human rights has gathered momentum in the latter half of the twentieth century through the proliferation of human rights as principles of broad value to all people.

The commitment to tackle human trafficking in Africa is enshrined in several binding declarative and legislative enactments. Ground works to combat trafficking were put in place in 1990 by the African Charter on the Rights and Welfare of the Child. A follow-up acknowledgement of this commitment was solidified in 2002 by the African Union during its labor and Social Affair session. In December 2001, the Economic Community of West African States (ECOWAS) in conjunction with the Plan of Action adopted in December 2000 by the Sub-Regional Consultation on the Development of Strategies to Fight Child Trafficking for Exploitative Labor Purposes in West and Central Africa, have set procedures for combating trafficking in Africa. The New Partnership for Africa's Development (NEPAD) is also participating in efforts to reduce human trafficking.

CAUSES AND TYPOLOGIES OF HUMAN TRAFFICKING

As a fluid phenomenon, it is difficult to come up with one-glove-fits-all causes of trafficking (Letsie et al. 2008; Trafficking-GB2ed-2005). Trafficking-GB2ed-2005 indicates that is particularly true in Africa, and because each country presents factors endemic to it, generalized proclamations of causes of trafficking would be erroneous. Among some of the causes that have been proffered are: "poverty, weak governance, armed conflict or lack of effective protection against discrimination and exploitation" (Trafficking-GB2ed-2005). While the focus is usually on those that supply trafficked victims, not much attention is paid to those who utilize the services of these victims. In economics parlance, Trafficking-GB2ed-2005 explains: "analyses of causes generally highlight the 'push factors'—on the so-called 'supply side'—and tend to neglect the demand dimension of the problem. However, 'pull factors' on the demand side are of equal salience for effective counter-active measures against trafficking in women and children" (6).

As Adepoju (2005) explains, many Africans gradually got to know about human trafficking from activists, the media, and NGOs around the 1990s and many paid little attention to the problem (Sawadogo 2012). Further, Adepoju (2005) explains that because many presidents of African countries did not find trafficking a punishable offense, there were hardly any laws against it. Nigeria, Togo, and Benin, appeared to have been the first countries in that continent to raise alarm on the issue given the transportation of children to work on farms. Increasingly, as the practice of trafficking of women and children across country borders became more entrenched, some political heads of states began to pay close attention to the problem by asking for legislation and public education of the problem. In Africa, blame fell squarely on poverty, and then upon closer look fingers were pointed at oppressive, hostile, and discriminatory cultural practices that place women and children in at-risk groups for trafficking. These factors are even more evident in local settings. There, incipient practices of female subjugation, with seemingly blasé attitudes toward female trafficking, mixed with pervasive poverty, provide fertile grounds for trafficking in women and children. As well, conditions that promote violence and deprivation expose women to further victimizations. Customary factors that relegate women to inferior roles, thus devaluing their worth in society, render them easy targets for recruitment, abduction, coercion, or deception into trafficking.

Adepoju (2005) and Sita (2003) explain that three types of trafficking exist in Sub-Saharan Africa: trafficking in children to perform domestic chores, farm work; trafficking in women and young boys and girls across borders for sexual exploitation; and trafficking of women from other African countries to South Africa to work in the sex industry.

The Palermo Protocol defines trafficking of children as:

> Trafficking of children shall mean the recruitment, transportation, transfer, harboring or receipt of a child for the purpose of exploitation. Exploitation shall include, at a minimum, the exploitation of the prostitution of others or other forms of sexual exploitation, forced labour or services, slavery or practices similar to slavery, servitude or the removal of organs.

With regard to child trafficking in West and Central Africa, Veil (1998) deciphers six types:

> Abduction of children, payment of sums of money to poor parents who hand over their children on the promise that they will be treated well, bonded placement of children as reimbursement for debt, placement for a token sum for specified duration or for gift items, and enrolment for a fee by an agent for domestic work at the request of the children's parents. In the sixth form,

> parents of the domestic workers are deceived into enlisting their children under the guise that they would be enrolled in school, trade or training.

These dynamics certainly do not include the more bizarre and recent cases of abduction of girls for the purpose of holding them as hostages or for selling them as bride wives. Sbs.com.au (2014) commenting on the nearly 300 Nigerian schoolgirls in Chibok abducted in April 2014 by the Boko Haram group in Nigeria states: "many have reportedly been forced to marry members of the Islamist sect. The case is hardly unique, experts told a ministerial meeting of about 50 African countries in the Ethiopian capital." This remains a tragic reminder of the roadblocks many girls in several countries in the developing world have to encounter in pursuit of education.

Besides the trauma of marrying a complete stranger, these children/girls are likely to suffer from post-traumatic stress disorder, depression, anxiety, and a range of other behavioral, health, and physical problems (Laufer and Shechory-Bitton 2013). These issues notwithstanding, these children are likely to be deprived of education and other social skills necessary for upward mobility.

Other causes of trafficking are associated with the absence of birth registrations and certificates. Without a valid form of identification children are vulnerable; they can't confirm who their parents are, where they were born, and can't conclusively state which country they are from. Thus they are prey for any trafficker. The lack of identification also makes it difficult for children to be reunited with their families, or to be sent back to their country of origin. Finding oneself involuntarily in a country other than one's own is already traumatic, being subjected to slavery thereafter generates a psychological paralysis accompanied by depression, anxiety, and other behavioral issues.

- Compounding issues of lack of identification is the problem of "transitivity." Transitivity involves situations where a victim may be trafficked to a country, or may migrate to a country, and then subsequently trafficked to another country. In the process, the victim, or authorities lose track of the victim's actual home of origin, and thus make it difficult for authorities to figure out where to ultimately repatriate the victim. Three forms of transitivity exist:
- Persons migrating legally from one country to another find themselves at risk because of poverty, discrimination, and marginalization and become trapped in a trafficking network.
- Persons trafficked from one country to another for particular purposes are later trafficked to a third country, for a different purpose. For example, a child may be trafficked the first time as a domestic worker, and trafficked later on as a woman, sold, or recruited into prostitution.

- Persons trafficked internally, from a rural area to an urban area, and later trafficked to another country for a different purpose. This creates a link between internal and cross-border trafficking (Trafficking-GB2ed-2005, 13).

Both UNICEF and Trafficking-GB2ed-2005 inform that at least 49 percent of African countries acknowledge that trafficking poses problems in their countries. These countries acknowledge that child trafficking is more insidious than trafficking in women because children are of enormous help in that they perform domestic chores, farm work, petty trading, and errands; and even when women are more trafficked countries consider child trafficking as worse.

Survey conducted in West and Central Africa shows that over 70 percent of the populations consider human trafficking to be a problem. Indeed a third of that population considers the problem of trafficking to be serious. Meanwhile, 33 percent of countries in East and Southern Africa find trafficking to be a problem. Information regarding human trafficking in North Africa has been sparse especially since the population of that region is either uninformed about the problem, or do not consider it to be a problem.

Trafficking African women for commercial sex to Europe, the Middle East, and within Africa seems to be rife in much of the continent. Earlier studies report that Nigerian women are usually taken to Europe, for commercial sex through Ghana; while Togolese women are trafficked to Gabon, Cote d'Ivoire, and Lebanon to work in the sex industry (Adepoju 2005; Taylor 2002). Adepoju (2005) reports that women are trafficked from Senegal, Liberia, Sierra Leone, Kenya, Ethiopia, Lesotho, Mozambique, Malawi, South Africa, Zambia, to destinations within Africa and abroad. Cameroon is also listed by U.S. State Department (2008) as both a source country, and a transit country for trafficked girls and women. These transactions in humans are done by syndicates that make travel documents for the trafficked women, obtain visas for them, and set them up with brothels in the destinations they are sent to.

The Freedom Project (n.d.) breaks down the various ways by which people become victims of trafficking:

- Many women and children are kidnapped into slavery
- Some children are sold to traders by their parents
- Some children are willingly sent with a trader by their parents, who have been promised that their children will receive a good education, an apprenticeship, or a good job and good prospects or even just adequate food. Traders can often be well-known locals or relatives, so the parents trust them.

- Some women are married, only to find that their marriage is a sham, and that their new husband has sold them into the sex industry.
- Some respond to job advertisements offering good pay for manual labor, only to find that they are imprisoned on arrival, subjected to vastly different employment contracts from what they had been led to believe, with no escape, and may be made to work for many years laboring for no pay at all.
- Many women apply to sham foreign job agencies or to study overseas, and go abroad willingly thinking they will receive education or have employment as a waitress or a nanny, etc., only to find when they reach their destination that the reality is very different, and that they are imprisoned, raped, and forced into the prostitution industry.

It is reported that Ugandan women who themselves are prostitutes sometimes entice girls to join the sex industry since the men prefer younger women. Some of these Ugandan girls and women are kidnapped from the northern parts of the country where there is political unrest to become sex slaves to rebel commanders, or at times, are commoditized as slaves to rich Sudanese men, and other rich men in the Gulf states (Adepoju 2005). Adepoju (2005) also reports that Kenyan girls are trafficked to Europe by syndicates operated by Japanese businessmen, and that women trafficked to Europe are usually transited through Kenya. Further, as Adepoju (2005) reveals, female orphans from Uganda and Kenya are "sold" to traffickers with the false believe that the girls will be given a better life.

Adepoju (2005) discusses a particularly heart-wrenching trafficking network and practice. He describes:

> Ethnically based criminal syndicates in South Africa's refugee camps recruit and transport their victims, usually married women from their home countries. In Lesotho, traffickers recruit male and female children, victims of physical and sexual abuse at home, or children orphaned by AIDS. Such children normally migrate from rural areas and border towns to Maseru, the capital, from where they are trafficked by mostly South African White Afrikaans who use force and/or promise of employment in Eastern Free State, asparagus farms in the border region, and Bloemfontein. At the destination, victims are locked up in private homes and starved of food while being sexually, physically, and verbally exploited. Sexually exploited, humiliated, and penniless, these young victims are later dumped at border towns to make their way back to Maseru. Long-distance truck drivers also traffic their victims from Lesotho to Cape Town, Zambia, and Zimbabwe, with the help of corrupt immigration officials at the border posts. (Adepoju 2005, 79)

The methods of obtaining victims for trafficking are varied. Deceptions, threats of witchcraft, magic, or some horrible aspersions are allegedly cast on the victims as tactics to make them compliant. Martens et al. (2003) explain how successful businesswomen in Malawi together with truck drivers recruit young victims by promising them study, marriage, or employment opportunities in South Africa. Many are eventually gang raped or murdered if they resist. Victims undergo malicious control and disregard for humanity; they get beaten down emotionally for so long so they do not even know whom to trust. Boys and girls younger than 18 years who are trafficked are made to engage in "pornographic sex acts" and posted on the internet. Some of these are pictures of children, and the children are sent to pedophile networks.

While many traffickers tend to be men, in Mozambique, they are mostly women who are in conspiratorial ventures with South African men who do the transportation of victims from the capital city of Maputo to cities in South Africa. There, victims are rendered completely helpless. All documents of identification and travel of the victims are confiscated by the traffickers. The victims are then sold to brothels as sex workers, or as wives to mine workers (Adepoju 2005).

To date, Adepoju (2005) is one of the few who provides the most comprehensive account of human trafficking in Africa; yet, while he is detailed in his account of human trafficking in Southern Africa, his research is scanty about this crime in other parts of Africa. This is no fault of his; little ethnographic research has been done in many countries in Africa. What is known is through archival or secondary data from at times unreliable police reports, or from NGOs, or some activist groups. Adepoju (2005) acknowledges that with regard to data on trafficking in many regions in Africa "a lot of grey areas exist between the concept of female migration for work, the aim being to improve the migrant's conditions and those of her family, illegal migration, smuggling, and trafficking of women" (85). Sawadogo (2012) concentrates on human trafficking in West Africa, and makes the stunning report that in 2008, of the 229 children trafficked in Benin and Gabon, 86 percent of them were females, and half of this number were under the age of 16. In an earlier study of three countries, it was evident that girls more than boys were more susceptible to be victims of trafficking.

Table 5.1 is from Sawadogo 2012, 97 (see United Nations Office on Drugs and Crime). It shows patterns more consistent with female trafficking than male in Benin, Nigeria, and Togo.

Despite attempts by NGOs, the United Nations, local governments, and activist groups to discourage the use of child labor, children are still widely used. Even though some countries like Gabon have enacted laws mandating school attendance for children, and strict labor laws, thus limiting child labor, a shortage exists within the country for cheap child labor. This thus enables traffickers to traffic children from Togo to work in Gabon.

Among the myriad of causes, many researchers believe that poverty and lack of education are paramount (Adepoju 2005; Letsie et al. 2008; Onuoha 2011; Sawadogo 2012; Temesgen 2014). Privations leave families with hard-

Table 5.1. Female and Male Trafficking in Benin, Nigeria, and in Togo

Gender and Age of Victims by Country							
	Benin*		Nigeria**		Togo***		Total
Gender	Minor	Adult	Minor	Adult	Minor	Adult	
Male	85	37	3	1	2		128
Female	112	65	16	10	17	20	240
Age	age and gender				6 (+3 girls)		24
Gender Unknown	Unavailable for 18 victims				age unknown		

*The Benin sample includes information on gender from 284 (182 children and 102 adults) victims interviewed and the information contained in the 13 case files.
** The Nigerian sample includes information on 30 victims interviewed.
***The Togo sample includes information on 45 victims obtained from case files. One of the case files involved 16 Nigerian girls and women stopped in transit through Togo. They were being trafficked to The Netherlands and Italy for work in prostitution.
Source: United Nations Office on Drugs and Crime 2006.

ly any choice but to give up children to a promising caregiver who transpires to be a trafficker. Traffickers misrepresent themselves as "employment brokers" and deceive unsuspecting victims into thinking that they will have gainful employment in the new land. This, with prevailing attitudes about the inferiority and the frailty of women and girls, objectifies them and exposes them to abductions and trafficking. When poverty is rife a paradoxical relationship sets in between a girl and her parents. On the one hand the girl is considered to be a financial burden, yet on the other hand, she is an asset in that she can be given up for early marriage. With early marriage the girl can be given away to an older man who in exchange can give the family cattle or money as dowry. This marital arrangement does not guarantee a good life for the girl; if anything, research has shown that in many situations the girl's impoverished circumstances persist based on abandonment, separation, divorce, or persistent torture by the husband. While many flee, some do find themselves working in sex industries to make ends meet as examples in Ethiopia and Kenya reveal (Trafficking-GB2e-2005). This is at times the fate of girls who flee their homes in order to avoid being sold by their parents as young brides. Whether the girl initially flees voluntarily and ends up being trafficked into the sex industry, or she is abducted and sold to marriage, trafficking of girls as an economic enhancement remains a practice among destitute families in several African countries.

The United Nations Inter-Agency Project on Human Trafficking (UNIAP n.d.), however, cautions about the assumption that there is a strong causal link between poverty, lack of education and human trafficking. Their cautionary note is backed by evidence-based research that suggests that in some places in Asia the assumption that poverty and lack of education as a cause for trafficking is weak. Instead, UNAIP indicates that in Northern Thailand where girls are more educated, they are also more susceptible to become victims of trafficking in that the pressure to earn money to make up for their educational expenses and to reward their families leads them to migrate and they are often trafficked to Bangkok, Malaysia, and Japan. UNAIP explains that it is not lack of education on trafficking that leads people vulnerable to trafficking (NGOs, activists groups, UN agencies, government agencies, put out plenty of warnings), rather economic disparities within and among nations necessitate migration. Migration as the organization acknowledges is by itself not tantamount to trafficking, if anything, it is a means to alleviate poverty; but differences in immigration policies and the job market have opened up opportunities for unguarded migration, and a flood of people who are open to exploitation and abuse. UNAIP concludes that "Human trafficking is not 'caused' by poverty, lack of education, lack of legal status, or any other vulnerability factor: human trafficking is caused by human traffickers—criminals who commit criminal acts against victims and vulnerable people."

In explaining the causes of human trafficking in Ethiopia, Temesgen (2014) highlights poverty as a main cause. He cites the absence of opportunities, unemployment, and dwindling social services as contributory factors. While these factors affect a good segment of the population, he concedes that girls fare even worse since they are disproportionately less educated, their skills in some trades are limited and not wanted, and because they have no assets credit is restricted, so they end up getting low-paying jobs as domestic workers.

Unsuspecting parents entrust children to others seemingly better off like relatives, friends, or strangers in hopes that the children will at least have a life free of perpetual poverty. Victims themselves willing to migrate based on promises of a better life unwittingly set themselves up for coercive measures to subsequently be used against them. The need for cheap laborers, the growing industry for pornography, and the increasing need for sex workers all make trafficking a lucrative venture. In Cameroon as the U.S. State Department states, laborers needed for agriculture and fishing industries, as well as for street vending, and spare parts shops make the trafficking of children from different countries in Africa a lucrative venture. Temesgen (2014) makes the point that being in a country illegally makes one vulnerable and thus easily amenable for use in any way even if in inhumane ways. Trafficking-GB2ed-2005 explains how an African woman who resided in Sweden lured a group of girls from Tanzania. On a visit to Tanzania she visited the homes of the girls and duped their parents into believing that she could offer the girls "educational opportunities" in Sweden. Naively, the parents believed the woman and entrusted their daughters to her. In Sweden, she forced them to work as prostitutes.

Traffickers are often hard at work trying at every turn to bolster their clientele. By using falsified information including false identities, and coercive practices they either lure victims or outright abduct them. At times, intermediaries are used to assist in the criminal enterprise.

Lutya (2012) explains deprivations alongside vulnerability as having a causal link with human trafficking. In this regard as Lutya explains, the dire straits in which these victims are: lacking food, shelter, medications, and just the basics for survival, make them more trusting or even gullible. They fall for any hint of sympathy, any promise of a better life, and sycophantic traffickers abuse the victims' vulnerability (Bernat and Zhilina 2010). Lutya (2012), reports that there were 148,000 households headed by children in South Africa in 2007 as a result of the passing of their parents from AIDS and other illnesses. These children are desperately poor, and thus are more susceptible to be lured by traffickers.

Even though HIV/AIDS has claimed millions of lives, many people still have skewed understanding of the disease. AIDS has been an epidemic in Africa; many children have been orphaned, and women have been left without husbands because of the disease. Traditional families in Africa tend to have men as breadwinners; consequently with husbands dead because of AIDS, women are burdened with the responsibility of taking care of themselves and of their children. In search of ways out of poverty, some women and children migrate to destinations they think are greener pastures. In these new destinations, they are trafficked in to sex industries where they are at times raped and tortured, and without protected sex, they are infected with HIV. Some of these women and young girls in foreign countries seek help from the governments in the countries where they are, or from NGOs and churches.

It has been known that in the Southern parts of Africa, some men believe that having sex with young girls is a cure for HIV/AIDS, or that it lessens the likelihood of contracting the disease. This ill-informed reasoning has trafficking for young girls increase significantly. The "virgin cure" as Lutya (2012) refers to this myth has also led to a rise in the abduction of girls on their way to schools. Prince (2009) explains that when young girls are abducted by older men for the purpose of curing them of HIV/AIDS, these girls are turned into child brides, and even when parents know what is going on, they ignore the inherent oddity of the situation after receiving gifts of money or goods (see also Oliphant 2009). In South Africa as the United Nations projects, about 79 percent of trafficked victims are used for sexual exploitation (Lutya 2012; Tyakume 2009). This number as Lutya (2012) acknowledges may be skewed because in South Africa, as in other countries, mechanisms of identifying and accounting for victims of trafficking have not been fully developed.

Lutya (2012), Onuoha (2011), Temesgen (2014), and U.S. State Department (2008) blame the persistence of trafficking on the absence of effective legislations and qualified and dedicated personnel to combat traffickers. It is for these reasons that the State Department places Cameroon on a Tier 2 Watch List. In South Africa as Lutya reports, while there is legislation that bans prostitution, compelling anyone to work as a prostitute, and the operation of brothels (Act 23 of 1957 Sexual Offence Act), law enforcement officers are lax in enforcing the legislation. As well, Gould and Fick (2008) confirm that even when police officers raid brothels in South Africa, owners open them as soon as the officers leave.

Temesgen (2014), states that in Ethiopia, inadequate legislation, improperly functioning agencies and processes, and an ineffective judiciary are the primary causes of human trafficking. Government inadvertence perpetuates the problem. In 2012, it was reported that 600 Ugandan women were trafficked to Malaysia to work in the sex industry. The women were deceived into thinking that they were going to Malaysia to get high-paying jobs. When the plight of the women was reported to the Ugandan government, the government's ignorance, real or staged became apparent. As Lutya 2012 reports: "James Mugume, the Permanent Secretary for Foreign Affairs, says the staggering figure of 600 women took government by surprise" (Trafficking was not an issue until we got this big problem of Malaysia, 6). Prior to the 600 women being trafficked, 100 Ugandans had been trafficked to Iraq (Lutya 2012). The Director of Interpol in the country carried out a similar display of ignorance about the trafficking of people in Tanzania, in 2011. The Director was reported to have said: "This is a new phenomenon in the country. Yes trafficking of people and sex labor slavery have been there but it has not exploded to this magnitude" (Lutya 2012, 8, quoting from the *Daily News* of Tanzania). As though this was not sufficient to make the government become more sensitive to the issue, the Home Affairs Deputy Ambassador downplayed it again after 20 Somali nationals who were being trafficked to South Africa via Tanzania were found dead from suffocation in a truck. When a citizen brought up the issue of human trafficking the Home Affairs Deputy Ambassador is reported to have said, "It wasn't a serious issue" (Lutya 2012, 9).

A similar characterization of the problem is explained in West Africa. Sawadogo (2012) explains that traffickers have committed their offenses almost carte blanche since trafficking was not considered a crime and even as of his writing many countries have done little to legislate and put in place proper enforcement mechanisms to prosecute and limit the prevalence of the crime. Sawadogo (2012) goes on to state:

> Most states, even now, have done little to integrate human rights concerns or strategies into their laws or policies relating to human trafficking or smuggling. With few exceptions, trafficking in human beings remains a relatively low priority among officials. So for criminal networks West Africa was a "haven" and still presents a comparative advantage in reducing risks and consequently maximizing profits via transnational trafficking in human beings. (103)

Conflicts in many African countries (Sudan, South Sudan, Northern Uganda, Somalia, and Democratic Republic of Congo) have also been blamed for the surge of human trafficking. With these conflicts, the proliferation of camps for soldiers and peace-keeping forces becomes necessary (Sidint.net, n.d.). Children are trafficked as child soldiers, as well as child sex slaves (Flint and De Waal 2008; Lutya 2012; Onuoha 2011; Sidint.net n.d.; Temesgen 2014; Turner 2008).

Children as well as adults are also trafficked for the purpose of harvesting their body organs. Victims are coerced or tricked into selling body organs by traffickers. Those targeted are usually destitute, marginalized persons, whose circumstances are dire thus leading them to accept the exploitation. Traffickers do at times rationalize the exploitation on the basis that consent was given and payment was made for the body part. This reasoning has not been found tenable giving the fact that the Palermo Protocol considers any "abuse of a position of vulnerability" (vulnerability including age, illness, gender, and poverty), as sufficient to nullify consent and establish trafficking. As a consequence of limited knowledge on the issue, there are no reliable data on the frequency of the occurrences of these acts and no reliable information on the breakdown of victims by gender, age, or race (see, coe.int. 2009). What has been surmised though is that the main cause for trafficking in human parts is the "shortage of organs to meet demand for transplantation, inequities in health care and poor economic and other conditions that put persons in vulnerable situations" (coe.int. 2009, 55). Regardless, Article 21 of the 1997 Convention on Human Rights and Biomedicine [CETS No. 164] states, "The human body and its parts shall not, as such, give rise to financial gain."

Regarding those most vulnerable to have their organs harvested, coe.int. (2009) opines that while data on this are scanty, one can extrapolate that because under normal and legal circumstances women are donors, it is likely that those trafficked for this purpose are women. Female organs are relatively free from renal diseases, and that makes female organs more desirable. This, as coe.int. (2009) confirms is the reason why women in some Asian countries are the primary donors. In India, as coe.int (2009) reports, a survey revealed that of 305 people who were commercial donors, 71 percent were females. These women indicated in an interview that they were donors because their husbands were breadwinners and suffered from health issues. The report also indicates that a couple of women indicated that they had been "obliged" by their husbands to donate their organs, and that because family members were present during the interview it was likely that many women were intimidated to be forthcoming about why they became donors. On a cautionary note though, coe.int (2009) points out that universally, women may not be primary organ donors because in Egypt for instance, men were primary donors. With regard to age donors, coe.int (2009) informs that it is mythical to contend that children are abducted for the purpose of organ transplants. Such kinds of transplants are rare as the organization notes because organs from children are only useful in other children and there isn't much of such demand; the process of extracting the organ and transplanting it to a recipient needs skilled medical intervention; and extracted organs have a very short life span, hence organs extracted from one country have to be in the recipient's country within 7 hours especially if it is a liver.

It is worthy of note that the problem for the donor does not end with the exploitation; studies show that there is decline in the overall health of the donor. For liver donors 58 to 86 percent of them experience such decline (Baudiani-Saberi and Delmonico 2008; Goyal et al. 2002). As well, depression and anxiety are other problems that donors experience. Coe.int (2009) also reports that some donors are stigmatized, shunned, and isolated, and worse of all the predicate reason why they were compelled to sell their organs, which is poverty, is never resolved. If anything, their circumstances, and that of their families deteriorate as health issues now beset the donor, and the little money they receive from the buyer is spent on health care.

Trafficking-GB2ed-2005 advices that "users" should be distinguished from traffickers. This, as the organization contends is crucial in order to comprehend the various methods used in their operations, and to fashion out programs of intervention. Users do act alone, but it is not uncommon for them to work in consort by associating with other illegal enterprises in order to have access to cheap labor, as for instance, displaced children and undocumented immigrants. As Trafficking-GB2ed-2005 reports, users are to a large extent unaware of and at times disinterested in how trafficking is conducted and where the victims are from. Regardless of what users perceive their selves to be, they are in the business of exploiting vulnerable persons, and in that regard, they are really not different from traffickers.

Human trafficking is real; and just about every country is a source, a passage, or destination for trafficked persons. Unless there is a scandalous occurrence, as for instance, large numbers of people trafficked, little attention is paid to the issue. Sawadogo (2012) explains that human trafficking reduces the effectiveness of the social contract that citizens have with their leaders, diminishes the rule of law and the confidence that people place in their leaders, and thus prompts national tragedies. Governments simply pay lip service to the problem. The public is unaware of the severity and prevalence of the problem. Identifying, accounting for, and providing help for victims is sporadic, and mechanisms to assist victims are weak and ineffective. Most victims of trafficking are children, and that is the case in Cameroon as well. They are trafficked for sexual exploitation, for domestic servitude, to work as laborers in fields, and to be curbside beggars for their owners. Credible efforts to curb these crimes against children and to provide help for them begin with accounting for and keeping records of who they are.

Chapter Six

Crimes of Culture

Forced Marriages, Bride Price, Levirate, Female Circumcision, and Violence Against Women

FORCED MARRIAGES

Much has been written about female victimizations in Africa, particularly those that are rooted in custom, such as forced marriages, bride price, levirate responsibilities, and female circumcision (Bentheim 2010; Bunch 1990; Chigbu et al. 2010; Kaye et al. 2005; Kiragu 1996; Park 2006; Welch and Sachs 1987; Welstead 2009). It is worth noting that many of these practices are coming under severe scrutiny and criticism even in the countries where the practices still go on. Many proponents of the practices, who see them as embedded in custom and tradition, are gradually re-thinking their stances in light of education. Women's rights movements, non-governmental organizations, community groups, and other organizations are spreading awareness about the backwardness of the practices. Some countries such as Benin ban these practices outright, while some countries have legislations that punish the practices, even if the laws are not enforced.

According to ForwardUK, forced marriage is a union "conducted without the valid consent of one of both parties and is a marriage in which duress—whether physical or emotional is a factor" (Welstead 2009). Both adults and children as young as seven years old can be, and have been victims of this repressive practice (UNFPA 2005, Child Marriage Factsheet). A corollary of forced marriage, and occasionally independent of it is bride price. "Bride price is a sum, either in cash or kind, used to purchase a bride for her labour and fertility" (ForwardUK). Bishai and Grossbard (2010) explain that bride price "involves the payment of goods or cash from the groom's family to the bride's family at the time of the marriage" (1177). Data provided by Monekosso (2001) approximates that in Mali 72 percent, Niger 57 percent, Uganda 47 percent, Burkina Faso 44 percent, Cameroon 41 percent, Nigeria 37 percent, Central African Republic 39 percent, Malawi 36 percent, Liberia 32 percent, Senegal 29 percent, Togo 27 percent, Zambia 27 percent, Ivory Coast 26 percent, and Tanzania 26 percent of girls between the ages of 15–19 are forced into marriage.

IRIN Africa (2007), places the percentage of women married in Mali between the ages of 20–24 at 69 percent, and states that these women were married before they reached the age of 18. The same source reveals that one out of every ten girls who got married between the ages of 15–19 went on to have babies before they even got to be 15 (IRIN Africa, 2007). Even though accounts place the incidences of forced marriages very high in Mali, as a matter of fact, highest among African countries with data on the problem, on February 22, 2007, the president of the Malian Human Rights Association (*Association Malienne des droits de L'homme*, AMDH) disputed the claim, but conceded that the practice occurs in the country, but in far lower numbers (Refworld, 2012). However, on February 23, 2007, office of the Research Directorate received a letter from the president of the Association for the Progress and Defense of the Rights of Malian Women (*Association pour le Progres et la defense des droits et des Femmes Maliennes, APDF*), contradicting claims by the AMDH by stating that "forced marriage is commonplace in Mali even though the Malian Marriage and Guardianship Code prohibits such marriages" (Refworld, 2012). To further bolster the report of the APDF, on February 14, 2007, the president of the Sahel Association for Assistance for Women and Children (*Association du Sahel d'aide a la Femme et L'enfance, ASSAFE*) stated that "Malian women get married very young and very often without their consent" and that "they are often married at 12 years of age" (Refworld 2012, 1). In further support of the claims of the APDF, ASSAFE, a United Nations (UN) report on June 14, 2005, and that of the Population Council of September, 2005, were produced (Refworld 2012). Plan UK estimates that forced marriage rates exceed 70 percent in Mali, Chad, and Niger, because of "gender inequality," "poverty," "negative traditional or religious practices," "failure to enforce laws," and "conflicts, disasters, and emergencies."

The case of *Hadijatou Mani Koraou v. The Republic of Niger* (2008) (ECW/CCJ/JUD/06/08), brought to light the issue of bride price, forced marriage, and slavery in the Republic of Niger. Mrs. Hadijatou Koraou, the plaintiff was 12 years old in 1996 when she was sold to, and forced to be a concubine of a 46-year-old tribal chief, called Mr. El Hadj Souleymne Naroua. Hadijatou was used both as a slave and as a sex partner. She eventually bore four children with Mr. Naroua, two of whom passed away. In 2005, Mr. El Hadj Souleymne Naroua released her from the bondage of slavery but not from the forced marriage. In 2006, Mrs. Hadijatou Koraou sued to regain her freedom from Mr. Naroua. This lawsuit challenged the laws of Niger that enabled harmful and unconscionable customs and practices that promoted the crime of slavery, and the notion that women were inferior, and more or less men's chattels. Mrs. Koraou won her case and was awarded the equivalent of $19,000 in damages.

In Niger, 44 percent of women between the ages of 20–24 were less than 15 years old when they got married; while in certain parts of Ethiopia marriage by abduction is about 92 percent, and as an aggregate nationwide it is 69 percent (see UNA.GB Model U.N. n.d.).

The problem of early marriage remains steady in rural areas of the country. The Nigerien law allows 15-year-old girls to marry as long as they are "sufficiently mature," but in rural areas girls 12 or younger can be forced into marriage. Efforts are being made by the Ministry of Population, Women's Promotion, and Child Protection, in concert with women's associations to educate the masses about the problems entailed in forced marriages.

Bride price is usually associated with forced marriages and at times, it is independent of it. It entails either monetary or some kind of property by the groom to the bride's family. Oumo (2004) states that bride price entails a contractual exchange of money, livestock, or some other good given by the groom to the bride's family in consideration for the bride's domestic duties, and ability to procreate. Bride price has been associated with domestic violence because grooms consider it almost like purchase of the woman and since the bride's family usually spend the money or use the property, they are usually not able to refund it, should that be necessary. That being the case, the woman feels stuck in the marriage, and the man then thinks the woman is his to do whatever he wants with. Statistics with regard to bride price are not available, but the practice has undergone much scrutiny. Following a study by Kaye et al. (2005) in Uganda, they determined that not only was bride price linked to domestic violence, it also impacted the reproductive health of women. Research from July 2003 to March 2004 in the Wakiso district of Uganda, coupled with 14 in-depth interviews, and 10 focus group discussions, Kaye et al. (2005) found that "participants perceived bride price as indicating that a woman was 'bought' into the man's household, which reduced her household decision-making roles. It limited women's independence and perpetuated unequal gender power relations, especially regarding health-seeking behaviour" (300).

Other studies on bride price have also documented it as a contributory factor to domestic violence. Hague and Thiara (2009), for instance, document "significant" linkage between the practice and domestic violence, as well as with impoverishment and increase in HIV in rural parts of Uganda. From their research in Uganda, Hague and Thiara (2009) list several ways by which bride price impacts the lives of women participants in their study.

Among the examples are: women being excluded from inheritance because of bride price; husbands consider their wives as chattel, and thus engage in domestic abuse and violence, and subject their wives to "punishment"; women being abandoned, or maltreated because their part of the bride price contract was not fulfilled since they were unable to conceive or have sons; young girls forced to early marriages to generate income for their parents, and a myriad of other issues.

In Burkina Faso, domestic violence has been linked to forced marriages. In fact, studies by Kabore et al. (2008) of a focus group discussion of women between the ages of 25–49, reveal that:

> Forced marriage is still rampant all over the country, especially in rural areas. Early marriage is known for being prevalent in Sahel and in the East among the populations of the Fulani and Gurmanche. This type of violence, furthermore, may be even more prevalent than what is officially reflected in figures.
>
> In fact, during a focus group discussion, women explained that violence committed by men against their wives happened daily: "Violence is such a product of the habits of most of our men that we even consider such acts as part of their second nature. When we can no longer stand it, we bring it to daylight through disputes with blows and abuses on both sides. (16)

Besides physical violence, psychological violence has been recorded which includes "all kinds of insults and forms of humiliation; refusal of husbands to support their families; the practice of demeaning post-menopausal spouses or favoring younger spouses; the demeaning or the desertion of infertile women; the repudiation of women who have given birth to girls" (Kabore et al. 2008, 17–18). Those forced into early marriages are sometimes as young as 9–12 years, but it is not uncommon to find victims of this practice among other age groups throughout the country especially in the Sahel community (Kabore 2008).

Hurd (2010) reports that "girls as young as 14 are still being forced into marriage in some rural communities in South Africa, despite a campaign to end the practice." As Hurd recounts, some of the girls she reported about indicated that their families were instrumental in their abduction and early marriages to men they did not know. While the girls Hurd spoke with had left their husbands, they still wanted to be anonymous for fear that if their parents knew where they were, their parents will force them to return to their husbands. Hurd (2010) also indicates "hundreds of teenagers every year fall victim to what village elders defend as a 'tribal tradition,' most of them in East Cape."

Reports also reveal that in Burkina Faso girls are deemed to be "economic property" and the earlier they are married the better since their virginity will still be intact, and that in many villages of the country, kidnappings associated with early and forced marriages are very prevalent (Kabore et al. 2008).

Kidnapping, which should be a crime is considered in the villages an act of bravery, hence an ego bolster. Kabore et al. (2008) report that an unnamed official from the eastern part of the country explained to them that:

> Kidnapping a girl is showing to the community that one has become mature. Kidnapping girls helps one earn the social status of an accomplished adult. Very often, after kidnapping a girl, a man will raise a flag in his compound to serve as a testimony to the community that he is now to be considered among the strongest and most respectable men in the village. (24)

In Cameroon for instance, the Appellate Court refused to recognize a marriage of thirty years simply because bride price had not been fully paid at the inception of the marriage. According to the appellate court even though a marriage certificate had been issued, it "did not perfect what was already an imperfect union" (*Maya Ikome v. Manga Ekemason* (CASWP/CC76/85[un-reported] cited and discussed in *Time* 2012). The consequence here is that the woman could not lay claim to any property acquired during the thirty years marriage with her deceased husband. In those villages in Cameroon that require bride price, a child is only considered to be that of the father if the latter paid bride price. If the husband did not pay bride price, any offspring of the marriage are considered not his, but children of the bride's father or any man who subsequently pays bride price on the woman (Ngassa 1998). Further, upon divorce, if bride price is not refunded, any subsequent children the woman has with another man are presumed to be those of her estranged husband. In *Ngeh v. Ngome* (1963), for instance, Ms. Ngeh who left her husband, Mr. Ngome, and subsequently married and had twins with Mr. Ngeh, found herself in a contentious lawsuit with Mr. Ngome who claimed the twins as his because the bride price he paid was never refunded. Curiously, the lower court sided with him, upholding customary practice, but then the appellate court in overturning the lower court's ruling, declared that the lower court "allowed rules and regulations of native law and custom to so enslave him as to have caused him to close his eyes to biological and other realities" (Ngassa 1998, 47). As a widow, the woman has to return in full the bride price; failure to do so will lead to any children she thereafter gets to be presumed those of her late husband.

Ngassa (1998) who remains an avid advocate for women's rights in Cameroon states "One of the woman's greatest problems is the application of customary laws to the legal status of a woman as a contradiction to the direction of the law and social reality" (38). She further goes on to state that "However, the general tendency in all our customary practices which cut across the nation is to foster gender inequality and promote male domination and in so doing suppressing the woman, degrading her status and most often hurting her in her person and property" (39).

Typically, marriages in Nigeria are contracted under customary law, civil/statutory law, and Islamic (Maliki school of law) (Immigration and Refugee Board of Canada 2006). Even when the marriage is contracted under statutory law, customary law usually takes precedence in personal issues (see Danish Immigration Service 2005). Many forced marriages that occur in Nigeria are contracted in the rural areas and mostly in Northern states (Bamgbose 2002). Following the Maliki School of law, a father or guardian chooses a husband for his daughter after deciding on what is best for the daughter, and this may include monetary considerations (see Danish Immigration Service 2005). The *daurin aure* marriage practice in Northern Nigeria requires that the bride-to-be (that is, the girl) continues her academic pursuits, but typically, forced marriages among the Hausas involve girls below age of puberty, and who have not gone to school (see Danish Immigration Service).

Forced marriages among the Igbos and Yoruba of Nigeria have drastically diminished over the years, in part because teen marriages are detested, and because of Christian beliefs (Danish Immigration Service 2005). Forced marriages still take place in parts of the country especially in the Northern provinces (Alewo and Olong 2012). The practice persists in these areas because much premium is placed on the virginity of the woman (Alewo and Olong 2012), and since such virginity can be ensured from children and teenage girls, these underage girls and teenagers are forced into marriages. Forced marriages are ancillary to bride price.

Alewo and Olong (2012) state that in those parts of the country, as for instance Imo State, where the practice of forced marriages still prevails, a woman's worth is assessed based upon the amount of bride price. In turn, a man who pays an exorbitant price for his bride is deemed a "real man" (Alewo and Olong 2012). Such high prices for brides also mean that many women are left unmarried because many men are unable to afford payments. Some women resort to cohabiting with their lovers while their lovers work to raise the requisite funds for the bride price. The expectation after bride price is paid is that the woman bears children. In the unfortunate circumstance that the woman does not bear children, she and her parents may be forced to pay back the bride price. The 1999 Constitution of the Republic of Nigeria, section 34, guarantees the right of dignity of a person. As explained by Legalnaija (2012), the right to dignity prohibits "torture . . . inhuman or degrading treatment."

LaFraniere (2005) discusses forced marriages in Malawi by using known examples. She discusses how parents give female children to men decades older than the children as payment for debts. The case of 11-year-old Mwaka was quite disturbing, as she was made a second wife to a man who was about thirty years older than she was simply because her parents could not repay a loan of 2,000 Kwaha, the equivalent of approximately $16. Bravely, Mwaka was able to flee after six months to her parents who gladly took her back.

Edah, a 17-year-old Malawian girl was not so lucky. Her parents gave her away for marriage to a 63-year-old man, and threatened to starve her, or whip her to death if she was belligerent. The problem persists in the country because of famine that has rendered most people destitute, as Malawi's director of social welfare services, Mr. Penston Kilembe, indicates.

The government of Malawi has tried to curb the practice of bride price and forced marriages by training volunteers to intervene and protect young girls who are slated for early marriages. Forced marriages and bride price persist because of ignorance, poverty, and tradition. Mr. Mapendo Simbeye, the father of 11-year-old Mwaka who was given to a man decades older than she is as payment for a $16 debt said "I did it out of ignorance; I had five kids, no money and no food. Then Mr. Kalabo wanted the money back so I thought of selling the daughter. I didn't know I was abusing her" (LaFraniere 2005). Poverty persists in Malawi as does famine, and poor governance, and even with government's proposal for a legislation that will raise marriage age of girls to 18 years, Women's Rights advocates find no solace in this because most marriages in Malawi and in many other Sub-Saharan countries are customary/traditional. That being the case, the courts are usually leery to intervene in subsequent issues (see LaFraniere 2005). While poverty may be a reason for selling girls into marriages, it is even more painful when a girl-child is forced to marry a man old enough to be her grandfather or great grandfather, to enable her parents to pay dowry for the woman her brother chooses to marry. In essence, the girl is sacrificed for her brother (the case of Uness Nyambi [LaFraniere 2005]).

In 2012, an on-line news outlet in South Africa had the following caption "Young girls kidnapped and forced to marry HIV-positive men . . . because sufferers believe VIRGINS are a cure for AIDS" (see Mail Online, May 28, 2012). This type of forced marriage is different from forced marriages in which parents freely participate in the marriage arrangement either as a way to promote rapport between families, or for pecuniary benefits; here they are sometimes hoodwinked into consenting to have their children forced into marriage with disease-afflicted men. This is not to dismiss the fact that some parents in South Africa are motivated by greed or need to consent to such unconscionable marriages of their daughters (Mail Online, May 28, 2012).

The problem of forced marriages is dire in South Sudan. According to statistics provided by the government, approximately half of the girls aged 15–19 and some as young as 12 are married. As a consequence of early marriages, these girls miss out on formal education. Accounts suggest that school enrollment for girls is just about 39 percent (CBSnews.com, March 8, 2013). Even though the government, and the Child's Act of the country sets marriage age at 18, girls are still forced to marry for financial reasons and allegedly, "to protect girls from sexual violence and ensure that they do not bring dishonor on the family by getting pregnant out of wedlock"

(CBSnews.com). The consequences of girls marrying at such tender ages in the country include acts of violence perpetrated on the girls, and high mortality rates of young mothers during childbirth. Resistance to any marriage may result in savagery on the girl and even relatives who attempt to intervene on her behalf. As Columbia Broadcasting System (CBS) news reported on March 8, 2013, a 17-year-old girl in South Sudan was beaten to death because she refused to marry a man about the age of her grandfather. Another girl who Human Rights Watch refers to as 15-year-old Aguet N. was forced to marry a 75-year-old man after the man gave her uncles 80 cows. The girl and her mother resisted the marriage, and both of them were subjected to severe beatings (CBSnews.com).

According to LaFraniere 2005:

> Child marriages remain entrenched in rural pockets throughout Sub-Saharan Africa, from Ghana to Kenya to Zambia, according to UNICEF. Studies show that the average age of marriage in this region remains among the world's lowest, and the percentage of adolescent mothers the world's highest.
>
> Many rural African countries, steeped in centuries of belief that girls occupy society's lower rungs, are inured to disapproval by the outside world.

While Ghana strives to be progressive, it has been unable to ward off some traditional practices that much of the world abhors. According to Canadainternational.gc.ca, "A joint United Nations-Ghana Press release indicates that 25 percent of girls will be married before their 18th birthday . . . about 27 percent of women aged 20–24 were married before age 18" (canadainternational.gc.ca/Ghana).

In 2005, a survey was conducted in Ghana under the supervision of the National Council on Women and Development on the issue of forced/early marriage. The findings were:

> Girls marry at an earlier age than boys and that parents and other close relations were more likely to decide and choose partners for the girl-child than the boy-child. . . . 22 percent of the married females stated that their parents decided for them as compared to 12 percent of the males. In addition, 30 percent of the females reported that their parents and other close relatives chose their partners for them as compared to 16 percent of the males. (Ardayfio 2005)

Ghana does have laws that prohibit marriages entered into without the consent of a party (see Act 29 of the Criminal Offences Act 1960), as well as laws that forbid forced marriages of children (Act 560 of the Children's Act of Ghana). Yet, the practice continues to flourish, with just a 1 percent drop rate since 2003 (Canadainternational.gc.ca.). A 2013 report reveals that 108 girls were forced into marriage in three districts in the upper west region of the country between 2011 and 2012, but fortunately for the girls a Community Based Anti-violence team rescued them (see allafrica.com July 9, 2013). While some reports contend that the problem is more prevalent in the upper west region, the Minister of Gender in the country noted on August 26, 2013, "forced marriage has assumed a disturbing trend in Ghana, with the Upper East Region recording the highest rate" (gbcghana.com).

Other reports raise an alarm about the dwindling enrollments of girls in schools, and the blame falls squarely on forced marriages according to Integrated Social Development Center (ISODEC), an NGO operating in Ghana. The decline of enrollment is because parents are wary to send their daughters to school because teachers may intervene to prevent an impending forced marriage. Parents maintain that the practice is a cultural means of uniting and strengthening family friendships, a means of financial benefits, and a means of shifting the expenses of taking care of their daughters to a husband (ghanabusinessnews.com).

At a 2014 summit in Addis Ababa, the capital of Ethiopia, where at least 50 African heads of states and representatives from the United Nations gathered, a two-year campaign to ban marriages of girls under 18 was launched. Martin Mogwanja, deputy executive director of UNICEF, stated that 4 of every 10 girls between 20–24 years in Africa married when they were children (see sbs.com.au 2014). To this, The Regional Director of the United Nations Population Fund (UNFPA) added, "progress has not come fast enough. The consequences of inaction will see 16 million child brides in Africa each year" (sbs.com.au 2014). Countries that were pinpointed as those where the problem is entrenched are Burkina Faso, Cameroon, Chad, Ethiopia, Mauritania, Mozambique, Niger, Sierra Leon, Malawi, Zimbabwe, and Zambia (sbs.com.au 2014). As well, the Democratic Republic of Congo was portrayed by UNICEF as a nation where 70 percent of child brides are married into polygamous unions, and to old abusive men (see sbs.com.au 2014). Nena Tundu, an African Union Social Affairs Researcher cautioned that without checks on practices of child brides millions of girls are turned into slaves, and they are pressured to become mothers at very tender ages (sbs.com.au 2014).

LEVIRATE

Levirate relates to a custom whereby "widows are inherited by their late husband's brother or other kin" Kiragu (1996). Traditional forms of marriages that prevail in many parts of Africa remain anomalous to the western world. Polygamous marriages, marriages that are forced or that require bride price, levirate, and sororate (sororate is a marriage between a widower and his wife's sister) are some of the peculiar types of marriages that still prevail throughout Africa even if sparsely in some parts.

While the practice of levirate is entrenched in tradition, religious precepts are also influential even if secondary. For instance, Deuteronomy 25: 5–10 states that: "If brethren dwell together, and one of them die, and have no child, the wife of the dead shall not marry without unto a stranger: her husband's brother shall go in unto her, and take her to him to wife, and perform the duty of a husband's brother unto her." The word levirate derives from the Latin word "*levir*" which means "husband's brother" (Encyclopedia of Judaism 2006).

In a study by Plateau et al. (2000), 120 women in different regions of Burkina Faso were surveyed to gauge their attitudes toward levirate, polygamous marriages, as well as their attitudes toward bride price. Reasons that women gave for supporting the practice of levirate marriage overwhelmingly were that because the widow and their children stayed together, that "the psychological and material support of the widow and children is better ensured" (Plateau et al. 2000). Among the reasons the women gave for not finding levirate marriage a good practice are that the widows are not taken good care of by their new husbands, the women are not physically attracted to the men, and that there is no love in such marriages (Plateau et al. 2000).

Regardless, levirate marriage is still prevalent among certain tribes in Burkina Faso especially among the Mossi, Gourmantche, Lobi, Dagara, Samo, and Gurunsi (see Kabore et al. 2008). Even though the spread of HIV/AIDS has slowed the practice, it is still in existence. Reports suggest that women subjected to levirate obligations are denied rights of inheriting their deceased husband's property, and are subjected to abuse of all types including violence (Kabore et al. 2008). Widows who are intransigent by refusing to marry their in-laws face reprisals which may take the form of violence, or even refusals from taking showers, or having a haircut for as many as three years. These practices as Kabore et al. (2008) state occur among the Lobi/Dagara tribe.

In a survey in Senegal regarding attitudes toward levirate marriages Plateau et al. (2000) found that 109 women believed levirate marriage is good, while 64 found it to be bad. Six women who thought levirate marriage was good "conditionally" explained that it was "good if the woman is rather old (one opinion), if the woman accepts it (two opinions), or if the relationship between husband and wife is good (three opinions)" (Plateau et al. 2000). The Family Code of 1972, Article 110 forbids marriage between a brother-in-law, and sister-in-law, but allows for levirate and sororate marriages as long as the initial marriage ended because of death.

Customary law in some parts of Nigeria makes it possible for the practice to be in sustenance. Take the Yoruba, the Igbo, and the Hausa-Fulani for instance; the practice still prevails (see Bamgbose 2002), even though some reports state that it is waning (2002). The consequence of not engaging in levirate marriage is that the widow may lose financial support, custody of any children, emotional support, and in some instances, particularly among the Igbos, face "persecution" from their deceased husband's family (Bamgbose 2002, Nwosa 2005).

> Levirate marriage is considered a custom of the Yoruba, the Igbo, and the Hausa-Fulani . . . levirate marriages . . . are commonest among the [I]gbo. . . . Under customary law among the Yoruba. . . . A brother or son of the deceased husband . . . was traditionally allowed to inherit the widow as a wife. . . . The inheritance of the youngest wife of the deceased by the eldest son . . . continues to be practiced in Yoruba land. . . . Under Igbo customary law . . . a brother or son of the deceased Igbo husband . . . was traditionally allowed to inherit the widow as a wife. (Encyclopedia of Judaism 2006)

Even though HIV/AIDS epidemic and enlightenment have drastically curbed the practice of levirate responsibilities, it has not been eradicated. Oddly, formal courts promote this practice. In *Ogunkoya v. Omo Ogunkoya* (1988:6) (Alewo and Olong 2012), the Court of Appeal explained that following Yoruba customary practices, widows are chattels that are inheritable by family members of the deceased husbands. Women who do not sever ties with the family of the deceased are subject to having any children they have in a new relationship (even if the man has no affinity by marriage to the deceased man) to be considered the child of the deceased husband and not that of the new man. As Alewo and Olong (2012) state "the woman does not have a say whatsoever in the matter, her humanity and feelings are completely ignored. This is of course unfair to both her and the natural father" (136).

The state of Enugu, as the Immigration and Refugee Board of Canada (2006) reports, has enacted The Prohibition of Infringement of a Widow's and Widower's Fundamental Rights Law, 2001. Among the protections the law provides is the right for a widow or widower not to engage in a levirate marriage: "No person for whatever purpose or reason shall compel a widow/widower . . . to be remarried by a relative of the late husband/wife" (Immigration and Refugee Board of Canada 2006), and both punitive and monetary sanctions will be meted to those who compel anyone to engage in a levirate marriage. As well, The Widows Development Organization (WiDO) of Enugu endorses the rights conferred to widows by the Nigerian government. Some of those rights include:

- Assisting widows to obtain legal protection or redress when they have been dispossessed of their belongings and inheritance
- Enabling them to hire lawyers and negotiate with their relatives
- Creating an avenue to facilitate negotiations with the extended families
- Providing training for support groups in advocacy and campaigning

- Setting up Vanguard Team which engages in mediation efforts with the husband's relatives. (Immigration and Refugee Board of Canada, 2006)

The practice still persists in parts of Kenya. In the Maragoli tribe of the west, for instance, widows who re-marry, primarily do so to their late husband's brother; while among the Nandi tribe of Kenya's Highland, it is customary that the deceased's man's brother become the widow's husband, as marriage to any other man would be considered adultery. "In Kenya, levirate marriage has been manipulated to the point that 'wife sponges,' a type of levirate gigolos, are paid by the family-in-law to seize the property of wives who have just lost their husbands" (Sorosoro.org).

In South Africa, the practice is known as *Ukungena.* While the practice still persists, it is to be reckoned that occurrences of it are minimal. The decline is thanks in part to awareness brought about by women's advocacy groups, and in part due to fear of HIV/AIDS. Variations of the practice exist even if in small numbers throughout Africa. In Zimbabwe the "*Kugara nhaka,*" which is levirate marriage, still occurs among the *Shona* tribe. Among the *Shona*, only the younger brother can "inherit" the older brother's bride; the reverse is inapplicable. The practice still occurs in Somalia, South Sudan, Ghana, and Cameroon, and perhaps in several other countries for which there is absence of literature on the issue.

In Cameroon, levirate is practiced in the North West and Western provinces of the country, and sparingly in some other provinces, such as the South West. As Ngassa and Time (1999) state, in those provinces in Cameroon where the practice of levirate exists "once bride price is paid on the woman, she becomes not only the wife of her husband but family property and so even if her husband dies, she is bound to marry one of her deceased husband's brothers" (117). This is in accordance with tradition, and not formal law.

It is not just that the practice is wrong; it is also a manifestation of further abuse and suffering widows endure. By denying them any inheritance rights, and handing them down as pieces of property a life of emotional and psychological abuse is perpetuated. The Cameroonian case of *David Tchakokam v. Keou Magdeleine* (1998) loudly speaks to the abuse of a woman's dignity. In that case, the plaintiff sued his levirate wife for the court to determine among several things "whether the defendant having been an object of inheritance along with the deceased's estate could lay claims to any part of her deceased husband's estate," (Ngassa and Time 1999, 111–12). Referring to the woman as an "object of inheritance" is as the court stated "The very terms in which that question is couched are so objectionable as to make it one of the most unpalatable questions a Common Law Court could ever be called upon to answer" (Ngassa and Time 1999, 113). As Ngassa (1998) reports, many more levirate marriages occur, as well as ensuing abuses, than are reported.

As well, when abuse is detected and there is intervention some women eschew the intervention. In the case of *AE/K Estate of Ndjonchuit* (n.d. unreported in Ngassa 1998), a court's attempt at intervening on behalf of a widow who had been hoodwinked into handing over court documents of her deceased husband's property to her in-laws, who then convinced her to marry one of the in-laws, was to no avail.

Studies by Malungo (1999) indicate that levirate marriage appears to be accepted for reasons that include the idea that a man who marries a deceased family member's widow is simply just taking care of the widow for the late relative, that he is simply continuing the lineage of the deceased man, and that he is retaining property in the family. Malungo (1999) concedes that the reasons for the prevalence of levirate marriages in the country are more complicated than that. As Malungo states, males and females are inherited in Zambia, and that in some of the tribes the practice is matrilineal. Malungo (1999, 50) discusses how the practice of levirate marriage is accomplished in Zambia:

> After the burial, the man's family takes you to the river and put some mud on your face and chest, a sign of mourning. They also give you *kkuba* (maize stalk) which you carry while mourning. This *kkuba* symbolized your being lonely after the death of your spouse. From the river, you lie down at a crossroads, and one or two of your in-laws would jump over you while you recite your husband's ancestral name. This marks your final separation from him. The following day, your family would wash you and dress you smartly. At the same time, the husband's family would line up possible men, to sexually cleanse you and perform levirate marriage. Long ago, it was really remarriage. The two of you are given a house to sleep in that night, and you have also accepted to marry that man. The following morning, they take you behind the house; they roast some cucumber seeds, which make noise. This is the noise which chases *musangu*, your husband's spirit, as they make the noise near your thighs, which he was very much fond of. From there that is the end, that man has inherited even your husband's name.

In a subsequent article, Malungo (2001) uses both qualitative and quantitative strategies to provide more insight on levirate marriages in Zambia. First, Malungo explains why tradition in Zambia requires sexual cleansing of a widow prior to a levirate marriage. Malungo explains that the practice is necessary to prevent the widow from being ostracized, and from getting insane. However, as Malungo goes on to explain, based on findings from research participants, while they would like to continue customary practices, the fear of HIV/AIDS, education, wide spread of western religion, and modernized life-style, act as restraints to continuous sexual cleansing or levirate marriages. Other types of rituals as for instance, cutting the widow's hair, cleansing the widow with herbs, and other procedures are now preferred over sexual cleansing. Unfortunately, as Malungo points out, property of the deceased does not go to the widow, it remains under the dominion, control, and possession of the person that performed the ritual regardless of whether the widow marries that person or stays unmarried; this even though the 1989 Intestate Succession Act prohibits that type of "property grabbing." Among other problems that ensue from property grabbing as Malungo explains are the financial burden to both the immediate family and society at large who have to chip in to assist the widow either financially or emotionally. For those who still continue the ritual of sexual cleansing, deaths from AIDS have soared, as well as an upsurge of orphans (Malungo 2001). Malungo thus calls for government, religious, non-governmental organizations, and international organizations to intervene.

In Mali, the practice of levirate is common among the Supyire people. As Jemphrey (2011) explains, levirate marriages among the Supyire people provide permanence to a family structure; it is a means by which the levirate wives and their offspring get access to land and other property—things that provide them means of sustenance. As Schulz (2012) explains, the practice of levirate is acceptable because it serves as a guarantee that ownership of the deceased husband's property will remain in the family, and that the widow and her offspring with her deceased husband will continuously be taken care of as the bond with the deceased husband's family is maintained.

A Canadian Broadcasting Corporation reported the practice of widows inherited by their husband's family in Ghana in 2004 (refworld.org 2006). The Widows and Orphans Ministry (WOM) of Ghana, which acknowledged that levirate practices exist in the upper east region of Ghana, corroborated this information.

Sororate marriages also exist in Africa. A sororate marriage is one that entails a widower marrying his wife's sister. Sometimes, sororate marriages can take place even when there is no loss of life, but simply because a man's wife is unable to bear children (stopvaw.org).

FEMALE CIRCUMCISION

Lionnet (2005) explains female circumcision as "clitoridectomy, but can also be accompanied by the excision of all or part of the labia, and by infibulation (or stitching together) of the two sides of the vulva" (99). Althaus (1997) simply explains it as "the partial or total cutting away of the external genitalia."

According to Althaus (1997) and Toubia (1995), at least 28 countries in Africa, primarily those in the northern part of the continent, practice female circumcision. The practice is not limited to any religious or ethnic group. Althaus (1997) states that 43 percent to 97 percent of women in Central African Republic, Cote d'Ivoire, Egypt, Eritrea, Mali, and Sudan, have undergone the practice. Further, she indicates that about 94 percent of Malian women in their reproductive age have been circumcised; of that percentage only 17 percent of women are from the Tamachek tribe. Maluleke (2012) explains that the procedure of female genital mutilation occurs in the Tsonga and Sotho communities of South Africa. In some communities in South Africa as Maluleke explains, the procedure is considered the gateway to womanhood. Others also consider it a procedure that increases fertility, limits a woman's desire for sex, and thus limits promiscuity.

Female circumcision is also practiced in Burkina Faso. It is mainly considered to be a traditional ritual intended as rite of passage to adulthood. According to Kabore et al., all tribal groups, as well as all religious groups in the country perform circumcision on females. Statistics provided by Kabore et al. show that 77 percent of women in the country have in some way experienced genital mutilation. Statistics on the various tribes indicate that 81.5 percent of Mossi, 76 percent of Lobi, 69.6 percent of Bobo, and 39.1 percent of Gurunsi have undergone the procedure. Other data reveal that 30 percent of women between the ages of 15–49 have at least a daughter who has undergone the practice. As well data reveal that people of all denominations engage in the practice: 61 percent of animists, 32 percent of Muslims, 23 percent of Catholics, 14 percent of Protestants (Kabore et al. 2008).

Female circumcision is entrenched in tradition, and it prevails because of patriarchal norms that still control female sexuality (Althaus 1997). The assumption is that female circumcision reduces the urge to have sex, and for unmarried girls it means a prospective husband can rest assured of the purity of the girl; for married girls and women, the man can live with no worries about the wife having sex outside the marriage. In those cultures where female circumcision takes place, circumcised girls fetch higher bride price, and as some of the girls who have undergone the procedure contend, it helps preserve virginity and fidelity during marriage, and bolsters their husband's sexual satisfaction (Althaus 1997). On the other hand, the harms that ensue from the practice include excessive hemorrhage, urinary infections, abscesses, urethra stones, fertility/sterility problems, and even death (Althaus 1997).

Much has been written about female circumcision, and while it is an unusual practice, the debate seems to hinge on how the practice is reported. Walker (1997) for instance, in a novel claims that the procedure is performed "with rusty razors, tin-can tops, shared pieces of unwashed glass or a sharpened stone's edge" (Obiora 2005, 196). This and others are claims that Obiora (2005) vehemently abhors, and refers to as "replete . . . with pedestrian broadsides."

Steffen (2011) outlines some of the ribald assumptions that outsiders make about the practice:

Table 6.1. Regional Data on Female Circumcision in Burkina Faso (by Kabore et al. 2008, 22)*

No.	Region	Prevalence Rate (%)
1	North	63.08
2	Central Plateau	62.63
3	Sahel	57.34
4	Centre-East	56.2
5	Hauts-Bassins	54.69
6	Mouhoun	54.66
7	Centre-North	50.46
8	Cascades	48.13
9	Centre	45.58
10	Centre-West	44.77
11	East	37.75
12	Centre-South	37.65
13	South-West	31.92

*Source: The Inter-Agency Network on Women and Gender Equality Task Force on Violence Against Women. U.N. Org/Women Watch Task Force. Version anglaise de l'etude de base VEF 2009).

1. A sinister vestige of barbarism, which violates universal standards of modern civilization
2. An oppressive system of patriarchy which attempts to control female sexuality through physical violence
3. A culturally sanctioned form of torture which violates every human's right to bodily integrity and individual autonomy
4. A despotic assertion of parental power which places the emotional and physical well-being of children at grave risk
5. An alien practice of Islamic affiliation which African Muslims are transplanting to the West (4).

Althaus (1997) reports that many of the women who have gone through the process see it as a way of life; accordingly, they perpetuate the practice. Data from Eritrea suggest that because of medical issues that sometimes ensue, men are more open to have women abandon the practice than women are. On the contrary, Sudanese men favor the continuation of the practice (Althaus 1997). How the practice is construed and reported, and the connotations given to the practice generate a scintillating debate. Opinions and reports from many westerners are tendentious mainly regarding the practice as torture, or inhumane, abhorrent acts, while locals view it as cultural rites. Lionnet (2005) frames the debate as entailing "two apparently conflicting versions of human rights, one based on the Enlightenment notion of the sovereign individual subject, and the other on a notion of collective identity grounded in cultural solidarity" (99). This is not to suggest that the debate is exclusively between Western versus African viewpoints; even among Africans, the practice creates a divide in ideology.

Regardless of the thrust of the debate, Obiora (2005) maintains that:

> One cannot help but concede that there are substantial merits to some aspects of the campaign against female circumcision. Where there is *well-founded* evidence that some practices are harmful, the issue ceases to be whether the custom should be challenged. The issue becomes how to identify and execute the responsibilities of relevant communities for extenuating the danger of harm. (194)

The physical, health, social, and psychological impact of forced marriages, bride price, and levirate are sometimes difficult to discuss apart especially since sometimes the acts are interconnected. For example, forced marriages may generate bride price, and that may lead to domestic violence as well.

Physical Violence: Bentheim (2010), Beswick (2001), Hague and Thiara (2009), Kaye et al. (2005), Mongbo (2007), Park (2006), and a host of others have written about the different forms of abuse evident in these practices. As a consequence of the fact that women are objectified in the thinking of men, the acts of violence they perpetrate on women include: assault and batteries, rapes, mutilations, and loss of life. Even in the absence of empirical data, it is logical to assume that a marriage that one never wanted is devoid of affection, and absence of affection in any relationship may be a catalyst for violence. As Reddy (2008) states, researchers and activists have reasoned that, "forced marriage is both a type of 'honour crime' in itself, and the precursor to or result of other types of honour-related violence" (306). Welchman and Hossain (2005) share similar beliefs.

VIOLENCE AGAINST WOMEN

While each act of violence stands apart, it is difficult to fathom girls slashed with a hoe, subjected to constant beatings, and forced to have sex even when they are ill simply because the man feels entitled to so do since he "bought" the woman (Hague and Thiara 2009). Episodic analyses of the brutality perpetrated against girls and women forced to marry does injustice to those whose victimizations are not included in the narrative. However, just to highlight the depth of violence entailed in these customary practices, a couple of examples are included. The egregiousness of axing off the legs of a

12-year-old recalcitrant, Hauwa Abukar, in Nigeria by a man she was forced to marry exemplifies the extent of violence, and impunity since no legal action was taken against the man (Black 2001; Time 2013). In Mali, a 13-year-old forced into marriage died the night of her wedding following complications from sexual intercourse with her husband (IRIN Africa 2007). Since hardly anything is done to these men, abused girls and women just accept abuse as a way of life, and even when reports are filed, they are coerced into retracting the accusations (Center for Reproductive Rights 2003). This is not endemic to a particular country; it is prevalent in every country where forced marriages, bride price, and levirate are accepted.

Take Sierra Leone as an example: customary law permits the chastisement of women, and because they have to always seek parental approval, women are considered perpetual minors (Dossier of Claims: Sierra Leone). In 2007, Sierra Leone passed an act devoted to domestic violence. Those convicted of domestic violence can be sentenced to up to two years, with a fine of up to 5m Leones (Ford 2012). Abuse of women and girls reached epic numbers during the civil war (1991–2002). During this time as Physician for Human Rights reports, between 215,000–257,000 girls and women may have been affected by sexual violence. Following empirical research conducted by a United Nations mission in Sierra Leone in 2000, the following data were revealed: 73 percent of women interviewed, some 20 percent being girls ages 6–17, claimed having been subjected to human rights abuses, 47 percent had been raped, 20 percent gang raped, 41 percent were abducted, 3 percent forced to marry their abductors. Of marked relevance is the fact that the Appeals Chamber of the Special Court for Sierra Leone (SCSL) in 2008 was known to be the first international tribunal to recognize forced marriage as a crime by itself. The Appeals Chamber in *Prosecutor v. Brima, Kamara, and Kanu* (commonly known as the AFRC trial) declared that forced marriage is a separate offense from sexual slavery and is a crime against humanity. It is to be reckoned that the Appeals Chamber (Gong-Gershowitz 2009) upheld the lower court's sentences of fifty years each to Brim and Kanu, and forty-five years to Kamara. The Court surmised that while enslaving one for the purpose of sex is a "horrendous crime" forcing another into marriage "is even more gruesome because of the length of the association and its domestic nature" (UNA.GB Model U.N. n.d.). Ford (2012) reports "husbands, not strangers or men with guns, are now the biggest threat to women in post-conflict West Africa."

Wife beating seems to be a way of life in Cameroon. As Time (2012, 463–64) states:

> In Cameroon, wife beating has been accepted as part of the culture. This attitude sometimes influences the statutory courts to the extent that a judge will hold it is right for a man to chastise the wife. Most often the women run to

> the police who will treat the problem as a family issue and ask the women to return to their homes. There are no structures that can help to facilitate justice. Many women are hesitant to complain, for one thing they think nobody is going to listen to them; secondly, they don't want to be stigmatized by society. They are not encouraged to report. Most often, the courts learn of violence in the home only during divorce proceedings at that time the assault is not given the attention it deserves. As Ngassa (1998) noted, even the hospitals where the victims run to, never keep statistics and are not empowered to make reports on behalf of the victims. In the case of Ndenno c/ Mme Guamgne Alphonsine (no. 36 of June 27, 1996), the Baffoussam Court of Appeal dismissed the wife's claims that her husband used to strangle her until she succumbed to unnatural acts of sexual intercourse. The court held the assertions were not proven since there was no witness. It should be noted that domestic violence takes the form of physical violence, emotional and economic violence. (FIDA CAMEROON "Women Children and the Law" 1996)

In Burkina Faso as Kabore et al. (2008) report, domestic violence takes the form of "battering, rape, and early and forced marriages" (15). As these researchers acknowledge, early and forced marriages are quite prevalent throughout the country, especially in the villages, among the Sahel, the Fulanis, and the Gurmanche (Kabore et al. 2008). These authors also explain that official data are likely skewed because many incidents of early and forced marriages are not reported, hence the dark figure of crime (Kabore et al. 2008). The authors also report that following a focus group discussion of women ages 25–49, the women disclosed that violence perpetrated on them by their husbands occurs so frequently that their supposition is that male violence is an inherent trait (Kabore et al. 2008). As well, the society appears to have a twisted view of the impact of wife beating. As Kabore et al. report, wife beating is deemed to be a "favorite sport" in certain parts of the country, and that wife beating is for the most part considered to be "an accepted part of being a woman" even though the country's 1991 constitution prohibits domestic violence (Kabore 2008, 16).

Other researchers have intimated that forced marriage likely leads to a persistence of marital rape after all, since there was no consent to the marriage, it is hard to fathom consent to sexual relations (Reddy 2008; Siddiqui 2003). As well, attempts at severing such relations by escaping or asking for a divorce, exacerbates violence (See Time 2013; Bentheim 2010; Mongbo 2007; Siddiqui 2003).

There are no reliable records of the occurrences of domestic violence in Niger, but according to State.gov. (2011) wife beating is prevalent. Even though there are laws that punish acts of violence, domestic violence is not expressly prohibited. Long-seated traditions that allow a man to treat a woman in whatever way he deems fit surpass legislations that bar domestic violence (state.gov 2011). Further, because of ignorance of their rights, women seldom file complaints of domestic violence. "Charges stemming from family disputes were often dropped in favor of traditional dispute resolution mechanisms. While women have the right to seek redress for violence in the customary or modern courts, few did so due to ignorance of the redress offered by the legal system and fear of retaliation or being stigmatized" (state.gov 2011).

HEALTH AND OTHER PHYSICAL AND PSYCHOLOGICAL PROBLEMS

Bentheim (2010), Black (2001), Bunch (1990), Erez and Thompson (1996), Monekosso (2001), Oyebanji (1981), Welstead (2009), and others have documented extensively health issues associated with forced and levirate marriages (Time 2013). Among the health issues discussed are sexually transmitted diseases such as HIV and AIDS, and other infectious diseases (Bentheim 2010; Plan-UK.org). Sexually transmitted diseases are prevalent because many of the men are not only polygamists they are promiscuous as well (Plan-UK.org). To further retain their sexual autonomy by making them less desirable to other men, husbands impregnate their wives so frequently, even against a doctor's warning that the woman's life may be in jeopardy. For girls/children forced into sexual relations at such tender ages they may be susceptible to early deaths (Erez and Thompson 1996), or complications during pregnancies and childbirth (Bentheim 2010) especially when there is limited prenatal care. Without proper care and correct nourishment, Bentheim (2010) reports that young girls forced into marriage suffer from poorly developed pelvic bones, which may impede healthy and safe childbirth. Leserman (2005) concludes that there is a causal link between a history of sexual abuse and "poor health status, more functional disability, more utilization of health services, and more physical symptoms, particularly gastrointestinal, gynecologic, panic related, and headache" (912). Meanwhile, Yuan et al. (2006), assert that experiences of sexual trauma or its onset may be different among victims, and that how long such experiences take before they become evident or before they dissipate vary. Experiences may vary from "depression, suicidal thoughts and attempts, problem alcohol abuse, disordered eating behaviors and sexual dysfunction" (Yuan et al. 2006, 3). Others have written about the profound shame and guilt that children who have been sexually abused experience, as well as resentment to sex even as adults, or experiencing a diametrically opposite extreme—being quite promiscuous as they grow to adulthood (Smith and Segal 2012).

Campbell et al. (2002) conclude that "abused women have a 50 percent to 70 percent increase in gynecological, central nervous system, and stress-related problems, with women sexually and physically abused most likely to report problems" (1157). Their study was carried out in the United States, and participants were drawn from a diverse racial pool, from ages ranging between 21 and 55, and from all educational and income-generating background; but of more relevance is the fact that the health measure used in the study was the standard Medical Outcomes Study 36-Item Short-Form Health Survey, which has been proven to be reliable among different populations. Of remarkable interest the researchers found that women who had been subjected to sexual abuse regardless of whether they had also been exposed to physical abuse were more likely to have reported one or more episodes of chronic stress or central nervous system breakdown than women who were simply just victims of physical abuse. Remarkable too was the fact that women who reported physical abuse only, also reported at least one gynecological problem just as those who reported sexual abuse. In sum, women subjected to both sexual and physical abuse reported among other illnesses "headache, back pain, vaginal infection, and digestive problems" as most recurring problems (Campbell et al. 2002, 1161), while women who reported sexual abuse reported "sexually transmitted diseases, vaginal bleeding, painful intercourse, pelvic pain, urinary tract infection, loss of appetite, and abdominal pain." Studies done by Jina and Thomas (2012) in South Africa confirm many of the illnesses discussed in the study by Campbell et al. (2002), and expound on it by discussing mental-health issues as well.

As a consequence of women being objectified it seems obvious that physical violence apart, the impact of psychological turmoil cannot be underscored. This is the case not only for women but also for children born into these relationships. In abusing their wives, men develop a false sense of self, fueled by abused women's diminished self-worth. Psychological abuse may take the form of isolation, manipulating a victim's sense of fear, deprivation that may take the form of financial and sexual. This intersection between poverty and violence creates a rippling effect that impacts the women, their children, and the community.

As Time, 2013 notes:

> The physical and emotional abuses that accompany such marriages scar the women for life. They never can carve out their own identities. Children forced into marriage miss out on childhood as they assume the role of wives and mothers at the dawn of their lives. They are deprived of education, are forever subordinates, sometimes rendered too timid to ask for basic acts of civility and loyalty from their abusive and promiscuous husbands (see Bentheim 2010; Immigration and Refugee Board of Canada 2007). As Chigbu et al. (2010, 141) conclude, the leading cause in Southeastern Nigeria of high incidents in husbands' total monopoly in decisions regarding sex," "sex related verbal abuse," as well as "sex related physical violence, and forced sex" are a consequence of "a culture of male dominance." Their families give the women and children away, and because they are commoditized, it is futile to be recalcitrant. Attempts at escape only exacerbate their plight (see Welstead 2009;

> Black 2001) and, of course, they cannot run back home. Kaye et al. (2005, 302), in their ethnographic study in Uganda quote a Non-Governmental Organization (NGO) employee's observation: "men are dominant in decision-making. The woman has no power for anything. Where the man is suspicious or insecure, domestic violence is common." Another participant in the study states "Women lack power to make decisions in the home. The culture does not allow them to stand up to the men. The laws also support men." (Kaye et al. 2005, 302)
>
> Those women who have the fortitude to ask for a divorce must then fend for themselves and for their children. The children born into these abusive homes grow to know abuse; for those whose parents divorce, they lose the constant presence of their father. Some of these children are exposed to a lifetime of abuse, and hardships, and to a culture that they assume is a way of life. (275–76)

According to Pagelow (1984), the standard of living of an abused woman who leaves the abuser usually takes a downward tumble, and in the event that there are children in the relationship, their odds of falling below the poverty level significantly increase. To avoid this, as Pagelow explains is in part the reason why women stay in abusive relationships until the children reach adulthood. Others have found a link between children from broken homes and poor academic performance, low self-esteem, behavioral issues, poor social skills, defiance, distant, untrusting, separation-anxiety, tantrums, clinging, among others (Amato 2001; Hughes 2005; Pickhardt 2011).

Writing about what goes on in South Africa, Maluleke (2012) states:

> There is a proven link between a lack of education, underdevelopment and poverty. *Ukuthwala* deprives girl children of opportunities to educate and develop themselves. Furthermore, research indicates that the majority of the girls and young women that are victims of *Ukuthwala* are from poor families. Their lack of education and underdevelopment, due to *Ukuthwala,* deepens their poverty and perpetuates the cycle of poverty. In many instances the children born into poverty also tend to be poor. This contributes to the cycle of poverty in the communities, particularly rural communities, where *Ukuthwala* is rife. (12)

Besides the sorrow and despair that generally accompanies a broken relationship these emotions do sometimes translate to shame in instances where a woman leaves her marriage and does not refund the bride price. The shame is brought about because even after a divorce she remains the wife of her estranged husband since she still owes him the bride price, and even in the event of her death, her estranged husband has claim to her corpse over her current husband (see Ngassa 1998).

Other types of abuse women in Cameroon whose family received bride price are put through include:

> Being forced to sit in confinement on the bare floor for at least eight days, not taking a bath for at least eight days, not being allowed to communicate with anyone except through other widows, going on a "*moukoussa's*" (widow's) diet, paying for cleansing, not shaking hands for a whole year.
>
> The Awings of the Ngemba tribe force the widow to go naked from waist up . . . she remains naked no matter how cold. She may be allowed a covering at night if she pays a bribe or fine. The widow is forced to sit with her legs outstretched with her two big toes touching at all times and her right hand holding the left shoulder. By the time most widows get up they are unable to walk properly and have to be helped by the older widows.
>
> The Bakossi of the South West Province confine the widow in a room with a smoking fire which makes her eyes weep all the time. Some go as far as making the widow eat a frog or pay a fine in order not to eat it. (Ngassa 1998, 44–45)

These are not only shameful; they are psychologically devastating. Some other psychological problems adults who have undergone "long-term" sexual trauma experience as discussed by Yuan et al. (2006) include body dysmorphic disorders and body mutilation.

Forced and early marriages create an unfair burden to the young girl/wife who soon becomes a mother, and besides taking care of her baby, also has to cater after her husband and in-laws.

Part III

Recommendations

Chapter Seven

Recommendations

When this researcher posed the question of what could be done to improve women's economic situation to the research participants in Cameroon discussed in chapter two, not surprising, responses to this question were diverse. A former head of the Agency for Community Development, a woman in her 60s, explained that the Division of Social Affairs through outreach programs makes women know their rights, but conceded that because of inadequate funding, such outreach programs are available only to a small proportion of women. She recommended more funding for that agency to enable it continue to promote women's rights. The agency teaches women to realize that girls' education is just as valuable as that of boys. She also complained about traditional marriages in Anglophone Cameroon because they do not legitimize such marriages. She explained that traditional marriages in Francophone Cameroon are given more legitimacy because the couples receive marriage certificates, so in the event of divorce, the woman is not left without any means of support from the husband, but then as she said in Anglophone Cameroon, traditional marriages simply translate to what she described in pidgin English as "come we stay," in essence, just being a perpetual live-in girlfriend with no legitimacy. She advocated a change in laws so that traditional marriages and extended live-in situations that translate as common law marriages be recognized.

A retired primary school teacher at the focus group interview emphasized the need for formal education for women, and why government should invest more on adult educational classes so that women can at least benefit from that. She stated that education is necessary to enable women to know how to count their money, and how to invest it. She also said if a woman is educated, she will make sure that her children, and other family members get an education. The majority of women chimed in concurring that education is the main path to women's empowerment. As one woman concluded "what is necessary is that education the woman gets is able to give her a voice and something she can do to not sit there and be looking for the man to give her a franc."

Another woman opined that if women could learn about foreign trade and business in general, they might gradually get out of poverty.

A grade one teacher in her fifties addressed the importance of NGOs during the one-on-one interview. She said that while NGOs are helpful in steering women toward action-oriented paths, they are not as action oriented as local activists groups because the government puts much constraints on them. "They end up just having much paper work, and nothing much to show for as success." The teacher suggested that government lift barriers that hamper the work of NGOs because they "have good ideas to help women become more independent." She also spoke about the scarcity of technology in most schools in Cameroon, especially in Anglophone Cameroon, and how that impedes modern day research. She asked for computers even if used ones in the libraries, as well as internet services in schools even if for just a few hours. She emphatically explained that computers and internet services are no longer luxuries. They are quite integral to modern-day learning, and information gathering. She also added that most schools especially elementary schools do not have libraries, and even secondary schools with libraries are poorly stocked, so even used books donated to schools will improve learning.

An elderly woman during the one-on-one interview applauded the efforts of some female lawyers in the South West Province of the country. She said female lawyers hold meetings with women every month end to educate them on marriage issues, what to do as a married woman, on healthcare, and how to save and invest money. She said the lawyers educate women on "how to take control of their lives so that they are not made stupid by men." The lady explained that while those lectures are mostly in urban settings, she thinks that if they could be extended to women in rural areas, women will be more empowered. The lectures are not paid for, but women contribute 1000 francs cfa ($2), simply for entertainment. The researcher asked the one female lawyer present during the interviews about what motivated female lawyers to begin this initiative. The lawyer said that abuse of women was rampant, and since many women were timid to file complaints, and cultural norms stifle their ability to do so it was necessary to let women know that abuse was unacceptable, and that they could always file reports against abusive men. She also strenuously advocated that government repel laws that promote capricious customary practices, and laws that either directly or indirectly promote practices that are unfair toward women.

A woman in her forties explained during the interview that while she wasn't trafficked, but living with an aunt when she was not even a teenager was an experience that she will never put any of her children through. She explained how even though she was just about the age of her aunt's children, she was responsible for their care, doing their laundry, and cooking for them, and while they went off to secondary schools, she stayed working for her aunt. She said she felt less of a family member but more of a slave. She recommended that those who take in children as domestic help need help; because she rhetorically asked "what makes one person's child better than that of another?" When asked what type of "help" she was suggesting, she said counseling so they know how to treat other people's children well. She said while she has forgiven her aunt, she hasn't forgotten the years of suffering. She did indicate that for children and women who live and work for wealthy relatives for no pay, the relatives at least should have an obligation to do something for the children or women, send them to trade school, save some money for them to start a life after leaving the services of the relative, at least do something to better the life of the servant. Asked why she had to live with her aunt and not with her parents, she said her parents were poor and had many children, and they thought her aunt who had a better job would help take care of her and give her a better life. It is noteworthy that the practice of wealthy family members taking in children of poor family members is common in the country.

The oldest of the participants, a lady in her seventies, explained that while she understands that poverty also calls for ways of survival, she recommended counseling because parents ought to know that a parent should never sacrifice a child for their needs. She recommended some type of punitive sanction, and restitution imposed on men who marry young girls especially if they do not enable the girl to acquire an education, or fail to do something that improves the girl's quality of life.

One of the women indicated that women in some parts of the country especially the francophone parts of the country appear to be more successful in lobbying for government assistance; consequently, they have more advanced appliances, tools like ploughs, and other equipment to facilitate farm work. She went on to suggest that such lobbying skills should be disseminated to women in other parts of the country in hopes that government will give similar attention to them as well. As she said, "because we are still more of an agricultural country, we need these tools that help us produce more and better crops." Also, as she went on to say, better roads especially in the Southwest region is a dire need. The lawyer agreed with the woman, and explained that anything that will help limit time poverty will go a significant way to help women, and to bolster the economy in general. Below are recommendations that have been put forth by NGOs, and researchers on the issues.

POVERTY

On poverty, the recommendations comprise making available to women better training programs, equipment, transportation, establishing empowerment groups for women, and gathering reliable data that can help in assessing improvement levels of women.

As a fluid experience, what poverty is varies from person to person, from time to time, and from society to society. Wilson (1997) explains that the difficulty of finding work, the difficulty in getting transportation to work, the paucity of programs that train potential workers account for poverty among denizens in ghettos in the United States. Jacob (2005) takes well the point, and further expounds on it by explaining that ghetto residents are in no way responsible for these problems, rather the whole system is to blame. The current study and many others have not ignored Jacob's premise.

Abdourahman (2010), explaining time poverty in Africa takes issue with patriarchal divisions of gender roles. He explains that when women's domestic workload is lessened, women can then indulge in remunerated jobs and other more productive jobs. This, he contends benefits society as a whole and helps to attain a country's Millennium Development Goal (MDG). He recommends better and more efficient energy sources such as those needed for cooking and heating. He also recommends better transportation, clean water, good sanitation, and waste disposal systems as simple ways of getting women out of poverty. He stresses the need for time-use data through surveys so as to incorporate women's domestic work in national budgets and accounting classifications. Those kinds of data are crucial in putting together programs and policies that solidify women's economic and social rights (Abdourahman 2010).

Women can create empowerment groups that can lobby for their rights in both traditional settings and in judicial forums. As Scalise (2012) reports, "The Grassroots Sisterhood Foundation" collaborates with local women in the northern parts of Ghana to help improve their tenure security to land in various ways that include:

- Developing alliances with tribal chiefs, religious leaders, professionals, land agencies, and other groups in the community;
- Holding stakeholder forums; training women on their land, property and inheritance rights;
- And holding community conversations to raise the awareness of land and property issues among traditional and religious leaders (Scalise 2012, 59).

As a success story, Scalise (2012) recounts how using the above suggestion, a group of women was able to (even though it entailed persistence, and a little change out of their wallets to buy drinks) convince the Chief's elders, counselors, and ultimately the chief to bestow to the women 5 hectares of land. Each woman could bequeath her portion of land to her children.

As revealed to this researcher in 2014 during a focus group interview with Cameroonian women, a somewhat similar practice exists in the South West province of the country. Women are assisted by female lawyers through lectures to figure out how to take control of their lives in matters of finance, healthcare, property ownership, and education. They do not spend any money for these lectures, but women contribute about 1000 cfa. which is approximately $2 for each meeting just for entertainment and advancing camaraderie.

Some women in the focus group interview in Cameroon explained that devices like ploughs would go a long way to help them in their farms. They explained that women in some provinces in the country who have these devices have their work facilitated, and farm yields doubled. Those women with devices as was explained have much opportunity to lobby for funds for such equipment. The women explained that in the South West province where they reside farm work is still quite labor intensive, so women bind in groups of about fifty to till soil for one woman and then move on to the next. Farm machinery would go a long way to ease up life for these women and to reduce the amount of energy and time they spend in doing farm work just for subsistence and petty trade. As well, equipment that helps process and preserve farm products such as cassava and yams will go a long way to help women. It behooves mentioning that products like cassava and yams that are locally produced in most African countries are processed and preserved abroad in countries like the United States and sold back to the producing countries at exorbitant prices. Solar dryers used in preserving crops have been found to be more efficient, more hygienic, and less time consuming than when such crops are left out in the open to have the sun preserve them as commonly done by most small-scale African farmers. Mulokozi (2000) had since written about the noticeable hike in produce preservation in Tanzania following the advent of solar dryers in the country. Many more of his findings are discussed below.

The World Bank suggests getting frequent reliable data in order to be able to assess progress and to implement and evaluate policies. Accurate statistics are necessary in estimating a country's GDP, and in order to understand poverty. Citing Malawi, the World Bank discusses problems inherent when data are not consistent and reliable. Reports by different agencies in the country, including the Ministry of Agriculture, the National Census of Agriculture and Livestock, and National Statistical Office, in 2006–2007 regarding maize harvests provided divergent data ranging from 1.6 tons to 2.6 tons per hectare. Such a huge disparity in numbers made it difficult to determine progress not only in approximating annual yields but quality as well (Worldbank.org 2013).

Technology, as the Worldbank.org 2013 states, can be instrumental in collecting data. Giving the fact that a good percentage of Africans rely on mobile phones as a primary medium of communication, this is a potential data collection medium especially as it relates to household surveys.

The use of simple technological gadgets like handheld Global Positioning Systems may help in identifying locations of crop yields (WorldBank.org 2013).

Improving soil quality is also crucial in increasing both the quality and quantity of crop yield. High levels of productivity will have an immediate effect of combating hunger, and a long-term effect of reducing poverty. With increased crop production, farmers will not only plant for subsistence, they will get involved in export. During a one-on-one interview with women in Cameroon in 2014, one woman in her forties explained that crop improvement was necessary to alleviate poverty. She explained that since cocoa farmers rely on productivity level and quality, there has to be better ways of achieving that. She explained how overused the soil is, and how farmers set some of the farms on fire hoping that when new crops are planted they will do better. Better ways of improving soil quality using modern products and modern devices to facilitate fertilizing huge farms are desperately needed. The woman said that when cocoa sales are low parents face the choice of sending either sons or daughters to school; invariably, she concedes, sons are sent.

As noticed in Cameroon during two visits to the country in 2013, and one in 2014 low-cost home devices like stoves that require less firewood but generate more heat, help reduce women's time and energy in fetching and splitting firewood, as well as time spent in fanning fires while cooking. The thesis is that equipment and devices that help reduce activities that constitute time poverty are much needed, as they in turn will help reduce poverty among women.

With regard to time and energy that women expend on farm work, tilling the soil, planting, taking out weeds, harvesting, and all else, better tools and equipment, fertilizers, pesticides, and other things that dramatically can cut down human labor will enable women to devote time to other activities. Using Tanzania as an example, Mulokozi (2000) explained how the use of food processing technologies substantially saved time women used for drying food, and also helped retain the nutritional value of the foods. Typically in many African societies, in order to preserve grains, vegetables, crushed roots like cassava and cocoyam, and other farm products like plantains, women dry them on mats for several days and at times weeks. Sometimes, animals, birds, and bugs feast on them, contaminate them, and their nutritional value is compromised based on the effects of direct sunlight, and other elements. Better ways of preserving crops will reduce time and energy that women exert in the process, and will also help to retain the nutritional value of the crops. Mulokozi discusses how the Tanzania Food and Nutrition Centre (TFNC) in collaboration with other organizations in the country manufactured solar dryers that facilitated the drying process of foods and kept the integrity of the foods intact. In order to test the efficacy of the dryers a comparison was made between two groups of women—those that used the dryers, and those who maintained the status quo. At the end of one year, it was discovered that women who adopted the solar drying process produced on an aggregate 55 liters while those who did not produced 33 liters. Those who used the dryers as Mulokozi reports dried different types of vegetables, and in bigger quantities. Of more relevance is the fact that foods that were dried using solar dryers provided more vitamin A than those that were dried through direct sunlight. In terms of time management, if women could have access to these technologically improved equipment and devices, women could use their time and effort for other projects including going to school to pursue an education or to learn a trade.

Another woman in the one-on-one interview conducted by this researcher in Cameroon in 2014 explained that Cameroonian women might escape poverty by getting knowledgeable about trade and business in general. She said:

> Many Cameroonian women are not business minded, and have not left their towns or villages where they live. They do not know the foreign markets, have not established clientele abroad; and those women who know and have these connections are reluctant to share because they worry about competition. Training women on how to conduct foreign trade will greatly increase their income. The vegetables they produce can be shipped to foreign markets in Gabon and Nigeria, and other countries.

When asked by this researcher whether getting formal education, teaching a woman a trade, or as the researcher jokingly asked marrying a rich man can be most helpful in lifting women from poverty, one of the participants during the interview without reservations said "education." She continued to state that:

> Education is the best because modern world education, reading even little and counting money is enough. It is not the level of education a woman gets, what is necessary is that education the woman gets is able to give her a voice and something she can do to not sit there and be looking for the man to give her a franc.

RESTRICTED PROPERTY RIGHTS

Benschop (2002, 50) explains that three main things are necessary to promote women's property rights. They are: "ensuring gender-sensitive legislation; promoting judicial capacity and effective litigation; and advancing public awareness and understanding." She elaborates these further by explaining that in environments where women's property rights are tenuous the following should be done:

> Reforming inadequate or discriminatory legislation, attending to the divide between customary and statutory law, sensitizing chiefs, elders, and community residents to gender aspects of property issues, and working to ensure that women have local access to legal channels and resources [may strengthen women's rights]. Engaging men and boys at every step along the way, especially through activities oriented to gender awareness and human rights education, is vital since the realization of women's property and inheritance rights requires a fundamental transformation of social norms surrounding gender relations and power dynamics. (Benschop 2002, 50)

Others have echoed Benschop's points. Maluleke (2012) suggests a review of customary law to eliminate or refine archaic customs and traditions.

Writing about the Cameroonian woman and the law, Time (2012) recommends that formal courts should in upholding the constitution of a country (and most constitutions proclaim that everyone is equal before the law), not uphold any customary laws that go against equity, well-founded conscience, and public policy, and of course those that are tendentious. She also advocates that traditional leaders take the lead in ridding their various constituencies of repugnant and invidious customary practices. She requires that as a signatory to many international conventions that advance human rights such as the Convention on the Elimination of all forms of Discrimination against Women, Cameroon should comply with such mandates. Time (2013) opines that it is not that there is the absence of laws; the problem is that there is an absence of enforcement claws. The very fact that those who promulgate laws and are responsible for enforcing them are mostly men makes it somewhat challenging for them to get rid of laws which for the most part give them dominance over women. This fact Time (2012) admits when she explains the role of "custodians of customs." It follows that if society is really serious to observe the rights of women it should to a large extent integrate women into those male dominated decision making positions.

When this researcher asked Cameroonian women during a 2014 focus group interview about their property rights, one woman in her sixties said that:

> Many women rent land, and some own it. You pay rent for land first, and then plant crops, so if the crops don't do well, it is your loss. Boys get preference for land, but now things are changing. People now see that in many families it is the girls that end up helping their father and mother, so especially for girls who do not get married, some families prefer to give them title to land.

When asked what she thinks could be done to change prevailing attitudes about female ownership of land and other property, unequivocally, her response was that those who still harbor beliefs that a male child is better than a female are "backwards." She said education, letting people know that "God gives you a child whether boy or girl for a particular reason. They come to this world not knowing anything. All they eventually get to know is what society teaches them, so if you tell them from early on that everyone is equal, that is how they will live their lives."

Inheritance rights as it relates to widows were also discussed during the focus group interviews. When asked what steps the women recommend could be taken in order to stop widows and girls from being stripped of their inheritance rights, one woman pithily said "prayers, so that people can be enlightened. There needs to be constant conversations on this issue so that eventually people can become more sensitive towards women. Widows need to be assisted; they have already lost a husband, why take away the things they can use to help themselves and their children?" Another woman was less placable. She advocates punitive sanctions and fines for family members who would want to circumvent the law in order to cheat a widow and her children out of property.

In summary, recommendations to help alleviate issues of property rights among African women are:

- Reforming invidious laws.
- Rewriting or rewording poorly written laws relating to property rights.
- Reviewing customary and statutory laws and eliminating those that create a divisive environment.
- Stimulating chiefs, elders, and other community members to be mindful of women's human and property rights.
- Facilitating women's access to legal avenues to lay claim on what is rightfully theirs.
- Educating/orienting men and boys on gender issues and rights, especially property rights.
- Educating the masses about the necessity of living wills, and the need for courts to respect and enforce them.
- Empowering women to be able to speak out, speak up, and fight for their rights.

HEALTH CARE

The World Bank and many western countries have invested in health care in many African countries as discussed above in chapter two, but much of the time some countries cannot account for the money (see BBC News/Africa/

Cameroon corruption hinders AIDS fight 2007; Castro-Leal et al. 2000) early on reported that health subsidies to Africa go to help the rich more so than the poor. In fact they report that subsidies to the poorest of the poor are substantially less than subsidies made to the rich. In essence, help that is intended for the most needy seldom is directed to meet its target. Budgetary allocations are in part to blame as reported because in some countries like in Ghana, a huge chunk of the medical budget went to a teaching university in Accra and on hospital services (Castro-Leal et al. 2000), but not to patient care. As a solution, Castro-Leal et al. (2000) propose limited spending on hospitals and more spending on primary facilities.

Many of the illnesses that afflict a good number of Africans are preventable diseases such as malaria, diarrhea, respiratory illnesses, and as Castro-Leal et al. (2000) contend, such illnesses could be treated or prevented at primary-level facilities if those facilities are accessible to the masses, and if they are well equipped, stocked with the necessary medications, and staffed with well-trained professionals. It is noted in chapter two that many patients live in remote areas, with no roads or unbelievably horrid paths on which they have to trek for miles to get to the nearest medical facility which at times is a miserable dispensary with hardly anything inside but an old worn-out bench. Many patients end up going to a traditional/native doctor. If public transportation is improved, including better stocked, better furnished medical facilities, and better trained staff, the number of unnecessary and premature deaths will be significantly decreased.

Income inequality in the majority of African countries is massive and as discussed in chapter two, women are disproportionately disadvantaged. Going to consult at a clinic or hospital means incurring a financial hardship, and when placed together with other needs, women invariably put themselves up as the sacrificial lambs. They forego medical treatment in order to meet the needs of their children and their entire family. As Castro-Leal et al. (2000) explain, following longitudinal studies conducted by Litvack and Bodart (1993) in Cameroon, and that by Gertler and Molyneaux (1997) in Indonesia, when medical facilities increase charges/fees without enhancing services or improving the quality of what patients get, the poor are likely to discontinue visits to the facility, or may not even venture to that facility. It is thus recommended that if hospitals and other medical facilities need to increase patient charges, such charges must be "introduced carefully" and "they should be accompanied by improvements in both access and quality" (Castro-Leal et al. 2000, 71). As well, it is necessary to monitor reactions of poor people when there are hikes in health care charges, and especially the decisions or alternatives they pursue thereafter (Castro-Leal et al. 2000).

Recommended also is the need to closely watch household reactions to health care costs, and to disseminate information to poor people that even with increases in health costs, prompt intervention in their health care at a higher cost is better than sacrificing their health for other household expenses. In summary, Castro-Leal et al. (2000) state:

> For Africa, at least, the message is that reallocations of public expenditures are not sufficient; policies must be based on a sound understanding of the factors that govern household decisions about health care and of the means by which subsidized services can lead to better outcomes for the poor. (72)

Others like Saraladevi et al. (2009) have suggested the following initiatives to bolster Africa's health care system: recruit and train efficient staff, provide attractive incentives to stop migration of qualified professionals; if sponsored for foreign training there must be mandatory requirement to go back home at the completion of the training. They also suggest retention incentives, better pay, tax breaks, and opportunities for upward advancement (Kingue et al., 2013).

Specific programs that are geared toward women require significant public funding for women's health care, prenatal and peri-natal. Sex education programs need to be added to elementary and secondary schools curricula, as well as in adult classes, and efforts should be made to disseminate health-related information to women with no formal education. Better planning and focus needs to be put in place to address the needs of women with life threatening illnesses such as HIV/AIDS. Programs should be established to address sexual abuse of girls and women. Such programs should comprise training for law enforcers, that is, the police and prosecutors so that they are sensitive to reports about sexual abuse. Other recommendations include the hiring, deployment, and retention of health workers in not just the cities but in more remote areas as well (Buchan et al. 2013). Buchan et al. (2013) contend that there is a correlation between the availability of health workers and decent health services. The authors explain that having trained medical practitioners in remote places is of utmost relevance since approximately half of the world's population resides in rural areas but only one-quarter of the world's doctors serve this half.

Food subsidies over years have proven to be a good resource in helping to abate health issues stemming from malnutrition. Aid money that goes directly to the neediest of households will also help alleviate the plight of the most destitute. This can be assured by entrusting NGOs not government with the money to allocate to the neediest persons.

Many countries in Africa, if not most, still do not have a system of health insurance. Only patients who have the required cash amount can pay for their health care. Governments need to figure a way of providing health services to families, and to establish health insurance programs and coverage.

Train health extension workers. These are low-level professionals who have a short training who can work in mobile clinics to assist in creating awareness of health, nutritional needs, and other benefits to pregnant women. These types of programs are yielding progress in Ethiopia (voanews.com 2010).

In order to minimize the effects of HIV among women, the following are recommended:

- Promote and protect women's rights
- Increase education and awareness among women
- Provide access to contraception and microbicides
- Provide access to post-exposure prophylaxis to prevent HIV exposure becoming an infection
- Provide medical care to prevent MTCT of HIV (Avert.org n.d.).

With regard to HIV/AIDS the UNAIDS program bases its recommendation on evidence-based program results. As such the following are some of the recommendations they make: (1) make available sex education so as to promote safer sexual behavior. (2) Put in place intervention programs that empower youths to be discreet in the choices they make regarding their sexual, reproductive health, HIV, and gender party status. (3) Implement preventative HIV infection programs including sex education programs' accessibility to reproductive health services. (4) Promote programs and activities that engage vulnerable groups in participation in health conscious activities.

FAMINE, WARS, VIOLENCE, AND DISEASE

In discussing solutions to famine in Somalia, Oxfam.org (2011) comes up with three broad ideas:

- Production solutions: accelerate investment in African food production. There must be more support for smallholder farmers and pastoralists, such as hardier crops, cheaper inputs, and disaster risk management.
- Access solutions: first, it is necessary to provide more aid and budgetary investment into physical infrastructure that comprise roads and communications. Second, there has to be public assistance such as grain reserves to rectify market failures until such markets recover.
- Response solutions: concentrate more on guaranteed social protection which entails year-round food and insurance assistance to enable emergency supply even in times of dire need.

Some, like Professor Jonathan Cook (Welsh 2014) has argued that predicate problems like obstructing supply, poor management, and the paucity in innovative agribusiness that are deemed to be easily addressed by training

Africans in business schools, are not capable of providing the panacea that Africa needs. Instead, he proposes that the solution lies in opening business-oriented schools that are a combination of "research and development" based agricultural schools and business schools. Notable, in Cook's research is his finding that of the 774 programs in African universities that are concentrated on business training degrees, a minuscule number of them have programs that concentrate on "agribusiness and supply-chain management."

To enhance his recommendation Cook explains that graduates from agribusiness schools should be able to strike deals with foreign investors, deals that specifically are geared toward investments in agriculture, and to which a significant proportion of the deal directly benefits Africa. To this end are also the needs for sustainable development ventures. As a continent with approximately 60 percent of untapped land, and with the rush by the Chinese and Indians to get a share of this, business scholars such as Professor David Abdulai of the University of South Africa, advises that investors from these countries should be able to push forward ideas of sustainable development (Welsh 2014).

Zoundi (2011) contends that short-term humanitarian aid to famine-stricken areas is fine, but of more importance are programs that address the crux of the problem. He places responsibility on African leadership to tackle famine. Here is some of what he thinks African leadership should do:

- End the vicious cycle of armed conflicts and political instability
- Put in place government-sponsored agricultural and food policies which attract sustainable investments in order to ensure their implementation.
- Raise agricultural productivity and develop adaptation and migration measures in response to climate change impacts (including means to reduce the vulnerability of the region's pastoral populations).
- Incentivize local food production.
- Reinforce the regional market.
- Reinforce the early-warning and alert systems for drought, food security, and armed conflicts.

Zoundi (2011) also explains the need for African countries to comply with or follow the lead of the Charter for Food Crisis Prevention and Management that challenge African governments and intergovernmental institutions to look for sustainable solutions to take care of the underlying issues responsible for food shortages. Such solutions include, but are not limited to making the availability of food a right following government classification as specified by law, available funds, and needs based.

Scarce resources have been known to be in part the catalyst of conflict (the Darfur conflict). Hastily, it should be mentioned that Verhoeven (2011) prefers that in a discussion of conflict of Darfur, other factors that prompted the conflict should be taken into account rather than just connecting the climate-related changes to the conflict. While the World Bank and western countries act generously to African demise, African leaders themselves have exercised less than brilliant judgment in providing long-range solutions for their countries' problems. While their environments have been hard hit by ecological devastation, Pearson (2011) states: "local and national administrations have stood back, watched, or even abetted efforts to dam or curtail the flow of forested rivers into the regions where people need water for their very survival." Pearson (2011) contends that planting thousands or "millions of trees" may help with environmental changes; but diverting water sources simply to irrigate plantations may hamper efforts of saving lives.

Poverties.org (2013) reveals that as a consequence of negligence and mismanagement of handling resources and poor economic development there are currently "three times" more victims of famine than was the case twenty-five years ago. The organization provides the following recommendations to deal with famine:

- The need for a tailored plan to develop agriculture: The best type of aid to offer is one that will provide assistance for Africans to engage in agriculture and sustainable development strategies. Thus aid should always be part of a wider poverty reduction plan as it's the only way to prevent these food crises and famines from happening over and over again. . . . Eastern Africa needs to follow a plan tailored to the region and its terrible weather. Specific crops, specific agricultural techniques and technology are needed. . . . Develop trade within Africa, especially with neighboring countries that aren't affected by the disaster. . . . Experts should work so that the development spark spreads around to other neighbors.
- Bringing African farmers in world trade: The UN's World Food Program (WFP) [should continue to run] training programs—such as Purchase for Progress—that help African farmers get quality crops as well as increase their productivity and income [so as to make the farmers more competitive in the global market].
- [Limit] humanitarian aid: [Even though food aid may be needed in the short term during] emergencies, long-term plan is also vital. . . . In the end it's also the local countries' responsibility to implement a sound famine prevention strategy that includes: weather and crop monitoring; risks and aid management as well as a response strategy to make the best use of all their resources.
- Using strategies that work: Another of the World Food Program's projects consists in buying food for regional farmers (in Ethiopia for example) at a fixed price so that they support the development of a local economy. . . . Being sure that you'll sell your crops for a specific amount of money gives farmers a guarantee that income will be steady so that they can invest in

new technology (machines, better crops, etc.). Then little by little, the agriculture is modernized (Poverties.org).

With regard to sending humanitarian aid to Africa in times of crisis, Poverties.org makes the following recommendations:

- It needs to arrive in a timely fashion;
- In predictable amounts;
- It needs to be properly targeted.

The organization also makes recommendations on how to tackle the problem of limited fertile soil in East Africa. It proposes the introduction or widespread application of "green revolution." Alongside this, the organization recommends "the use of modern techniques with chemical or other improved fertilizers (though expensive) and high-yielding, stress-resistant crops among other things" (Poverties.org 2013).

In a 2000 issue Foreignaffairs.com admits that while Africa is primarily responsible for solving Africa's problems, it admits that "preventing wars, rather than fighting them" is always the best policy to apply. Foreignaffairs.com explains that if the cold war could be won peacefully, Africa's conflicts can also be resolved peacefully. However, the organization is also quick to admit that because of the "weak authoritarian" governments in Africa, there is the absence of leadership to spearhead such an endeavor. The organization explains that because African institutions are notorious for nepotism, systemic poverty, and entrenched income disparities, it is easy to see how conflict is just a heartbeat away. Nonetheless, the organization recommends that any efforts to contain wars in Africa must begin with addressing these issues. The organization recommends that as the most progressive country in Africa, South Africa should be projected as the broker/intermediary, as long as it receives the backing of the United States, business organizations, and other entities.

Elbadawi and Sambanis (2000) explain that because Africa's civil wars are a result of "poverty, failed political institutions, and economic dependence on natural resources…the best and fastest strategy to reduce the incidence of civil war in Africa and to prevent future civil wars is to institute democratic reforms" (244). These researchers propose that the following democratic reforms are necessary:

- Promote inter-group cooperation
- Fashion out specific political governance and economic management institutions
- Make sure ethnic groups feel adequately represented by their national political institutions

- Make certain that the economy provides opportunity for productive activity (Elbadawi and Sambanis 2000, 244).

In a blog published by World Resource Institutes in 2009, Peter Veit, elaborates on how "resource wars" can be stopped in Africa. As a start, Veit explains that two-thirds of poor people reside in countries that have vast amounts of extractive resources. Unfortunately, they hardly partake in the wealth of their countries (Hoefler 2008). Lifting people from chronic and entrenched poverty has been a consistent suggestion in ridding Africa of some of its wars (see discussions above). In this vein, Veit suggests two broad actions and elaborates on each. They are:

- Help governments establish fair distribution policies: U.S. development assistance can work with governments to develop extractive resource revenue management and distribution policies that create economic, political, and other incentives in support of poverty reduction, a priority national policy objective in most developing countries . . . equitable access and fair distribution can be more effective than economic growth alone in reducing poverty.
- Strengthen democratic institutions and support good governance: U.S. development assistance must also strengthen other centers of power that can press for such reforms and check the authority of the executive branch. Among these other power centers are the legislature, civil society organizations and citizens. . . . Working with the popular media to educate the public on policy processes can engage citizens in government matters. Promote accountability. Accountability requires information on institutional performance, and the power to sanction poor decision and discipline behavior (Veit, 2009).

Using South Sudan as a case study, Kevlihan (2013) explains that in times of conflicts healthcare is crucial and having a grip on how to provide social services and medical supplies to the populace is of utmost importance especially since a lot of hoarding and red taping occur during this time. How to overcome these obstacles in order to provide much needed preventative and urgent medical care is vital in order to save lives. Overcoming these in the town of Malakal in Sudan was instrumental in saving thousands of lives (Kevlihan 2013). Financial support from the international community and operational support from NGOs are critical at this time. In addition, immunization of children even before the brunt of war is felt in an area is crucial. Kevlihan (2013) also recommends that potential risks to medical staff be taken in to consideration; as well he recommends accountability with regard to where and when medications and other medical supplies are dispensed. Further, he recommends open and honest communication with local government and security forces on plans to provide medical services to mothers and children first before intervention can be extended to the entire population.

Vaccinations and medications for transmittable diseases aside, Dugassa (2009) explains that when women's health is considered in light of human rights, then embarking on treatment will first require an understanding of the underlying factors that put women at risks for such diseases. These underlying factors as Dugassa (2009) outlines are:

- Lack of control over sexuality and sexual relations
- Poor sexual and reproductive health
- Neglect of health needs
- Clinical management based on research on men
- Harmful cultural practices
- Stigma and discrimination
- Lack of access to education
- Sexual abuse and all forms of coerced sex (696).

Giving that women's health issues are inextricably tied with these social realities, Dugassa (2009) suggests that social reform should take precedence over "technical fixes."

With regard to Ebola, Baker (2014) recommends that more staffed Ebola treatment centers be opened, and such centers should have sufficient beds for patient load. With regard to staffing, Baker recommends that there be at least "four highly trained" staff members for each patient, that includes a doctor, a nurse, disinfectant person, and a janitor trained to dispose risky materials. Foremost, Baker recommends that aid in whatever form should not arrive too late, and aid workers should not leave too soon.

Zelikovsky (2014) explains a "commonsense" approach in dealing with Ebola. She advocates a multi-dimensional approach that includes "prevention, treatment, containment, and eradication." In discussing communicable diseases such as influenza, Kamradt-Scott (2012) provides the following advice "international organizations, governments, local authorities, industry, and even individuals all have a role to play in planning and preparing for the . . . pandemic" (97).

GOVERNMENT FAILURE

How African societies can put together good governance is not especially daunting, if only those they "willfully" choose to do the right thing. As the most progressive country in Africa, South Africa has demonstrated through its leaders especially the late President Mandela that there can be good governance in Africa. Good governance begins by the leader making himself not only a leader but also a steward of the people. In this regard, he does not look at what he alone can benefit from, but how he and his people can lift themselves from any adverse circumstance. For developing countries this means, getting out of poverty and systemic corruption. A blogger (whose identity nor address was revealed) on the web page of Global Economic Symposium (2014) made the suggestion that good governance can be achieved by "strengthening peer review, establishing international agreements on state and business transparency, and monitoring through the recipients of aid." The blogger goes on to explain that peer reviews by other African countries, and a review process that involves private think tanks, should incorporate opinions of those in the society.

Lee (2013) advances "New Governance" as a movement that encourages diverse institutions and citizenry to participate in solving issues that affect them. New Governance requires the need by stakeholders to disperse functions and powers and to have persons or organizations monitor and provide feedback on how things are run—a process Lee (2013) states is also known as "learning by doing." For New Governance to work, Lee explains that two mutual and inseparable factors must exist: all involved must work toward the same goal, and each involved must recognize the contribution of each participant to effectuate a common goal. While Lee does not propose New Governance as a solution to the poor governance that exists in Sub-Saharan states, the principles which she outlines are robust enough to be recommended to African states especially those that grapple with entrenched poverty. As Lee (2013) explains, New Governance:

> Supports the development of holistic, creative, cross-disciplinary, cross-jurisdictional, and cross-institutional solutions, which seem necessary to address complex problems like poverty and economic development. New governance theory also supports greater access to decision-making processes by marginalized groups, promoting their ability to influence law and policy and to help reform the social-welfare programs to better respond to their needs. (412)

Promoting good governance as a means to reform may take the following process as Lee (2013) explains:

- Destabilizing event creates a common goal and motivations: Here, as Lee explains, when stakeholders vehemently oppose the status quo through cohesive and constructive protests and resistance, opportunities for changes may ensue.
- Participants define a common goal: Participants have to agree on a common goal through concerted efforts by all. In order to accomplish this, they need opinions from the populace. Such opinions can be made known through surveys, polls, town meetings, and by soliciting testimonials from the population.

- Architect imposes a common goal: A leader decides on a common goal especially when there are divergent goals. Caution has to be exercised as Lee states so as not to engage in "a command-and-control structure."
- Architect creates motivations: After agreeing on a common goal, Lee recommends that the participants must maintain a healthy motivated attitude so as to accomplish the goals.

While Lee's new governance ideas have now and then been used successfully in the United States by different stake holders, such as Cincinnati's (Ohio) "police reform initiative" one wonders if this could be applied successfully in Africa especially since many of the rulers are dictatorial in how they rule their countries. But then, look at South Africa; who could have believed the turn of events in that country from an apartheid rule, to now a nation that is the envy of Africa. Lee (2013) concludes her discussion on new governance by dismissing the pessimism that may veil her ideas, and proclaiming that, "reversing long-standing inequities will require as many tools as can be imagined, and New Governance is one" (440). It requires just one leader choosing to do the right thing; Late President Mandela decided to do just that.

Addressing poor governance as some like Otu (2012) and Time (2012) explain, there must be mechanisms in place to address impunity. This too can only be achieved if there is adherence to the rule of law. Knowing how the rule of law has been notoriously eschewed in many African nations, it will take only a concerted effort through separation of powers to bring defiant persons to justice. Replacing inept leaders has been problematic in many African states since many leaders are known to win elections through chicanery, with that cycle of election grabbing persisting as they stay in power for life. Perhaps getting more neutral observers from the international community to observe and supervise elections in problem African countries may be useful in ascertaining that the people's choice for a leader prevails. President Jimmy Carter, former president of the United States, has led this type of endeavor before, but then for how long can people be monitored especially if the "watchmen" subsequently have to return to their homes? Having people engaged by voicing opinions on how government is run without fear of reprisals is a useful start in ensuring that the new ruler does well for his people. Shanta Devarajan, Chief Economist for Africa at the World Bank, explained how the incessant demands by Africans in some countries for their governments to be transparent and accountable has been useful in Kenya and Ghana. Devarajan (2011) states: "Kenya's open data initiative and Ghana's petroleum revenue management bill are but two examples of citizen-led efforts to 'tie government's hands,' to avoid or reduce the possibility of elite capture that characterized economic policy in the past."

EDUCATION

PlanInternational.org (2012) outlines a series of policy recommendations on tackling problems related to education in Africa. Foremost, the organization invites governments to take a lead in the movement to create equal opportunities for both genders to obtain an education. To achieve this end, government will have to introduce legislations that advocate gender equality. As well, governments will have to increase budgets for education, not only for infrastructure, tuition, and school supplies, but also for reasonable remuneration of teachers to ensure recruitment and retention of effective teachers. Lastly, government should engage in collaborative work with the larger community to strive for parity in boys' and girls' education.

With regard to legislation, PlanInternational.org (2012) suggests for governments to "undertake a gender review of government education sector plans." In this regard, governments should put in place policies that make sure that every child gets at least a 9th grade "quality" education. This quality education should take into consideration the following:

- Girl-friendly educational environments: This is to "ensure safe and supportive learning environments for girls." This requires that schools implement policies that incorporate students' opinions, and allow girls to actively take part in decisions made about them as they relate to school violence and abuse, and to ensure that codes of ethics that bind teachers to exemplary behavior and accountability are put in place.
- Provide sufficient numbers of trained, motivated and resourced teachers. Here, incentives such as reasonable pay packages and good work environments are to be put in place so as to attract and retain good teachers and in particular female teachers. Teachers have to be trained on sensitivity issues especially as they relate to gender differences, and in particular on children's rights.
- Examine and revise the curriculum and teaching materials: The intent here is to ascertain that school courses are not gender biased, and that contents reflect the needs of girls.
- Strengthen comprehensive sexual and reproductive health education: To be effective, this mandate has to be incorporated in school curricula and teachers and school administrators have to undergo requisite training in this.
- Expand flexible and non-formal education options: Here the purpose is to give girls who become mothers while in school opportunity to get back to school so they can receive formal education.
- Strengthen public service information campaigns and community advocacy: This will help everyone in the community ward off those cultural

biases against girls, those that are insensitive to forced marriages, forced sex, and other demeaning acts against girls.

- Strengthen the enforcement of policies to enable pregnant girls and young mothers to stay in schools.
- Take appropriate measures to prevent child marriage: This should be done through legislations, and policies that can be enforced, and that have punitive sanctions.
- Ensure effective education policy dissemination and implementation: Government should promulgate policies that are reasonable and that can be easily implemented. How these policies will be monitored and assessed should be clearly stated.
- Monitor and improve learning outcomes. Improve funding to support girls' education: Here PlanInternational.org (2012, 46) makes six suggestions:

    a. Review current budget allocations to fill funding gaps identified by the gender review of Education Sector Plans.
    b. Allocate at least 11.4 percent of the national budget to pre-primary, primary, and lower secondary education.
    c. Fund at least 9 or more years of compulsory free education for all and progressively eliminate other cost barriers to girls.
    d. Protect national education budgets from austerity measures, recognizing that education underpins economic growth.
    e. Improve the planning and management of education and ensure transparency, accountability, and zero tolerance of corruption.
    f. Strengthen the tax base at all levels to fund increases in the education budget.

- Support the development of an effective post-MDG framework that maintains a strong priority on education as a goal which:

    a. Takes an equity approach and includes gender equality indicators, both quantitative and qualitative.
    b. Redefines basic education to include post-primary.
    c. Emphasizes quality of learning in addition to enrollment and access. (45–46)

First, educating mothers on the benefits of educating their children is vital. Awareness advocacy and empowerment seminars are critical in building girls' self-esteem, and assuring families of the benefits of educating girls. PlanInternational.org (2012) informs that in countries like Ghana, Sierra Leone, Liberia, and Togo, Plan's *Girls Making Media* project has created girls' clubs with mentors who are specialized in gender and children's rights. At least one million girls in the four countries have been empowered through messages they get from media outlets such as television and radio. Credit has been given to the program for elevating girls' self-esteem, and for refining parents' attitudes about their daughters, and having girls able to express their opinions on issues concerning them and their communities. In Sierra Leone, with the direction of PlanInternational.org, students dramatize the downside of child marriages, they give media talks on the consequences of forced and child marriages, and with collaborative efforts from members of the community, positive results are being reported as girls are resisting early marriages.

With regard to early pregnancies, such advocacy groups as *Girls Making Media* should actively address transactional sex, and the consequences entailed in engaging in unprotected sex. Teachers too need to be counselors for these girls by providing sex education classes or lectures. For teachers who abuse their authority by soliciting sexual relations with students, there should be consequences such as job termination, and criminal sanctions. That is likely to serve as a deterrent to others. PlanInternational.org recommends committees that comprise students, community members, and members of Parent Teacher Associations, to discuss students' issues including early pregnancies, and readmission to school after the babies are born. Such committees have been reported by PlanInternational.org as successful in Ethiopia, and have been instrumental in having policies in the country designed to advocate the return of girls to school after their babies are born. Other countries like Mali and Liberia have implemented liberal policies to accommodate young mothers who elect to return to school. For instance, such mothers are exempted from manual labor and sports, and are allowed to leave class to breast feed, and may not be penalized for going late to school.

With costs of education rising annually, countries are coming up with ingenious ways of cutting such costs. Zimbabwe, for instance as PlanInternational.org (2012) explains, has introduced the Basic Education Assistance Module (BEAM) which provides financial assistance to families and children having difficulties paying fees and other costs of education. This has been instrumental to the enrollment and retention of students in schools. Other programs like bursary help needy students. Programs like these have been reported to be very helpful especially to girls in Kenya and Malawi (PlanInternational.org 2012).

Providing meals for children also appears to be costly for many African families, and many children have reported hunger as an issue that inhibits their studies. Hence, school programs that incorporate meal plans will help with enrollments and retentions. PlanInternational.org (2012) informs that in countries such as Guinea-Bissau, Ghana, and Mali where school programs that offer meals to students have been introduced, a boost in enrollments and retentions not only of boys, but of girls as well has been seen.

The solution does not lie solely on subsidizing or providing women's income, it goes deeper into cultural norms that still do not put as much value on girls' education as they place on boys'. Such subsidies should only be made to those women who are determined to make sure that their daughters stay enrolled in school. Families have to be educated on the fact that making sacrifices to take care of siblings is just not for girls to do. Boys too can be caregivers and teaching boys to be caregivers will facilitate work at home. Establishing welfare programs for children, programs such as day care for children and the elderly, should be introduced with government subsidizing the programs. This will free girls from the role of being the constant caregivers of these vulnerable groups, and enable them to enroll in schools and take classes on a regular basis.

Siteresources.worldbank.org (2013) suggest the following reforms to the educational system in Cameroon:

- Broadening the role of PTA so they can scrutinize the educational system and call for accountability.
- Have inspectorates held to account if they don't do proper inspection of teachers and school management. Set standards for evaluation have to be put in place.
- Make the process of hiring of teachers transparent, introduce a system of rewards and awards to bolster moral.
- Improve the process of funds allocation, and not create a system of one budget fits all.
- Provide media access to what is ongoing. Exposing corruption may be a deterrent.

With regard to addressing sexual harassment, sensitivity training, empowerment seminars/workshops for girls to bolster self-esteem, are viable options. Lambert et al. recommend scholarships for female students, textbooks that focus on gender education, designating a "girls' education week," improving school safety, and building female sanitary units. Lambert et al. (2012) explain that during their menstrual circle, some girls stay at home because of shortages of toilets or those designated for girls only.

"Stop violence against girls in school: A cross-country analysis of change in Ghana, Kenya and Mozambique" is an initiative spearheaded by Actionaid and financed by UK's Big Lottery Fund. The initiative is set in place to empower girls to pursue education and to enjoy life without worries of violence. In schools, the move has been to divert teachers from harsh corporal punishments such as whipping/caning to more positive ways of disciplining. Progress is gradual since teachers still prefer to subject students to spend long periods of time kneeling or squatting as punishment. Success has been experienced with girls through Girls' clubs in Ghana, Kenya, and Mozambique, as they increasingly demonstrate more knowledge, and confidence, in the activities they engage in, and in their responses to inequality, and to violence (Actionaid 2013).

ECONOMY

In 2003 Ayodele stated that Africa should be mindful that "if you want something done well, do it yourself." He explains that Africa to a large measure has brought upon itself its own problems, despite blames levied on the Western world (Arnold 2001; Sender and Smith 1986; Warren 1980). He is of the opinion that Africans themselves could reduce these problems, and key to doing this is by increasing economic growth through relaxing policies that impede trade. Mwaba (2000) seems to agree with Ayodele's line of reasoning. Indeed, Mwaba (2000) maintains that while trade opportunities may provide a necessary short-term solution, what would be more advantageous in the long run to accelerate export growth is to relax policies such as tariffs. This is a premise that Mihalakas (2011) also endorses. Mihalakas (2011) maintains that if the consensus is that trade promotes economic growth, it makes sense to get rid of barriers that impede such growth. A Free Trade Agreement (FTA) that concentrates on Intra-African trade, as Mihalakas contends might with commitment from the African Union lead to success as it has for South and East Asia. Mwaba acknowledges that some whom he refers to as "protectionist scholars" are opposed to liberalizing trade because it does not enhance growth and may even lead to a decline in growth if pursued by African countries. Berry (1991) holds similar views. He argues that markets with less restrictive barriers may be detrimental to "African Social realities."

Thirlwall (2000) explains that if each country increased productivity in the crop or product that they are most endowed with, then "specialization on the basis of comparative advantage enables the maximum to be produced from a given amount of factor resources. Production increases, consumption increases, and therefore global welfare" (8). Thirlwall further explains that while there is no guarantee that each country will benefit similarly (doctrine of comparative advantage) whether each country will benefit is based on the exchange rate of products/goods, on the trade terms determined by the countries involved, and if the countries involved maintain the acceptable resource level commensurate to their specialization.

Brautigam and Knack (2004) conclude that "aid dependence" translates to "aid interdependence." This dynamic as Brautigam and Knack explain does not work because in many of the states that aid money has been given, there is little to nothing to show for as results, as such change in disbursement of aid needs to be made. They advocate three main changes: (1) the need for donors to be more selective in which country gets aid, and for aspiring countries to be more competitive. In this regard, a few steps have to be taken such as selecting countries for aid only if the country has demonstrated performance with previous aid, as well as specifying the intended use for the aid such as health care. Incentive like loyalty to a donor country, and buying products or services from a donor country should not be the determining factor for aid recipients. Instead a system of competitive proposals from governments, NGOs, private sectors with a clear goal and objectives for the aid money, and a system of accountability should be the determining factors for aid. (2) Donors and recipients need to understand that aid is a temporary means of development and not intended to be a constant and non-stop flow of cash to the recipient country. Therefore, donors should put in place a strategy for determining countries that qualify for aid, strategies for deciding aid amount and duration of aid, strategies for accountability of aid money, and strategy for determining if use of aid money matched stated objectives. (3) Donor countries should assist the recipient countries to figure out ways of bolstering means of expanding savings, acquiring bonds in international bond markets, ways of diversifying foreign investments, as well as diversifying exports.

The economy of African states cannot get to a satisfactory level without the various countries addressing the issue of poor governance. Outlined in the section of Government Failures are recommendations on addressing it. Corruption, mismanagement, and defalcation have been discussed as some of Africa's biggest encumbrances to progress. It follows that before African nations can figure out how to grow their economies they must first contain corruption, mismanagement, and embezzlement. To do this also requires separation of powers of the three bodies of government (Cheema 2005; Otu 2012; Time 2012). Separation of powers does not simply mean having autonomous heads of departments, it means each branch having the capacity to prevent any one entity to exert unfettered powers. When such checks and balances are adhered to, it enables law enforcers to prosecute and convict those found guilty of corruption, and to be able to put in place mechanisms to seize assets linked to corrupt practices. Whatever sanctions put in place to address issues of graft must be effective to act as a deterrent. Beccaria (1963) had long ago stated that for punishment to be effective three factors must be present: certainty, celerity, and severity. The drift here is that impunity can be addressed only when those who amass a country's wealth for themselves through chicanery can be dealt with through the full force of the law. Kahan (1996) advices that "when society deliberately forgoes answering the wrongdoer through punishment, it risks being perceived as endorsing his valuations, hence the complaint that unduly lenient punishment reveals that the victim is worthless in the eyes of the law" (598). Economic sanctions as Ruback et al. (2014) explain, serve three functions: "punishment, deterrence, and the restoration of justice" (406). Without the threat of punishment being real, they acknowledge, law-breakers are not going to be deterred. Further, as they explain, restitution helps provide some justice to the victim and it further helps in making the offender appreciate the harm caused and the need to make up for that harm; and finally, it helps in reintegrating the lawbreaker into society.

Restructuring government also requires transparency and accountability among the three facets of government. Without this impunity will persist. Anti-corruption rallies, town meetings, education, flyers, radio and television propaganda, are just steps, even if baby steps to refocus the minds of people toward doing the right thing. The president of Cameroon set up an Anti-Corruption Commission in March 2007. The intent is to abate corruption in the country through television programs, flyers, workshops, and subjecting guilty persons to shaming by publishing their names (see Sa'ah's J. report in Cameroon dances to anti-graft beat 2007). This is a positive step, but these commissions or workshops have no rigor if purging corruption is not vertically and horizontally effected. The little thief has stolen, but the huge embezzler has ripped off society, so incarcerating the little thief, and then turning a blind eye on the recalcitrant corrupt manager, judge, politicians who fatten themselves with ill-gotten gifts, corrupt deals, and embezzlement of public funds only helps sink society into a deeper economic abyss.

Much of Africa's economy is agrarian based. Transitioning from this to a manufacturing economy is in part necessary, but then a country has to figure out what most helps in increasing the country's gross domestic product. Some like Gleave and Morgan (2001) explain that concentrating on agriculture serves some African countries well. Stagnation or lack of diversification may not. In 2014, the Gulf Cooperation Council countries (Bahrain, Qatar, Oman, Kuwait, Saudi Arabia, and the United Arab Emirates) met to discuss how their economies could grow. After hearing from experts and scholars, an agreement was reached that in order for the various nations to attain a desirable economic growth, they have to diversify their economies to not rely mainly on oil supply. The consensus was that a country that diversifies its economy is less likely to experience economic upheaval. The benefit of diversification is that when there is a negative price shift on a heavily relied-on product a country can remain viable by falling back on other products or means of income. The point here is that African countries can follow the path that these Arab nations with diametrically opposed economic circumstances are willing to take. These Arab nations are by far better off than most if not all African countries, yet they are willing to put heads together so to speak, to figure out how to get better economically.

With regard to nations that rely extensively on agriculture for their economic growth, massive yields are necessary to remain economically viable. Following projections by the United Nations Food and Agricultural Organization (FAO), if desertification is not stopped in Africa, the continent will lose about two-thirds of its arable land. Africa Renewal (2012) explains that desertification requires that farmers refrain from misusing land by using unsuitable fertilizers, or by planting crops that are not conducive to growth based upon soil type.

Desertification can be stopped as botany.uwc.ac.za states, by growing more plants without their destruction by man and animals. Soil has to be mulched frequently, and people have to make a concerted effort to manage the land. As reported, all African countries are members of the United Nations Convention to Combat Desertification (UNCCD). This organization has established the National Action Programs (NAPs). These programs are to address desertification issues and methods of tackling it with NGOs, local and community leaders to monitor such programs. NAPs programs are to be in charge of poverty reduction strategies. Five Sub-Regional Action Programs (SRAPs) and a Regional Action Plan (RAP) were put in place in 1999, with the focus of implementing programs that deal with: "integrated water management, agro-forestry and soil conservation, rangelands, ecological monitoring and early warning systems, new and renewable energy sources and technologies, and a sustainable agricultural farming system" (UNCCD.int n.d.). Further, UNCCD came up with decision 3/COP 9, whose mandate is to make sure that countries are cooperating with one another and programs are well coordinated. UNCCD.int (n.d.) confirms that decision 3/COP 9 is instrumental for:

- A regional consultative committee established in November 2012 in Algiers to guide and support regional coordination.
- A regional work program drafted as a practical framework for joint activities and coordination within the region.
- A regional coordination unit (RCU) for Africa hosted by the African Development Bank in Tunis.

Growing Africa's economy also depends on improving the infrastructure, telecommunications, and opening up avenues that attract foreign direct investment. Facilitating sending and receiving mail, and products, and in this context business mail, and other shipments is crucial. Even though many transactions can be facilitated through e-mail, e-shopping, e-commerce, and what have you, there is still the need for the physical presence of operational centers that are accessible in all ways. Electricity blackouts, dead telephone lines and connections, water shortages, and despicable roads hamper trade and development. These have to be in order to attract trading partners, and to participate in trade with those partners. Of most importance is the necessity to have good roads, good railroads, reliable shipping lines, and good air systems. In a focus group interview with Cameroonian women in 2014, some brought up the issue of exceedingly bad roads as an impediment to trade. They made the point that if just small pliable roads were constructed farmers will be able to transport their crops to markets where they can be sold. One woman made the comment that she purposely has limited the size of her farm because what good is it having huge crop yields and no means of taking them to big markets where they can be sold.

A country's economy cannot flourish when the private sector is lagging. Privately owned businesses, small businesses, particularly those that impact the lives of women and children are crucial. In a document written by the United Nations Development Program (UNDP) (n.d.), the point is poignantly made: "sustained economic growth reduces poverty. The link is equally clear between economic growth and strong private investment" (7). The UNDP (n.d.) goes further to state:

> Put simply, an innovative private sector can find ways to deliver low-cost (even sophisticated) goods and services to demanding consumers across all income ranges. It can sell to the urban distressed area as well as the poor rural village or town. It can develop distribution links to the consumer in the village and so be better able to harness knowledge about the actual needs of this segment of the market. It can keep costs low though outsourcing, for greater flexibility. The private sector can thus alleviate poverty by:
>
> - Contributing to economic growth.
> - Empower poor people by providing them with services and consumer products, increasing choices and reducing prices. (8)

HUMAN TRAFFICKING

Three main avenues have been advocated and are being advocated in this study to combat human trafficking: prevention, prosecution, and protection.

Prevention: Temesgen (2014) proposes that to the extent that trafficking is a function of social inequality, the root causes of poverty have to be addressed. In this regard, he recommends that micro-credits should be given to women to assist them in starting small businesses. To effectuate this, literacy programs for women who did not have the benefit of formal education will be vital. Literacy skills should not be limited to just the ability to read and write; they should encompass the ability to run their businesses, manage their finances, invest and diversify investments. Mindful of the fact that the stock market and such intricate investment ventures are not common in Africa, such financial education may not be the best route. The point here is that making women develop a robust money mindset, help them figure out how they can increase cash flow, and how they can become more competitive in their business ventures are what are of primary relevance. Many African women hoard money under mattresses, in obscure and odd places, but seldom save money in banks where at least some profit can be generated. Many others participate in contributing to a monthly fund with other women and each month one woman receives a lump sum based on what each participant contributed. The money that the woman receives by and large goes to keeping the household solvent, but does not ensure her financial security. It is thus important for women to be educated on how to clarify their financial goals, how to invest the money they make, how to navigate through trade unions, and how to make informed decisions about their lives.

The European Union, the European Commission, the International Organization for Migration, and the International Police Organization have in various ways, especially through assisting police in different countries, worked to prevent human trafficking through funding awareness campaigns, providing technical cooperation, establishing regional networks to combat trafficking, convening conferences, workshops, and coordinating transnational law enforcement efforts to fight human trafficking (Sawadogo 2012). These efforts while laudable, need to be intense and persistent to be effective.

Following reports and accounts from Ethiopian women who had been trafficked to the Middle East and had found a way to return to Ethiopia, the government decided to take measures to counter trafficking, including severe punitive sanctions for traffickers. These are the initial measures the government took: The Ethiopian consulate opened a shelter in Beirut, Lebanon, to help Ethiopian victims of trafficking who had nowhere else to go. The government established the Private Employment Agency Proclamation, with a special committee to probe on the trafficking of Ethiopian women to the Middle East. The agency's 104/1998 is focused on safeguarding rights and dignity of Ethiopian workers particularly those sent abroad. It also requires that anyone with ambitions to open a private employment agency prepare an official contract of employment that needs to be forwarded to appropriate authorities.

Agencies that are in the business of hiring and sending workers to foreign countries are required to comply with the following:

- Ensure that the employment contract fulfills the minimum working conditions set in Ethiopian laws;
- Be responsible for ensuring the rights, safety, and dignity of the worker;
- Have a branch office or representative in the receiving country;
- Provide orientation for the worker before he or she is sent abroad, concerning the work and the country;
- Notify the nearest Ethiopian Embassy of the worker's presence;
- Deposit guarantee funds in a recognized financial institution; US $30,000 if up to 500 workers can be placed by the agency, US $40,000 for between 500 and 1,000 workers and US $50,000 for more than 1,000 workers. (Trafficking-GB2ed-2005, 25).

Theoretically, these initiatives make sense, but in practice they are seldom implemented because but for one private agency that registered as a company that sends workers to Lebanon, all others including traffickers still engage in covert operations (Trafficking-GB2ed-2005). It follows that preventative measures have to be scrupulously implemented otherwise little or no inroad will be made to curb trafficking.

Not to be ignored are ways of combating the demand side of trafficking. The fact is clear; the ability to predict who a trafficker is or will be is limited. The consequence of this in the context of law enforcement and corrections is certainly daunting, but not insurmountable. Relations between the police and the citizenry in African societies have not been known to be cozy (Diekola and Adebayo 2014; Nunzio 2014). Regardless of such precarious relationship, research shows that citizens working collaboratively with police solve a good number of crimes (Schmerler et al. 2006). Establishing a community policing system whereby citizens can feel comfortable to work in tandem with police to address trafficking by addressing the predicate causes of trafficking requires trust from both sides. This trust should not be limited to discussing trafficking issues; it should extend to victims feeling comfortable to run to the police for rescue or safe haven. In this regard, problem-oriented policing which is critical in having police and community in concert, solves problems, needs to be implemented in every society. It has been stated "Engaging the community without problem-solving provides no meaningful service to the public. Problem-solving without [partnerships] risks overlooking the most pressing community concerns. Thus the partnership between police departments and the communities they service is essential for implementing a successful program in community policing" Schmerler et al. (2006, 3).

It is fitting to insert a caption of the Diffusion of Innovation (DOI) theory here after all people and the community at large are free to adopt or disregard any innovative programs that purport to promote progress. "`Innovation' is an idea, practice, or object that is perceived as new by an individual or other unit of adoption" (Gayadeen and Phillips 2014, 228; Rogers 1995, 11), while diffusion relates to the process of introducing the new idea or practice to people in the community. A simple Google search on any topic on Africa yields recommendations on how the continent can improve and become more competitive in the global community. Certainly African leaders and governments are aware of the majority of these recommendations and do at times adopt some. The extent of success of innovative programs varies across societies. A few reasons account for this: (1) government leaders allow lower agencies to circumvent normal working of programs (2) the absence of proper partnerships between agencies and communities (3) the absence of credible and reliable agents. Rogers (1995) opines that a "powerful way for change agents to affect the diffusion of an innovation is to affect opinion leader attitudes. Persuading opinion leaders is the easiest way to foment positive attitudes towards an innovation" (eprints.dinus.ac.id, 7). As a global calamity, it makes sense for African leaders to adopt programs that show promise in combating human trafficking, and to engage the community in the venture.

Punishment serves several purposes. Whether it is intended to deter or it is meant as retribution, its infliction is a sound and definite reminder that society will not tolerate any breaches of its laws. Whether the response of the justice system to traffickers will deter or curb trafficking is left in the air. As Andenaes (1983) states:

> There is a long way to go before research can provide quantitative forecasts. The long-term moral effects (both good and evil) of the criminal law and law enforcement are especially hard to isolate and quantify. Some categories of crime are so intimately related to specific social situations that generalizations of a quantitative kind are impossible. An inescapable fact is that research will always lag behind actual developments. When new forms of crime come into existence, such as hijacking of aircraft or terrorist acts against officers of the law, there cannot possibly be a body of research ready as a basis for the decisions that have to be taken. Common sense and trial by error have to give the answers. (596)

Prosecution: In order to combat trafficking in Africa, it is necessary for the various nations to cooperate by putting together transnational initiatives to arrest and prosecute traffickers. Prosecuting traffickers should pose no legal quagmire since several international conventions lend support to legal prosecution of culprits (see for example, Convention against Transnational Organized Crime (CTOC) (2000) and its Protocol to Prevent, Suppress and Punish Trafficking in Persons, Especially Women and Children (2000)—the Palermo Protocol; Convention on the Rights of the Child and its Protocol on the Sale of Children, Child Prostitution and Child Pornography (2000); the International Labor Convention Number 182 on the Prohibition and immediate action for the elimination of the worst forms of child labor (1999). Regional Charters also reinforce the need to apprehend and prosecute traffickers. The African Charter on Human and Peoples' Rights (1981) and the African Charter on the Rights and Welfare of the Child (1980); the Economic Community of West African States (ECOWAS) adopted a Declaration and Plan of Action against Trafficking in Persons (2002–2003). Among the actions listed in the plan are for member nations to (1) criminalize traffickers (2) create an ECOWAS Coordination Unit to work with National Task Forces (3) protect and support victims (4) raise awareness regarding trafficking (5) advocate cooperation among border control agencies (6) have member states collaborate with the United Nations in collecting data relating to trafficking. Since then, member states have had meetings to assess success in their endeavors and have since added the need to cooperate with NGOs, IGOs, as well as civil society organizations.

In addition, the ECOWAS Court of Justice in Abuja, Nigeria, has jurisdiction to review cases that involve:

- An alleged failure by a Member State to comply with Community law
- A dispute relating to the interpretation and application of Community acts
- Dispute between Community institutions and their officials
- Community liability
- Human rights violations
- The legality of Community laws and policies. (see Ijrcenter.org, n.d.)

In adjudicating cases relating to human rights violations, the Court complies with the dictates of the African Charter on Human and Peoples' Rights. The Court's expanded powers to handle cases on human rights violations was accorded in 2005 following the adoption of a Supplementary Protocol A/SP.1/01/05, preceded by Protocol A/SP/12/01 on Democracy and Good Governance. Not to be ignored are the Convention on Mutual Assistance in Criminal Matters (adopted July 29, 1992, in Dakar) and the Convention on Extradition (adopted August 6, 1994, in Abuja). Some of the cases the Court has handled that are pertinent to human rights are: *SERAP v. Nigeria* (2009). In this case the Court made it clear that citizens had a right to education. Indeed, Femi Falana, the Solicitor for SERAP, stated "This is the first time an international court has recognized citizens' legal right to education, and sends a clear message to ECOWAS member states, including Nigeria and indeed all African governments, that the denial of this human right to millions of African citizens will not be tolerated" (*SERAP v. Federal Republic of Nigeria and Universal Basic Education Commission* ECW/CCJ/APP/08/08). In *Hadijatou Mani Koraou v. The Republic of Niger* (2008), after finding out that the complainant was held in slavery for nine years from the age of 12 and forcefully made to marry and bear four children with her slave master, the ECOWAS Court of Justice held that all states are required to eliminate slavery, and because the Nigerien government failed to protect her, the government of Niger was ordered to pay reparations to the woman in the amount of 10 million francs CFA, about USD 23,100. In handing down this judgment, the Court explained that the government of Niger was required both under international and national law to eliminate any forms of human rights violations including slavery, and that any appearance of passivity, acquiescence on the part of the state would not be condoned (*Hadijatou Mani v. Koraou v. The Republic of Niger* 2008; ECW/CCJ/JUD/06/08 of 27 October 2008).

The Convention on Extradition permits courts in member states to arrest, prosecute, and enforce any sanctions administered to traffickers. Morocco,

Mali, Senegal, Nigeria, and Burkina Faso have enacted laws against trafficking, even though there are nuances in the definitions of trafficking amongst the countries. Even without specific laws directed at trafficking, just about every African country has laws that criminalize behavior akin to trafficking, or has laws that protect citizens against those types of predatory offenses. The following enactments are addressed in just about every African country:

> (1) Prostitution and related activities (pornography, incitement to prostitution, sexual relationship with minors, etc.); (2) child exploitation, abandonment and mistreatment of children, and abduction; (3) right to integrity (slavery, torture, unlawful detention); (4) child labour and employment regulations; (5) immigration (Trafficking-BG2ed-2005, 20).

Take Cameroon for example, the U.S. State Department reports, "Cameroon does not prohibit all forms of trafficking, though it criminalizes child trafficking and slavery through its 2005 Law Combating Child Trafficking and Slavery, which prescribes a penalty of 20 years imprisonment." (U.S. State Dept., 2008). Countries vary with regard to the emphasis they place on curbing or stopping human trafficking. While the punishment for child trafficking in Cameroon seems to be reasonable, the U.S. State Department also reports that the government of Cameroon "did not show evidence of progress in prosecuting and punishing trafficking offenders or protecting victims." While Cameroon prohibits forced labor as stated in Article 2 (3) of Cameroon's Labor Code, the fine for violations is just around $100–$3,000. The country's Article 346 of its Penal Code makes it a criminal offense to procure aid, facilitate, or profit from the prostitution of a minor less than 16 years old. The punishment for violating the code carries a punishment of between 1–10 years. In 2008, the Ministry of Justice opened a data center in efforts to keep track of the number of trafficked victims. The center only became operational in 2012, but has remained inefficient. In that same year, the National Commission on Human Rights and Freedom in conjunction with the United Nations provided funds for law enforcement officers and magistrates in the country to participate in a seminar on anti-trafficking, and how to investigate and prosecute traffickers. With regard to an overall statute that criminalizes trafficking in general, the U.S. State Department makes it clear that Cameroon fails to prohibit every type of trafficking. The U.S. State Department reveals that because of its lax enforcement of traffickers, many crimes go unaddressed. The following is narrated by the U.S. State Department:

> The government [of Cameroon] did not report any prosecutions or convictions of trafficking offenders during the year, though it reported that it investigated three trafficking cases, one of which was conducted jointly with the Beninese authorities, and arrested one suspect in September 2008. Three suspects arrested in January 2008 for allegedly trafficking seven children have not yet

> been prosecuted. A suspect arrested in December 2007 for trafficking a child who died in his custody remains out of bail. A Yaoundé [capital of Cameroon] court in 2008 held hearings on six additional trafficking cases derived from arrests made in 2007; the cases remain pending in the court system. The government did not investigate traditional leaders in the Northern Provinces suspected of keeping hereditary servants in conditions of involuntary servitude.

In order to properly combat trafficking in Cameroon, the U.S State Department recommends:

> Increase efforts to prosecute and convict trafficking offenders; educate police, judges, lawyers, and social workers about the law against child trafficking; finalize and enact the draft law criminalizing the trafficking of adults; investigate reports of hereditary slavery in the Northern province; and develop and implement formal procedures through which law enforcement and victim protection officials may systematically identify trafficking victims among vulnerable populations and refer them for care.

Following a 2001 meeting of foreign affairs ministers of member states of the ECOWAS, a declaration and action plan to combat trafficking of humans which included passing laws against trafficking, providing training for law enforcement and judicial officials in the prosecuting of traffickers, and protecting the rights of victims was arrived at (Sita 2003). In 2002, delegates from West and Central African countries agreed to put in place laws that improve the well-being of child victims of trafficking, as well as laws that facilitate the return of trafficked children to their countries of origin. In essence, governments throughout Africa are open to enacting laws that punish traffickers and that protect the rights of victims. The problem is that effort at enforcing them is weak.

The South African Law Reform Commission has as one of its objectives the investigation of trafficking in humans. In this regard, the Commission ensures that traffickers are brought to justice, and that any punishment meted is effective. As well, the Commission has come up with specific legislation for the protection of victims. In this process, everyone with a stake in the issue is welcome to participate including civil society. The process requires that during investigations anyone with information or expertise connected to the investigation may provide knowledge on the process. The Commission puts together a project committee that comprises people that are knowledgeable about the issue at hand.

The National Assembly of Senegal since 2003 put in place legislation to address sexual exploitation of children and to have civil society (*partie civile*) comprising victims of trafficking participate during criminal proceedings against traffickers.

The practice of having victims participate in criminal proceedings has received mixed reviews. On the one hand, those who think it is a way to give victims a stronger voice in court applaud the process especially since victims usually just play the role of witnesses (Jorda and de Hemptinne 2002). Moreover, since increasingly both national and international law and several NGOs are inclined to give gravitas to victims' views, the role of victims in criminal proceedings was included in the Rome Statute of the International Criminal Court (the Statute) (Baumgartner 2008). On the other hand, concerns have been raised about the extent of victim participation in criminal proceedings, and whether such participation is fair, efficient, and if it serves the interest of justice (Raushenbach and Scalia 2008).

Measures to address trafficking in Africa take two dimensions: international and regional measures tend to emphasize prevention, while national policies emphasize prosecution (Britton and Dean 2014). These authors suggest that in order to tackle human trafficking in Africa, national policies have to incorporate preventative measures. Such preventative measures that provide opportunities for women to obtain upward mobility, economic viability, and human dignity are essential in order to minimize the predicate issues that promote human trafficking.

Protection: Solving poverty also entails introducing a variety of job skills training to disenfranchised persons, and other social welfare benefits to enable them get a leg up in society. For those who have already been victimized by traffickers adequate reintegration programs, counseling services, shelters and other assistance should be made available to them to attenuate the pain and suffering they have undergone. Data collection is crucial as data helps inform on who are susceptible, where and when people are likely to be victimized, as well as who the likely victimizers can be.

The safety of victims should be guaranteed, not only after they have been rescued from their captors, but also during the time they are made witnesses for the state during prosecutorial or legislative proceedings. As displaced persons, and moreover crime victims, adequate care should be taken to gradually reintegrate them into normal life and proper repatriation to their countries of origin should that be a viable and safe option.

Victims should be provided referral services to appropriate authorities and agencies that will assist them in obtaining the requisite help needed to attain vocational or educational training. A conscientious effort has to be made constantly to separate the victim from her captors because due to constant brainwashing, victims acquire a distorted loyalty to their captors. Prolonged and intense intervention programs are always required to ward off victims from the loyalty they have acquired toward their traffickers.

The dynamics and causes of trafficking are diverse and complex, as such in order to better curb the problem, public awareness and assistance should be heightened. Increasing awareness necessitates the introduction of radio and television programs, town hall meetings that focus on risk factors, and characteristics of offenders and victims. Programs of this nature may play important roles in offsetting some of the more immediate attempts at either recruiting potential victims, or foiling some recruitment in progress. These programs will also help put unsuspecting parents on alert, but this also suggests that they need to be coupled with job opportunities for parents and women, and indeed everyone of working age since studies show that traffickers thrive on the vulnerability of others.

Further, since the most susceptible groups are children and women, women should create women's groups that meet frequently to discuss pressing issues. Such support groups should expand support to entail information sharing on sex education, HIV prevention, sexual exploitation, and avenues to explore in case of victimization, or threats of victimization. As well, teachers should be vigilant in noticing changes in students' attendance, and performance as these may be indicative of problems at home; problems that may make the child more susceptible for early marriage or for parents handing the child over to nefarious persons. Children should be encouraged to speak out when they sense difficulties at home. They should be made to know that they could confide in their teachers, and to friends who will be able to alert teachers, police officers, social workers if available, or anyone who can intervene on behalf of the child. Student clubs, even if sports clubs, debate clubs, and whatever clubs students choose to participate in should also have as an extended agenda even if unrelated, the responsibility of looking out for one another. Such associations should also discuss issues that impede their safety and wellbeing, and form among themselves a cocoon that shields them from predators. Having lived in Africa, it is not uncommon for neighbors to look out for one another, and it is not uncommon for a family to take in a child who is wanting in parental care and guidance.

The role of churches and other religious affiliates is also crucial in that religion helps the soul of believers. It acts as a deterrent to wrongdoing to those who believe in it, and also acts as a positive force in reinforcing good behavior, and good will toward one another. It thus makes sense for civil society to collaborate with religious groups to advocate the prevention of harm to others. As an urgent need, it is prudent to consider all potential sources of help. NGOs have been known to play the extended role of crisis interveners even if not part of their responsibilities, so engaging them in the fight against trafficking is not only sensible, it is necessary. They, in particular can lend their experiences in acting as counselors, and conduits of peace restoration in the community. Their presence as non-affiliates of government also puts them in positions to pressure governments to put in place legislations that prevent, counter, and protect victims of trafficking, as well as pressure governments to put in place programs to help returnees of trafficking from abroad.

CRIMES OF CULTURE: FORCED MARRIAGES, BRIDE PRICE, LEVIRATE, FEMALE CIRCUMCISION

Over the years piecemeal attempts at reducing the prevalence of these crimes have been ongoing in many African countries. These crimes which are embedded in long cultural practices are seen by many locals as a way out of poverty or at least as a temporary relief from poverty. As discussed in chapter 6, while culture defines a people and thus should be respected, it is clear that when the culture is repressive, it should be abandoned. Forced marriages, bride price, levirate obligation, and female circumcision have been severely denounced by civil society, thus it is time to once and for all get rid of them.

As signatories to many international conventions and charters such as the United Nations Convention on the Rights of the Child, The Convention against Torture and Inhumane Treatment, The Convention on the Elimination of all Forms of Discrimination against Women, The African Charter on the Rights and Welfare of the Child, The Universal Declaration of Human Rights, one would imagine that endorsees of these conventions and charters (most African countries are) will be inclined to abide by their principles, but that is not the case. It is this author's thinking that the United Nations should figure out how to humiliate countries that blatantly disregard the mandates of these conventions. Economic sanctions are not advocated since it is usually the disadvantaged who feel the brunt of such sanctions.

Many nations legislate against such practices, but because those nations that have been pinpointed as flag bearers for crimes of humanity lack enforcement claws, nothing for the most part is done against violators, and because customary practices occasionally take precedence over statutory laws, impunity prevails. As an example, in Cameroon (Cameroon is a signatory to the conventions and treaties listed above) law 69/DF/544 of 12/19/1969 passed in French speaking Cameroon, and its equivalent in English speaking Cameroon, law 79(4) of 6/29/1979, give weight to customary practices that are not contrary to statutory laws and that do not enervate statutory laws. *Time* (2012) reports that in Cameroon, it is not unusual to find out that occasional deference is given by statutory law to customary law even when those customary laws are outright repugnant. For example, she discusses a Cameroonian case from the South West province, *Maya Ikome v. Manga Ekemason* CASWP/CC76/85 (unreported). In that case, the appellate court decided against recognizing a 30-year-old marriage because bride price had not been paid in full. As the court reasoned a marriage certificate "did not perfect what was already an imperfect union" (Time 2012, 465). The imperfection is partial and not full payment of the dowry (case discussed in chapter 6). At times too, poorly worded statutory laws may be instrumental in bizarre judicial outcomes. In Sierra Leone, customary laws acquiesce child marriages despite the existence of the Prevention of Cruelty to Children Act in the country that prohibits sexual intercourse with girls younger than 14 years. As well, in spite of the Act, parents occasionally give their daughters as young as 9 years old to older men for bride price (Erez and Thompson 1996). Park (2006) confirms the existence of child marriages and other customary practices that devalue women in Sierra Leone.

Accordingly, the following recommendations are offered: invidious laws should be stricken out, poorly written laws need to be rewritten, and there must be a review of customary and statutory laws in order to eliminate those that perpetuate marginalization, subjugation, and divisiveness. Criminal sanctions in conjunction with civil action are also vigorously advocated. It is also necessary to figure out ways of enlightening chiefs, elders, community delegates, and even members of the judiciary on women's and human rights.

Marriage to a child even if approved by custom is a crime. Forced marriages even when the victim is an adult is a crime, and such marriages should be nullified. Article 16(2) of The Universal Declaration of Human Rights states that, "marriage shall be entered into only with the free will and consent of the intending spouses." As well, the United Nations Convention on the Elimination of All Forms of Discrimination against Women, General Recommendation No. 21 states, "a woman's right to choose a spouse and enter freely into marriage is central to her life and dignity as a human being." Unfortunately, as a consequence of limited or lack of any formal education, many women are not aware of their rights, and even if they are, are not aware of any recourse. The absence of consent should nullify a marriage, and in the case of minors since the law presumes that they cannot give valid consent, a case of non-consent can be easily established. Further, when there is proof that the minor was coerced by parents or some cultural requirement, lack of consent should be implied. That should be the case as well, if the minor or woman is vulnerable based on some disability, impairment, or mental illness that makes it such that she cannot understand what she is signing on to. Munby J., an English Judge explains that it is reasonable to infer non-consent when the person is "(i) under constraint; or (ii) subject to coercion or undue influence; or (iii) for some other reason deprived of the capacity to make the relevant decision, or disabled from making a free choice, or incapacitated or disabled from giving or expressing a real and genuine consent" (*Re SA* Vulnerable Adult with Capacity: Marriage 2006, 1 FLR 867, para.77). He further expounds on his thinking by offering the following guidelines:

> Where the influence is that of a parent or other close and dominating relative, and where the arguments and persuasion are based upon personal affection or duty, religious beliefs, powerful social or cultural conventions, or asserted social, familial or domestic obligations, the influence may as Butler-Sloss, LJ put in *In re T* (Adult: Refusal of Treatment), be subtle, insidious, pervasive and powerful. In such cases, moreover, very little pressure may suffice to bring

> about the desired result. (*Re SA* Vulnerable Adult with Capacity: Marriage 2006, 1 FLR 867, para.78)

Munby, J. (2006) adds the following factors among others that can vitiate even an adult's consent "effects of deception, misinformation, physical disability, illness, weakness (physical, mental or moral), tiredness, shock, fatigue, depression, pain or drugs" (1 FLR 867, para.78).

Even after nullifying forced marriages, further measures should be taken including restitution to help the girl/woman transition into a normal life alone or with offspring of the marriage. A woman in a focus group interview this researcher conducted in Cameroon recommended, without reservations, the imposition of criminal sanctions on men who marry little girls especially if the man did nothing to improve the girl's stance in life. As Bentheim (2010) and Black (2001) explain, many of these women/girls forced into marriages are financially dependent on their husbands, and money earned if at all during the marriage has been exploitative following forced labor. Not only is alimony in order, child support payments must be mandatory—a point some women in a focus group interview in Cameroon made in 2014. Since mechanisms for such monetary collections are not in place in many African countries, and even if in place are not effective, it is recommended that effective and accountable mechanisms be put in place. Without such measures impunity will persist, and children and their mothers will be left chronically destitute.

The decline of forced marriages among immigrants in England is said to have occurred in part because of the Forced Marriage Protection Order (FMPO) enacted in 2008, as a novel part 4A of the 1996 Family Law Act (Gill 2008). The act is intended to protect victims, potential victims, and family members of victims, and organizations that provide help to victims of forced marriages (Gill 2008). While there is a little disparity in dates and other minute details about the Forced Marriage Act (for example, BBC News UK Politics (8 June 2012), suggests that the Forced Marriage Bill led to the Forced Marriage Act of 2008, but Welstead (2009), and Legislation.Gov.UK place the date of the Forced Marriage (Civil Protection Act) at 2007, no overarching substantive difference is obvious. Welstead (2009) explains:

> After wide reaching consultation, the Forced Marriage Unit was set up in 2005 as a joint venture between the Home Office and the Foreign and Commonwealth Office. Its remit is to assist all those who are at risk of a forced marriage, or have actually been forced into one, either in the U.K. or abroad. It also takes responsibility for providing information for social workers, teachers, health professionals and police who come into contact with cases of forced marriage. (57)

The crimes discussed in this chapter are in some aspects cultural induced, but then as the Forced Marriage Protection Act in England shows, laws can modify culture, and at times override, and even declare some cultural practices repugnant. The hope is that many African societies can follow the lead of England especially since based on tradition in African societies, suing family members for issues that are considered cultural are seldom heard of. Suing a parent for instance, is almost a taboo, and such mentality makes it less likely for parents to desist from noisome practices. No wonder when Ms. Nafisatu Laushi, a Nigerian girl, sued her father for forcing her to marry a much older and undesired man, her case made headline news (BBC News, September 7, 2002).

Giving that culture unites just as much as it may cause dissension, law enforcement and legal intervention are crucial mechanisms in bridging differences. Yet, these entities at times promote dissension or perform just marginal protectionist functions—functions so diametrically opposed to what they are supposed to do. Ngassa (1998) and Time (2012) report that wife abusers now and then evade prosecution because police officers regard their reports of abuse as domestic issues better addressed between the spouses. With despair, women resign to their lot in life, and shy away from complaining even to those who are best equipped to help them. Not having a place of refuge for women is quite disconcerting especially with the revelations made by Time (2012). She explains that in Cameroon, abused women who run to the police and to hospitals for help are turned away, and because there are no shelters for battered women they head right back to the homes where they continue to receive abuse. Victims and recalcitrant victims should have safe places of refuge established either by government or private agencies. Flavia's (1997) words resonate here:

> If oppression could be tackled by passing laws, then the decade of the 1980s would be adjudged a golden period for the Indian women, when protective laws were offered on a platter. Almost every single campaign against violence on women resulted in new legislation. The successive enactments would seem to provide a positive picture of achievement . . . crime statistics reveal a different story. . . . The deterrent value of the enactments was apparently nil. Some of the enactments in effect remained only on paper. (521)

The lesson here is that there needs to be a reawakening so to speak, a movement toward enlightenment where gender differences ought to be respected, and where law enforcers can set aside gender or customary biases and replace them with more constructionist perspectives. Opening shelters, creating awareness, and creating support networks are just steps society has to take forward.

The United Nations Convention on the Rights of the Child, Article 19 states:

> State parties shall take all appropriate legislative, administrative, social and educational measures to protect the child from all forms of physical or mental violence, injury or abuse, neglect or negligent treatment, maltreatment or exploitation, including sexual abuse, while in the care of parent(s), legal guardian(s) or any other person who has the care of the child.

Child protection services, shelters for children are not available in many African societies, and even when available, they are quite few and such shelters are run-down buildings with poorly remunerated staff, ill prepared for the tasks they are challenged to handle. The United Nations advises that if nations want to adequately tackle victimization of children and social marginalization of women a holistic strategy must be put in place. The "holistic strategy must be mainstreamed and coordinated both vertically, and horizontally and integrated into national efforts to prevent and address all forms of harmful practices" (United Nations, CEDAW, 2014).

The United Nations' point is well taken especially as reports show that a significant part of women's awareness and assistance comes from NGOs. It is documented that much of the help in promoting literacy among women in rural areas is usually spearheaded by NGOs. That is the case among the Hausas of Nigeria (Jaulmes 2007), and among the Kom tribe of Cameroon (Sil International 2010). The benefits of education cannot be overemphasized. Education be it technical, trade skills, or college/university training empowers women. Women and Literacy explain the benefits of education. Foremost, the organization highlights the relevance of literacy in informing women's choices be that in regards to when/if to get married, family size, health care matters, and other vital choices that affect them (Sil International 2010). These points were brought up during a focus group interview with some Cameroonian women in 2014. One of the women in the group explained that educated women know how to negotiate family size with their husbands; and since many have jobs, they settle on having fewer children. Cullen and Agnew (2011) explain that "parent education" in conjunction with "parent management training programs" are deterrents to adult offending. It follows that if educational opportunities are opened to everyone the more informed people will become, and thus the less incidences of bride price, forced marriages, levirate obligation, and female circumcision.

Education, private, and government interventions are good steps in empowering women, but then women have to be represented in all works of life in order to have their perspectives known and addressed. Time (2012) explains that in every African society the role of "custodians of culture" is crucial. These are people who interpret and uphold customary practices. As Time (2012) explains, most custodians of culture are men, and this is especially true in Cameroon. She also explains that a significant part of the custodians' jobs are rights based. Decisions handed down by these custodians of culture invariably following tradition are binding, and without women's voices the process seems invidious.

It is thus recommended that society understand the importance of women's perspectives and make every effort to incorporate women and their voices in decision making. As well, African societies that are still hesitant to shake off repugnant and discriminatory practices against women should realize that society never prospers when some sector is left behind. In 2013, Cameroon elected 70 senators, 17 of whom were women. The president of Cameroon subsequently added to these numbers 27 men and 3 women. Opinions have been mixed, some viewing this as a significant step in bridging women's rights, others as just tepid strides (Fonjock and Endeley 2013), while others see a society where women are still marginalized, not solely because of the doing of men, but because some women are not yet willing to see another woman make decisions about their lives. Professor Claude Abe explains this phenomenon:

> Structurally, Cameroonian society sits between tradition and modernity. As a result, there are many persistent and long-standing elements from tradition that continue to play a part in our society. . . . There is one category of women who remain stumbling blocks for other women—they are not prepared to vote for a woman simply because she is a woman—politics also requires a lot of money. Invariably, the majority of women are financially dependent on men and this limits their ability to get involved in politics. (World News 2013)

The preceding reveals how entrenched cultural beliefs and ideologies are, and how they influence rational thoughts. Educating, empowering women, as well as boys and men on human rights, and equality, is most useful in warding off some of the gender-biased beliefs that society nurses. Holding town meetings, rallies, radio and television discussions on gender issues are likely to properly inform the masses in ways they can understand about the oppressive aspects of some cultural practices, and the need for people to be treated with compassion and dignity. See canadainternational.gc.ca (2013) who working with Ghana through radio were able to bring to light the problem of forced marriages in Ghana, and provide a forum to address the issues and offer at-risk girls a place to turn to. A caller to the station, a victim of the practice herself stated:

> My parents gave me out for marriage to a 47-year-old man at age 13. It was seven years of hell and bondage and I would not wish for any girl to go through such an ordeal. I have been prevented from seeing my children for two years now, but thanks to your program, I now know where to turn to for assistance.

Some places to turn to include: Commission for Human Rights and Administrative Justice, the Domestic Violence Unit of the Ghana Police Service, the International Federation of Women Lawyers, Ghana (FIDA-Ghana), and Women in Law and Development (WILDAF).

It makes no sense that in this day and age girls and women are commoditized, exploited, and subjected to barbaric mutilation in the name of culture; and what is even more troubling is that the state by not strenuously barring such practices in essence silently acquiesces their persistence. Punitive sanctions alone will not do, there has to be a cultural or attitudinal change. Ruback et al. (2014, 410) discuss the effects of attempts to change behavior. They explain that there could be four responses: "compliance, internalization, no change, or reactance." Compliance is spurred by the need for rewards and the avoidance of punishment. However, they caution that this can only be effective if there is certainty that such rewards or punishment are imminent, or are definitely going to occur (Kelman 1958). They further the discussion by explaining that compliance may sometimes occur if the person whose behavior needs to change is simply just aware that he/she is being observed (Bateson, Nettle, and Roberts 2006). They reiterate the point that a vast majority of studies are definitive in their conclusions that simply making threats of punishment with little or no intention to carry them out is ineffective in changing behavior (Hollin 2002; Meier and Johnson 1977; Ray and Kilburn 1970; Tyler 2001; 2011). Internalization, as Ruback et al. explain can more effectively create change of behavior in a person if the person faithfully believes that a change of behavior is necessary, and is the right thing to do. Regardless of any persuasion to change behavior, this change of behavior prompted by internalization may also occur just from the need to "change self-image" (Ruback et al. 2014; Cialdini 2001). Ruback et al. (2014) explain that at times, people stick to their old ways, and regardless of any type of intervention, no shift of behavior is observed. For these types of people, a combination of different factors, perhaps punishment and counseling, and even restitution may be the panacea. Reactance, as Ruback et al. discuss, sometimes has a contrary effect in that the person whose behavior needs change decides against such change simply as defiance based on free will to do what he/she so pleases. As a definitive finding, Burger et al. (2010) conclude that intervention by itself has no deterrent effect. It follows that to abate these oppressive behaviors a combination of actions must be taken. There is no quick fix; what is germane is that people accept the need for change, and make visible, consistent efforts toward change.

In discussing reintegrative shaming Braithwaite (1989) in essence proposes a positive way by which lawbreakers in communitarian societies can self-correct when shame is applied in a judicious manner. This idea is premised on that the wrongdoer is made to know of his wrongs and let to take responsibility for his actions as society moves forward to reintegrate the person in society if full acceptance and an about turn are made in behavior (Braithwaite et al. 2006). Braithwaite's stance is that failure to shame those who prey on others furthers their criminal behavior. His assumption is that if society makes wrongdoers know how disgusting their acts are (shaming them) they will be less likely to continue their offending patterns. This, as Braithwaite posits, is likely to be effective in cohesive and more homogenous societies. Shame, as Braithwaite suggests, is the highest deterrent for persons who worry about their image or those who have a stake in society.

In the context of African societies, shame may work for some kinds of crimes like property offenses especially in villages, but for those culturally accepted behaviors, such as early marriages, bride price, levirate, female genital circumcision, wife beating, it is unlikely to see how shaming changes attitudes. There has to first be a change of cultural beliefs and acceptance of the new way of behaving. This new way of behavior has to completely supplant the old way of life for deviation to subsequently lead to shaming.

Restorative Justice attempts to introduce a more conciliatory process of dealing with criminals and offenders. This method of controlling criminal behavior and redressing the victim is as Johnstone and Van Ness (2006) state intended to replace "punitive justice and control . . . with community-based reparative justice and moralizing social control" (5). The concept works reasonably well for some types of criminals and crimes. The hope of restorative justice is to create some sense of community re-cohesiveness after the offender would have destabilized it. In essence, to make good of the wrong caused to the community. I see this meaningful to parents who traded their children for money or goods. What they did was cruel and they need to face their children to atone for their shortcomings. I see this too as an extension of what men who married children and young girls, and wife beaters, have to do. In doing this as Ronel (2013) explains is to respond "to the emotional, social, and material needs of the victim of the offense, paving the way for the reintegration of the perpetrators after they take responsibility for their actions." (342)

Conclusion

This volume was undertaken to bring to light some of the issues that African women undergo. Writing a book serves several purposes. Sometimes the intent is for entertainment as for instance, adventure, mystery, and romance; and at times, the intent is to educate on historical occurrences, or folklore, and at times it is to bring to the forefront of popular discourse some critical or timely issue. This volume is of a serious type. It is intended to expose to readers the plight of African women. Much of the time when people hear of Africa, it is portrayed as a continent where one goes for a safari, but mostly it is in a negative light—poverty, diseases, children malnourished, a continent seemingly a throwback to ancient civilization, benighted, or a continent deeply in slumber, almost like the fairy tale of the sleeping beauty, but without a prince to wake up the continent with a kiss. Some parts of the continent are waking up to see things the same, some with positive significant changes, some with slight changes, and some even seeing that their nightmarish stupor is true, things got worse.

How Africa can get out of the slump has been quite an engaging conversation. While some of Africa's problems have been blamed on colonization, some think that the continent is trapped in poor governance. Africa first must want to change. The aphorism that no one wishes better for you than you wish for yourself is true to Africa. In discussing Africa's problems Ayodele (2003) advises that: "if you want something done well, do it yourself." Tony Elumelu, a Nigerian philanthropist, echoed similar sentiments when he said "no one can develop Africa but us [Africans]." He unabashedly proclaimed this in 2012 in Washington, DC, at the annual Global Philanthropic Forum of international business leaders, philanthropists, and developers (Forbes.com 2012). Transparency and accountability are crucial. Africa cannot prosper when corruption, mismanagement of funds, graft, extreme greed, and lack of accountability are considered a way of life even as they continue to enervate the economy and the lives of its people.

Foremost, there is no way a country or continent can compete or catch up with others when its people, even if one segment like women, increasingly wallow in poverty, the majority of them living below the poverty level. How can Africa catch up with other continents when the infrastructure in most of its countries, its healthcare and educational systems increasingly are so substandard? It cannot, when it is clear that in some parts of Africa people's meager strivings are eradicated by violence, needless conflicts, and droughts. No doubt life for many has become a dystopia.

No one wants to be needlessly hard in one's criticisms about the sluggish growth of many of the countries in Africa, except one is oblivious of what goes on in the continent. There is no denying that imperial rule devastated Africa in many ways. Some other countries in other parts of the world experienced oppression as well. In Africa, South Africa suffered the scourge of apartheid for so long, yet it is setting the example of what it means to move on. Africa cannot keep pointing fingers (unless it forgets to see that many more fingers are pointing back at it). So many have written that even though the Western world is at times blamed for Africa's tribulation, Africa by and large perpetuates its problems (Arnold 2001; Ayodele 2003; Sender and Smith 1986; Warren 1980), and that it rests on the various governments to grow their economies.

The majority of Africans are hardworking, indeed unremitting in their work ethic, and that is true even with the diasporas. African women carry a lot on their heads and backs both figuratively and realistically, and many have done quite admirably in the professional paths they have carved out for themselves. Those who work at home work extra hard, harder than anyone can even imagine or give credit sufficient to portray their efforts. If only the leaders of Africa could try harder to weed out corruption, mismanagement of funds, greed, and all those impediments to progress, and engage in introspection (because you cannot clean the neighborhood without cleaning your own house first), maybe thereafter things may become brighter for Africa. A fainéant lifestyle is not one attributable to the majority of Africans, but that is not reflected in how the continent is showcased. Tony Elumelu (Forbes.com 2012) while acknowledging that Africa is now considered to be the world's fastest growing economy also declared that Africa can benefit from both an economic and a social burst, but that can be done only with the right leaders in place, and a robust private sector instead of from benevolence from the West: "There is a social and economic impact to be derived, but it needs to be done with the right approach—with African leadership and with the private sector, rather than from charitable orientation." Decades after decades since independence of African countries from colonization, Africa is still heavily reliant on the Western world for aid, and way back in 2001, Arnold

(2001) expressed a disconcerting outcome of this reliance when he made it known that by Africa accruing huge debts that could not be repaid, Africa was digging itself in to a colossal economic abyss, and a perpetual dependence, if not a parasitical dependence on the West, with the hope that the well from which the aid comes from will never dry up.

Elumelu (Forbes.com 2012) explains that even though the idea of charitable donations for worthwhile courses is something African philanthropists are not oriented to do, he sees that happening if legal structures to oversee that donations are channeled to generate developments within the continent are put in place. He is right, without such legal structures in place (hoping that those in charge are themselves free of corruption) it will be difficult for those philanthropists to give their money away knowing that the intended purpose for the donation will never be met.

Education is justified on the basis that its benefits are far reaching not only for the individual but also for the society at large. It provides one a competitive edge in society, longer life expectancy, and a better way of fending for oneself and for those one cares about. The quality of life of the individual spills to the betterment of society in that better and informed decisions are taken regarding healthcare, family size, volunteering, and contributing to good courses in society. Julius Nyerere, a former, and late president of Tanzania, explained the benefit of education is that it helps in the cultivation of youths so that they can eventually help in the growth and betterment of society (1970).

Fighting human trafficking is indeed a global effort. There is the demand side and the supply side, and the reasons for this despicable crime are multiple and complex. Better comprehensive methods to combat the crime on both the demand and supply side, including protection, and prevention are necessary. This is a global crisis and while many of the transactions especially trafficking of children take place within the continent, the numbers of transactions that are transcontinental cannot be put in abeyance. Bertone (1999) states:

> The patriarchal world system hungers for and sustains the international subculture of docile women from underdeveloped nations. The women themselves, who are forced or lured into trade, believe that providing international sex services and sex tourism outfits is the acceptable order of things. The men accept the world order as well, regardless of their background. (7)

The validity of this characterization calls for debate. Do these women accept "the order of things" or are they simply desperate women who due to privations see no way out of their circumstances? Conventional wisdom shows that caught in dire situations humans will take the route to survival. All things being equal, no one would want to be subordinate to another and worse even when such subordination involves degradation. Young girls and women moved from their familiar environment and taken somewhere where they are totally dependent on another never gives them the independence of rational free choices. That said, the starting point to address human trafficking is to acknowledge it as a profound problem, then put in place credible preventive, prosecutorial, and remedial or intervention programs. National, regional, transnational forces, and even community watch groups should one and all pitch in to stop the widespread prevalence of this atrocity. Adequate reporting, and a reliable data pool are necessary in this venture.

Culture identifies a people and some aspects of it distinguish a set of people from another. To the extent that the culture of a people promotes healthy values, it is an endearing concept. Flynn (2009) explains that "collectivist cultures" like those in African countries advocate high degrees of conformity, and this expectation and the culture itself are transmitted from generation to generation through "cultural socialization." Values as Flynn (2009) explains "refer to intangible qualities or beliefs accepted and endorsed by a given society. . . . Values share the following characteristics and qualities:

- Values tend to be unobservable
- Values tend to be confused with other social and psychological phenomena; and
- Values tend to have historical and cultural variability."

Flynn (2009) goes on to distinguish norms from values in that "norms refer to conditions for social relations between groups and individuals, for the structure of society and the difference between societies, and for human behavior in general." As Flynn further clarifies, a person can hold a specific value but groups hold norms. The drift of this discussion is that one can create a dichotomy between one's values and group norms. So, even when there have been long lasting practices people can, and do break from them, and that is honorable if the value is destructive. Commoditizing a child, marrying a child, regardless of the circumstance, is a most disreputable value. Subjecting girls and young women to genital mutilation, levirate relations, and polygamous marriages is a value (or norm if you wish to further the discussion) that can be warded off, and one person after another shaking off the practice will lead to such norms being dismantled. It is the twenty-first century; and even though societies have their various norms where there is a fusion between practices that most see as antiquated and those that meet the requirements of civilization, as for instance, letting children be children and protected by their parents, having them go to school, have them grow up to be adults and make their choices, in the interest of rightness, civilization should prevail.

Back to poverty and the backwardness of Africa as these consume the rest of this conclusion. Africa cannot thrive without deep institutional changes. Changes that provide equal rights and opportunities to women and men; watch groups including the media that can freely monitor and responsibly air the shortcomings of political, financial, private sectors, and indeed all branches of government without reprisals. Professor Richard Mkandawire, director of Partnerships, Resource Mobilisation and Communications (NEPAD) Africa, poignantly explains that no country has ever prospered by relying solely on foreign aid—a premise that resonates among many. More telling is the facts that in 2011, Liberia was given $765 million dollars for development aid, an amount that is reported to have constituted 73 percent of its gross national income (see OECD as reported in The Spectator, on 1/25/2014). Yet, Liberia remains severely impoverished. The Egyptians recognized that aid alone could not build a nation and eradicate poverty when they made their concerns known during the Arab spring protests in Cairo that began on January 25, 2011, and lasted for 18 days. Protesters fed up with corruption, mismanagement, poverty, and with power in the hands of just a few for decades, demanded a change. Without a change of ideology, and without the willingness to really want significant positive change, much of Africa is likely to remain atavistic.

In a paper written by Chinua Achebe, one of Africa's great writers, in order to implant on the minds of Africans the need to get out of its metaphoric slumber, Achebe (1968) writes:

> We all know the little joke of the African in London who ordered coffee and then stormed out of the restaurant when he was asked "white or black." To be able to make such jokes against ourselves is of course a most welcome sign of self-confidence. At the same time, to sneak through life swallowing real insults is to compromise one's self-respect. Whether we like to face up to it or not Africa has been the most insulted continent in the world. Africans' very claim to humanity has been questioned at various times, their persons abused, their intelligence insulted. These things have happened in the past and have gone on happening today. We have a duty to bring them to an end for our own sakes, for the sake of our children and indeed for the safety and happiness of the world. (162–63)

References

Abdourahman, O. (2010). Time Poverty a Contributor to Women's Poverty? *The African Statistical Journal*, Vol. 11, 16–37.

Abe, C. (2013). Looking to Cameroon's women senators. www.finalcall.com/artman/publish/world-news-3/article-9964.shtml. Retrieved June 18, 2013.

Achebe, C. (1968). The duty and involvement of the African writer. In C. Wilfred and M. Kilson, *The Africa Reader: Independent Africa*. New York: Vintage Books.

Achieveinafrica.wordpress.com. (2009). Facts on education in Africa/Achieve in Africa. http://achieveinafrica.wordpress.com/2009/04/15/facts-on-education-in-africa. Retrieved 2/9/2014.

Acker, J. (1992). From sex roles to gendered institutions. *Contemporary Sociology*. Vol. 21, No. 5, 565–69.

ACON Chief Economist's Office. (2009). Financial crisis impacts Africa. http://www.doc.google.com/viewer?a=v&q=cache:tG9S5ENCEPY;internet. Retrieved 10/15/2013.

Actionaid.org. (2013). http://www.actionaid.org/publications/stop-violence-against-girls-schoolcross-country-analysis-change-ghana-kenya-and-mozambique. Retrieved 5/29/2014.

Action.org. (2013). http://www.actionaid.org/sites/files/actionaid/svags_endline_study_report-executive_summary_english_october_2013.pdf. Retrieved 5/29/2014.

Ademiluyi, I., and S. Adedamola. (2010). Gender analysis of political participation in Nigeria. *Journal of Law and Psychology*. ISSN: 2078–1083, 55–60.

Adepoju, A. (2005). Review of research data on human trafficking in sub-Saharan Africa. *International Immigration*, Vol. 43, Issue 1–2, 75–98.

Adler, F. (1975). *Sisters in Crime: The Rise of the New Female Criminal*. New York: McGraw-Hill.

African Charter on the Rights and Welfare of the Child, OAU Doc. CAB/LEG24.9/49 (1990), entered into force Nov. 1999. http://www.1umn.edu/humanrts/afchild.htm. Retrieved 2/6/2014.

Africa Check. (2013). *Factsheet South Africa: Official Crime Statistics for 2012/13*. http://www.africacheck.org/factsheets/factsheet-south-africas-official-crime-statistics-for- 2012/2013. Retrieved 8/6/2014.

Africa Renewal. (2012). Desertification a threat to Africa's development. http://www.un.org/africarenewal/web-features/desertification-threat-africa%E2%80%99s-development. Retrieved 8/7/2014.

———. (2014). Famine in Somalia. http://www.un.org/africarenewal/we- features/famine-somalia. Retrieved 8/8/2014.

Agnew, R. (2001). Building on the foundation of general strain theory: Specifying the types of strain most likely to lead to crime and delinquency. *Journal of Research in Crime and Delinquency*, Vol. 38, no. 4, pp. 319–52.

———. (2005). *Why Do Criminals Offend? A General Theory of Crime and Delinquency*. New York: Oxford University Press.

Akers, R. (1998). *Social Learning and Social Structure: A General Theory of Crime and Deviance*. Boston: Northeastern University Press.

Alewo, A., and M. Olong. (2012). Cultural practices and traditional beliefs as impediments to the enjoyment of women's rights in Nigeria. *International Law Research*, vol. 1, no. 1, 134–43.

Allafrica.com. (2013). Africa: Can Africa's natural resources lift people out of poverty? Winnie Byanyima, 9/7/2013. http://allafrica.com/stories/201305091074.html. Retrieved 3/5/2015.

———. (2013). Ghana: 108 girls forced into marriage in region. http://allafrica.com/stories/201307100884.html. Retrieved 12/29/2013.

———. (2013). Sudan: Floods, flies, fever and famine in Darfur Camps. http://allafrica.com/stories/201307250097.html. Retrieved 1/9/2014.

Allais, C. (2013) Human trafficking: Some research challenges for South Africa. *Acta Academia*, Vol. 45, No. 3, 268–90.

Althaus, F. (1997). Female circumcision: Rite of passage or violation of rights? *International Family Planning Perspectives*, Vol. 23, No. 3, 130–33.

Amato, P. (2001). Children and divorce in the 1990s: An update of the Amato and Keith (1991) meta-analysis. *Journal of Family Psychology*. Vol. 15, 355–70.

Amenga-Etego, R. (2013). Categorization of women and human rights issues. *Crosscurrents*, 138–47.

Andenaes, J. (1983). Deterrence. In S. H. Kadish (ed.), *Encyclopedia of Crime and Justice*. New York: Free Press.

Anderson, C. (2011). The moral arc of the universe bends long but it bends toward justice: The search for justice in international law. *The Journal of Diplomatic History*, 35 (5), 787–91.

Andrews, D. A., and J. Bonta. (1998). The Psychology of Criminal Conduct (2nd ed.). Cincinnati, Ohio: Anderson Publishing Company.

———. (2006). *The Psychology of Criminal Conduct*. 4th ed. Cincinnati, OH: Lexis Nexus.

Ardayfio-Schandorf, E. (2005). Violence against women: The Ghanaian case. University of Ghana, Family and Development Programme. Paper presented at the Expert Group Meeting of the United Nations (UN) Division for the Advancement of Women in collaboration with the Economic Commission for Europe (ECE) and the World Health Organization (WHO) held in Geneva, Switzerland from 11 to 14 April 2005. Retrieved 12/29/2013.

Archieve.unu.edu. (n.d.). Overall status of women in Africa. http://archieve.unu.edu/unupress/unubooks/uu37we0t.htm. Retrieved 05/14/2016.

Arnold, G. (2001). *A Guide to African Political and Economic Development*. Chicago, IL: Fitzroy Dearborn.

Asante, R., and E. Gyimah-Boadi. (2004). *Ethnic Structure, Inequality and Governance of the Public Sector in Ghana*. UNRISD, United Nations of Research and Development.

Asifatu, S. (2012). Economic digression in developing countries: Implications of poor governance, corruption, and absence of independent judicial systems. In C. Okafo, *Grounded Law: Comparative Research on State and Non-State Justice in Multiple Societies*, Ch. 14, 345–65, UK: Wildfire Publishing House.

AVERT.org. (2013). Impact of HIV and AIDS in sub-Saharan Africa. http://www.avert.org/impact-hiv-and-aids-sub-saharan-africa.htm. Retrieved 8/11/2014.

———. (n.d.). Women and HIV/AIDS. Http://www.avert.org/women-and-iv-aids-htm. Retrieved 8/14/2014.

Ayodele, T. (2003). Trade and development—Trade, not aid: What Africa needs. *National Review*. http://www.findarticles.com/p/articles/mi_m1282/is_17_55/ai_107223567. Retrieved 7/27/2007.

Ayodele, T., F. Cudjoe, T. Nolutshungu, and C. Sunwabe. (2005). African perspectives on aid: Foreign assistance will not pull Africa out of poverty. Cato Institute, http://www.cato.org/

publications/economic-development-bulletin/african-perspectives- aid-foreign-assistance-will-not-pull-africa-out-poverty. Retrieved 6/10/2014.

Bachelet, M. (2011). Confluence of famine and conflict devastating for women and children in Somalia. http://www.un.org/africarenewal/web-features/confluence-famine-and-conflict-devastating-women-and-children-somalia. Retrieved 1/9/2014.

Baker, A. (2014). Racing Ebola. What the world needs to do to stop the deadly virus. *Time*. 43–45.

Bamgbose, O. (2002). Customary law practices and violence against women: The position under the Nigerian legal system. Paper presented at 8th International Interdisciplinary Congress on Women hosted by Department of Women and Gender Studies, University of Makerere.

Bandura, A. (1977). *Social Learning Theory*. Englewood Cliffs, NJ: Prentice Hall.

Bardasi, E., and Q. Wodon. (2010). Working long hours and having no choice: Time poverty in Guinea. *Feminist Economics,* Vol. 16, no. 3, 45–78.

Bargai, N., G. Ben-Shakhar, and A. Y. Shalev. (2007). Posttraumatic stress disorder and depression in battered women: The mediating role of learned helplessness. *Journal of Family Violence*, Vol. 22, 267–75.

Barnett, J., and W. Adger. (2007). Climate change, human security and violent conflict. *Political Geography*. Vol. 26, No. 6, 639–55.

Barro, R. (2001). "Human capital and growth," *American Economic Review*, Vol. 9, no. 2, 12–17.

Bateson, M., D. Nettle, and G. Roberts. (2006). Cues of being watched enhance cooperation in a real-world setting. *Biology Letters*, 2: 412–14.

Baum, S., and K. Payea. (2004). *Education Pays 2004. The Benefits of Higher Education for Individuals and Society*. Washington, DC: College Board.

Baum, S., J. Ma, and K. Payea. (2013). *Education Pays 2013. The Benefits of Higher Education for Individuals and Society*. Washington, DC: College Board.

Baumgartner E. (2008). Aspects of victim participation in the proceedings of the International Criminal Court. *International Review of the Red Cross*. Vol. 90, No.870, 409–40.

BBC. Co.uk. (2005) BBC News/Business/Cameroon Uncovers Salary Scandal (2005). http://www.bbc.co.uk. Retrieved 3/2/2005.

BBC News. (2002). Nigerian girl sues over forced marriage. http://news.bbc.uk/2/hiafrica/2242.stm. Retrieved on 10/7/2010.

BBC News. (2007) "Cameroon sees $5 billion debt erased by World Bank and International Monetary Fund" http://www.news.bbc.co.uk/2/hi/business/4964808.stm. Retrieved 10/28/2008.

BBC News. (2013). How can Africa move away from aid dependence? http://www.m.bbc.com/news/world-africa-22270164,Retrieved 6/9/2014.

BBC News Africa. (2014). Drought threat looms over Kenya's Turkana region. http://www.bbc.com/news/world-africa-26478240. Retrieved 8/8/2014.

BBC News/Africa/Cameroon corruption hinders AIDS fight. (2007). http://www.news.bbc.co.uk/2/hi/africa/6198337.stm. Retrieved 6/9/2014.

BBC News/Africa/Cameroon dances to anti-graft beat. (2007). http://news bbc.co.uk/2/hi/africa//7131637.stm. Retrieved1/4/2008.

Beccaria, C. (1963). *On Crimes and Punishment* (Dei delitti e della pen). Translated by Henry Paolucci, New York, NY, USA: *The Liberal Arts Press*.

Becker, J., and U. Wagner. (2009). Doing gender differently—the interplay of strength of gender identification and content of gender identity in predicting women's endorsement of sexist beliefs. *European Journal of Social Psychology*. Vol. 39, Issue 4, 487–508.

Behrman, J., D. Crawford, and S. Nevzer. (1997). "Conclusion." In J. Behrman and S. Nevzer (eds.), *The Social Benefits of Education*. Ann Arbor: University of Michigan Press.

Benschop, M. (2002). Rights and Reality: Are women's equal rights to land, housing and property implemented in East Africa? Nairobi: *United Nations Human Settlements Programme* (UN-HABITAT), 1–84.

Bentheim, C. (2010). Forced marriage in Africa: Examining the disturbing reality. ConsultancyAfrica Intelligence. http://www.consultancyafrica.com/index.php?opinion=com_content

&view=articl e&id290. Retrieved 10/9/2010.

Berenbaum, S., J. Blakemore, and A. Beltz. (2011). A role for biology in gender-related behavior. *Sex Roles.* Vol. 64, Issue 11/12, 804–25.

Berg, B. (1995). *Qualitative Research Methods for the Social Sciences*. 2nd Ed. Boston: Allyn and Bacon.

Bernard, J. (1981). *The Female World*. New York: Free Press.

Bernat, F., and T. Zhilina. (2010). Human trafficking: The local becomes global. *Women and Justice*, Vol. 20, No. 10, 2–9.

Berry, S. (1991). Copping with confusion: African farmers' responses to economic instability in the 1970's and 1980's. Unpublished manuscript, Johns Hopkins University, Baltimore, Maryland, USA.

Bertone, A. (1999). Sexual trafficking in women: International political economy and the politics of sex. *Gender Issues*, Vol. 18, no. 1, pp.4–22.

Beswick, S. (2001). "We are bought like clothes": The war over polygamy and levirate marriage in South Sudan. *Northeast African Studies*. Vol. 8, No. 2, 35–61.

Bishai, D., and S. Grossbard. (2010). Far above rubies: Bride price and extramarital sexual relations in Uganda. *Journal of Population Economics*. Vol. 23, Issue 4, 1177–87.

Black, M. (2001). Wanted: The right to refuse. *New Internationalist*, Issue 337. http://ehis.ebscohost.com.proxy.lib.odu/ehost/detail?vid=2&hid=116&sid=alad3ef4–8. Retrieved 10//9/2010.

Blackden, M., and Q. Wodon. (2006). *Gender, Time Use, and Poverty in Sub-Saharan Africa.* Working paper 73. Washington, DC: World Bank.

Bloomberg Report. (April 11, 2014). Ebola Outbreak Empties Hotels As West Africa Borders Closed. In H5N1: Ebola: The economic impact continues. http://www.crofsblogs.typepad.com/h5n1/2014/04/ebola-the-economic-impact- continues.html. Retrieved 8/9/2014.

Blumer, H. (1986). *Symbolic Interactionism: Perspective and Method.* University of California Press.

Borman, K., M. LeCompte, and J. Goetz. (1986). Ethnographic and qualitative research design and why it doesn't work. *American Behavioral Scientists* 30(1), 42–57.

Botany.uwc.ac.za (n.d.). *Desertification.* http://www.botany.uwc.ac.za/envfacts/facts/dessertification.htm. Retrieved 8/6/2014.

Braithwaite, J. (1989). *Crime, Shame, and Reintegration.* Cambridge, MA: Cambridge University Press.

Braithwaite, J., E. Ahmed, and V. Braithwaite. (2006). Shame, restorative justice and crime. In F. Cullen, J. Wright, and K. Belvins (eds.), *Taking Stock: The Status of Criminological Theory* (397–417). Piscataway, NJ: Transaction Publishers.

Brautigam, D., and S. Knack. (2004). Foreign aid, institutions, and governance in Sub-Saharan African. *Economic and Cultural Change*. Vol. 52, No. 2, 255–85.

Britton, H., and L. Dean. (2014). Policy responses to human trafficking in Southern Africa: Domesticating international norms. *Human Rights Review,* Vol. 15 Issue 3, 305–28.

Buchan, J., I. Couper, V. Tangeharoensathien, K. Thepannya, W. Jaskiewicz, G. Perfilieva, and C. Dolea. (2013). Early implementation of WHO recommendations for the retention of health workers in remote and rural areas. *Bull World Health Organ*, Vol. 91(11), 834–40.

Budiani-Saberi, D. A., and F. Delmonico. (2008). Organ trafficking and transplant tourism: A commentary on the global realities. *American Journal of Transplantation*, Vol. 8, No. 5, 925–29.

Bullock, H., and Lott, B. (2010). Social class and women's Lives. *Psychology of Women Quarterly*. Vol. 34, 418–24.

Bunch, C. (1990). Gender violence: A development and human rights issue. *Human Rights Quarterly*, Vol. 12, No. 4, 486–98.

Burger, R., M. Louw, and C. Van der Watt. (2010). The challenge of poverty and social exclusion in post-apartheid South Africa—Considering the potention role of religious groups. In I. Swart, H. Rocher, S. Green, and J. Erasmus (eds.), *Religion and Social Development in Post-Apartheid South Africa* (61–73). Stellenbosch: Sun Press.

Burgess-Proctor, A. (2006). Intersections of race, class, gender, and crime. *Feminist Criminology*. Vol. 1, 27–47.

Cable Network News (CNN). (2014). WHO panel says unproven drugs are ethical as Ebola death toll tops 1,000. http://www.cnn.com/2014/08/12/health/ebola-outbreak. Retrieved 8/12/2014.

Campbell, J., A. Jones, J. Dienemann, J. Kub, J. Schollenberger, P. O'Campo, A. Gielen, and C. Wynne. (2002). Intimate partner violence and physical health consequences. *Archives of Internal Medicine*. Vol. 162, no. 10, 1157–63.

Canadainternational.gc.ca. (Sep. 13, 2013). Canada and Ghana take to the airways to fight early forced marriage, http://www.Canadainternational.gc.ca/Ghana/..../early_forced_marriage-marriage_force_precoce.aspx?. Retrieved 12/29/2013.

Castro-Leal, F., J. Dayton, L. Demery, and K. Mehra. (2000). Public spending on health care in Africa: Do the poor benefit? *Bulletin of the World Health Organization*, Vol. 78, no. 1, 66–74.

Catalyst. (2008). *Census of Women Corporate Officers and Top Earners of the Fortune 500*. New York: Catalyst.

CBSnews.com. Third of girls in 42 countries forced into child marriages—CBS News. http://www.cbsnews.com/news/third-of-girls-in-42-countries-forced-into-child-marriages. Retrieved 12/29/2013.

Cepd.org.za. (2009). Challenges facing education in South Africa. http://www.cepd.org.za/files/pictures/The%20challenges%20ffFacing%20Education%20Interview%20Nov%2009.pdf. Retrieved 6/2/2014.

Center for Reproductive Rights. (2003). Claiming Our Rights: Surviving Pregnancy and Childbirth in Mali, p.51. http://www.reproductiverights.org/document/claiming-our-rights-surviving-pregnancy-and-childbirth-in-mali. Retrieved 5/4/2014.

Charmes, J. (2006). A review of empirical evidence on time use in Africa from UN-sponsored surveys. In C. Blackden and Q. Wodon (2006). *Gender, Time Use, and Poverty in Sub-Saharan Africa*. World Bank Working Paper No. 73, Ch. 3, 39–72.

Cheema, G. (2005). *Building Democratic Institutions: Governance Reform in Developing Countries*. Sterling, Virginia, U.S.A.: Kumarian Press.

Chesney-Lind, M. (1989). Girls, crime and woman's place: Toward a feminist model of female delinquency. *Crime and Delinquency*. Vol. 35, 5–29.

———. (1997). *The Female Offender: Girls, Women, and Crime*. Thousand Oaks, CA: Sage Publication.

Chesney-Lind, M., and R. Shelden. (2004). *Girls, Delinquency, and Juvenile Justice*. 3rd ed. Belmont, CA: Wadsworth.

Chigbu, C., K. Ekeazi, C. Chigbu, and S. Iwuji. (2010). Sexual violation among married women in South Eastern Nigeria. *International Journal of Gynecology and Obstetrics*, Vol. 110, No. 2, 141–44.

Childinfo.org. (2012). Monitoring the situation of children and women. Childinfo.org: Statistics by Area—Maternal mortality—overview. http://www.childinfo.org/maternal_mortality.html. Retrieved 2/26/2014.

Christens, B., P. Speer, and N. Peterson. (2011). Social class as moderator of the relationship between (dis)empowering processes and psychological empowerment. *Journal of Community Psychology*. Vol. 39, No.2, 170–82.

Cialdini, R. (2001). *Influence: Science and Practice*. Boston, MA: Allyn and Bacon.

CIAWorld Factbook. (2010). www.cia.gov/library/publications/the-world-factbook/fields/2103.html. Retrieved 8/9/2012.

———. (2015). Maternal mortality rate 2015 country comparisons, ranks, By Rank. http://www.photius.com/rankings/2015/population/maternal_mortality_rate_2015_0.html. Retrieved 04/22/2016.

Cinoglu, H., and Y. Arikan. (2012). Self, identity formation: From the perspectives of three major theories. *International Journal of Human Sciences* [online]. (9)2, 1114–31.

Clasby, E. (2013). The current education system in Senegal: A closer look at the advantages and disadvantages of attending private Catholic institution in Dakar. Independent Study

Project (ISP) Collection. Paper 1259. http://www.digitalcollections.sit.edu/isp_collection/1259. Retrieved 6/2/2014.

Coe.int. (2009). Trafficking in organs, tissues and cells and trafficking in human beings for the purpose of the removal of organs. http://www.coe.int/t/dghl/monitoring/trafficking/docs/news/organtrafficking-study.pdf. Retrieved 7/11/2014.

Collier, P. (2007). *The Bottom Billion.* London: Oxford University Press.

Condry, J., and S. Condry. (1976). Sex differences: A study of the eye of the beholder. *Child Development*, 47: 812–19.

Connor, M., L. Schackman, and L. Serbin. (1978). Sex-related differences in response to practice on a visual-spatial test and generalization to a related test. *Child Development*, Vol. 49, 24–29.

Cornwall, A. (2005). "Introduction: Perspectives on Gender in Africa," in Andrea Cornwall, editor, *Gender in Africa,* London: International African Institute in association with Indiana University Press, Bloomington and Indianapolis, and James Currey, Oxford.

Cross, C., and D. Hornby. (2002). Opportunities and obstacles to women's land access in South Africa. A research report for the Promoting Women's Access to Land Programme, February 2002. See www.nlc.co.za/pubs2003/womenlandaccess/wlatoc.htm. Accessed, 10/20/2014.

Cullen, F., and R. Agnew. (2011). *Criminological Theory: Past to Present.* 4th Ed. New York, Oxford University Press.

Cunningham, A. (2006). The broader societal benefits of higher education. http://www.jcu.edu/academic/planassess/planning/…/Broader%20Social%20Benefits.pdf. Retrieved 3/28/2014.

Daly, K. (1997). Different ways of conceptualizing sex/gender in feminist theory and their implications for criminology. *Theoretical Criminology.* Vol. 1, 25–51.

Danchurchaid.org. (2007). Floods in Amhara and Gambella. http://danchurchaid.org/news/news/floods-in-amhara-and-gambella. Retrieved 1/8/2014.

Danish Immigration Service. (January 2005). Report on Human Rights Issues in Nigeria: Joint British-Danish Fact-Finding Mission to Abuja and Lagos, Nigeria. 19 October to 2 November 2004. http://www.udlst.dk/NR/rdonlyres/e7hlzlsv5my6htxfzro2b63qy4eqixyze2ihhfpt fs7exr4yd lez7nljgn7f4idhzwsgd2n2ebzfebl24dkbb7rqicg/Nigeria2005_web2.pdf. Retrieved 8/3/2012.

Davies, P., P. Francis, and C. Greer. (2007). *Victims, Crime, and Society.* http://www.corwin.com/upm-data/15711_01_Greer_Chr_01.pdf. Retrieved 05/08/2016.

Debatewise.org. (2014). Africa must solve its lack of good governance to pull itself out of poverty. http://debatewise.org/debates/950-africa-must-solve-its-lack-of-good-governance-to-pull-itself-out-of-poverty. Retrieved 10/19/2014.

Deegan, M. (2005). Transcending "The marginal man": Challenging the patriarchal legacy of Robert E. Park. In R. Dennis (ed.), *Marginality, Power, and Social Structure: Issues in Race, Class, and Gender Analysis*. 207–27, Amsterdam: Elsevier.

Denzin, N. (1978). *The Research Act*. New York: New York, McGraw-Hill.

Devarajan, S. (2008). Poverty in Africa and elsewhere: Africa Can End Poverty. http://blogs.worldbank.org/african/poverty-in-africa-and-elsewhere. Retrieved 6/5/2010.

———. (2011). Africa's year of living dangerously. *The Guardian.* http://www.theguardian.com/global-development/poverty-matters/2011/de/21/afric-economic-year-living-dangerously. Retrieved 1/4/2015.

———. (2012). What will it take to end poverty in Africa? / Africa can end poverty. http://blogs.worldbank.org/africacan/what-will-it-take-to-end-poverty-in-africa. Retrieved 10/13/14.

Diekola, A., and S. Adebayo. (2014). Predicting the effect of emotional intelligence, self-efficacy, job interest, life satisfaction and pay incentives as correlates of effective community policing in South-West Nigeria. *IFE PsychologIA*, Vol. 22, Issue 1, p. 170–78.

Dietz, A., R. Ruben, and A. Verhagen. (2004). *The Impact of Climate Change on Dry Lands: With Focus on West Africa.* Kluwer Academic Publishers.

Dimandja, A. (2004). The role and place of women in Sub-Saharan African societies. Global Action on Aging. www.globalaging.org/elderrights/world/2004/subsaharan.htm. Retrieved 07/17/2012.

Doener, W., and S. Lab. (1998). *Victimology*. 2nd ed. Cincinnati, OH: Anderson Publishing Co.

———. (2007). *Victimology*. 6th ed. Cincinnati, OH: Anderson Publishing Co.

Dugassa, B. (2009). Women's rights and women's health during HIV/AIDS epidemics: The experience of women in Sub-Saharan Africa. *Health Care for Women International*, Vol. 30, 690–706.

Dunne, R. (2005). Marginality: A conceptual extension. In R. Dennis (ed.), *Marginality, Power, and Social Structure: Issues in Race, Class, and Gender Analysis*. 11–27. Amsterdam: Elsevier.

Ehrhardt, A. (1977). "Gender development." Paper read at the summer program of the Institute for Sex Research, Indiana University, July 28, 1977.

Elbadawi, E., and N. Sambanis. (2000). Why are there so many civil wars in Africa? Understanding and preventing violent conflict. *Journal of African Economics*, Vol. 9, Issue 3, 244–69.

Ellis, A., C. Manuel, and C. Blackden. (2006). *Gender and Economic Growth in Uganda: Unleashing the Power of Women*. World Bank: Washington, DC

EM-DAT: The OFDA/CRED International Disaster. Data Base, Universit Catholique de Louvain, Brussels, Belgium.

Encyclopedia of Judaism (2002). Levirate Marriage. *The New Encyclopedia of Judaism*. The Jerusalem Publishing House, Ltd.

Eprints.dinus.ac.id (n.d.). http://eprints.dinus.ac.id/6353/1/7.Diffusion_of_Innovation_Theory.pdf. Retrieved 10/12/2014.

Erero, J., and T. Oladoyin. (2000). Tackling corruption in Nigeria. In K. R. Hope and B. Chikulo (Eds.). *Corruption and Development in Africa: Lessons from Country Studies*. New York: Palgrave.

Erez, E., and R. Thomspon. (1996). Victimization of women in African society. In C. Fields and R. Moore (eds.), *Comparative Criminal Justice: Traditional and Non-traditional Systems of Law and Control* (61–82). Prospect Heights, IL: Waveland Press.

Ezard, N., J. Haskew, L. Machibya, and R. Makou. (2005). Challenges to effective malaria control in refugee settings: Experiences from Chad and Tanzania, 2004. *Humanitarian Exchange*. No.31, 19–22.

Farmer, P. (1996). Social inequalities and emerging infectious diseases, *Emerging Infection Diseases Journal*. Vol. 2, No.4, pp 259–69.

Fishbein, D. (1990). Biological perspectives in Criminology. *Criminology*. Vol. 28, 27–72.

Flavia, A. (1997). *Protecting Women against Violence? Review of a Decade of Legislation, 1980–89. State and Politics in India*, Partha Chatterjee, Delhi: OUP.

Flint, J., and A. De Waal. (2008). *Darfur: A New History of a Long War* (Revised and undated edition). London/New York, NY: Zed Books.

Flynn, S. (2009). Culture and Conformity. Research Starters Sociology (Online Edition). http://www.academicpub.com/map/authors/Flynn%2C+Simone+l.html. Retrieved 1/8/2013.

Fon, D., and T. Edokat. (2012). Marginalization of women's role in Sub-Saharan Africa towards crop production: A review. *Agricultural Science Journal*. Vol. 2. No. 9, 499–505.

Fonjock, J., and J. Endeley. (2013). Women in Anglophone Cameroon: Household gender relations and participation in local government. *Africa Peace and Conflict Journal*. Vol. 6, no. 2, 102–17.

Forbes.com. (2012). Only Africans can develop Africa, says Nigerian philanthropist Tony Elumelu, a Nigerian. http://www.forbes.com/sites/mfonobongnsehe/2012/04/20/only-africans-can-develop-africa-says-nigerian-philanthropist-tony-elumelu. Retrieved 1/24/2015.

Ford, T. (2012). Domestic violence is biggest threat to West Africa's women, IRC says. www.guardian.co.uk/global-development/2012/may/22/domestic-violence-biggest-threat-to-west-africa's-women. Retrieved 8/4/2012.

Foreignaffairs.com. (2011). Ending Africa's wars. http://www.foreignaffairs.com/articles/562.45/john-j-stremlau/ending-africas-wars. Retrieved 12/28/2014.

Forward U.K. (n.d.). Erradicating child marriage in Africa. http://www.forwarduk.org.uk/key-issues/child-marriage. Retrieved 10/4/2014.

Fox, G. (1977). Nice girl: Social control of women through a value construct. *Signs*, 2(4), 805–17.

The Freedom Project. (n.d.). http://www.thefreedomproject.org/human-trafficking. Retrieved 8/8/2014.

Galarpe, K. (2013). Nearly half of women in developing countries do not get prenatal care conference report. http://www.gmanetwork.com/news/story/310444/lifestyle/healthandwellness/nearly-half- of-women-in-developing-countries-do-not-get-prenatal-care-conference-report. Retrieved 2/19/2014.

Gayadeen, M., and S. Phillips. (2014). The innovation of community policing and the COPS office: Does diffusion of innovation theory hold in a manipulative environment? *International Journal of Police Science and Management*, Vol. 16, No. 3, 228–42.

Gatut, B. (2013). Individual business and leadership weaknesses consequences on society welfare and poverty formation. *Studies in Business and Economics.* Vol. 8, Issue 1, pp.11–19.

George, S. (1990). A fate worse than debt, (New York: Grove Weidenfeld). In Global Issues. Structural adjustment—a major cause of poverty. http://www.globalissues.org/article/3/structural-adjustment-a-major-cause-of-poverty. Retrieved 6/7/2014.

———. (1992). *The Debt Boomerang.* (Transnational Institute Series), London, United Kingdom: Pluto Press.

———. (1993). The Debt Boomerang. *New Internationalist.* Issue 243. http://newint.org/features/1993/05/05/keynote. Retrieved 5/21/2015.

Gertler, P., and J. Molyneaux. (1997). Experimental evidence on the effect of raising user fees for publicly delivered health care services: Utilization, health outcomes, and private provider response. Santa Monica, CA, Rand Corporation (Unpublished Document).

Ghana.com. (2013). Child marriage on the rise in Ghana. http://www.gbcghana.com/index.php?id=1.1502173. Retrieved 12/29/2013.

Ghanabusinessnews.com. (2013). Forced marriages impede education in Karaga-ISODEC. http://www.ghanabusinessnews.com/2013/09/05/forced-marriages-impede-education-in-karaga-isodec/#respond. Retrieved 12/30/2013.

Gill, B. (2008). Family Law: Forced Marriages. The Law and Society Gazette. www.lawgazzett.co.ok/in-practice/family-law-forced-marriage. Retrieved 6/19/2013.

Gleave, M., and W. Morgan. (2001). Economic development in tropical Africa from a geographical perspective: A comparative study of African economies. *The Geographical Journal*, Vol. 167, no. 2, 139–162.

Global Economic Symposium (2014). Create good governance by strengthening. http://www.global-economic-symposium.org/knowledgebase/the-global-economy/empowering-the-world-s-poor-countries/solutions/solution_1-empowering-the-worlds-poor-countries. Retrieved 12/31/2014.

Goffman, E. (1977). The arrangement between the sexes. *Theory and Society,* Vol. 4, 301–31.

Goldberg, S. (1974). *The Inevitability of Patriarchy* (expanded edition). New York: William Morrow and Co.

Goldsmith, A. (2001). Foreign aid and Statehood in Africa. *International Organization*, Vol. 55, Issue 1, 123–48.

Gong-Gershowitz, J. (2009). Forced marriage: A "new" crime against humanity? 8 North West University Journal International Human Rights, 53. http://www.law.northwestern.edu/journals/jihr/v8/n1/3. Retrieved 10/9/2012.

Gordon, A. (1996). *Transforming Capitalism and Patriarchy: Gender Development in Africa.* Boulder, Co: Lynne Rienner.

Gould, C., and N. Fick. (2008). Selling sex in Cape Town: Sex work and human trafficking in a South African City. Pretoria/Tshwane: Institute for Securities Studies.

Gove, W., and R. Carpenter. (1982). *The Fundamental Connection between Nature and Nurture: A Review of the Evidence.* Lanham, MD: Lexington Books.

Goyal, M., R. Mehta, L. Schneiderman, and A. Sehgal. (2002). Economic and health consequences of selling a kidney in India. *The Journal of the American Medical Association*, Vol. 288, No. 13, 1589—93.

Grana, S. (2002). *Women and (In) Justice.* Boston, MA: Allyn and Bacon.

Gupta, S., H. Davoodi, and R. Alonso-Terme. (2002). Does corruption affect income inequality and poverty? *Economics of Governance*, Vol. 3, Issue 1, 23–45.

Hague, G., and R. Thiara. (2009). Bride-Price, Poverty and Domestic Violence in Uganda. http://www2.warwick.ac.uk/fac/soc/shss/swell/final_report_bride_price_poverty_and_domestic_vi.pdf_adobereader. Retrieved 8, 3, 2012.

Herrera, J., and C. Torelli. (2010). Domestic work and informal sector employment in: What is the trade-off for women? International conference; "The informal sector and informal employment: Statistical measurement, economic implications and public policies, 6–7 May 2010, Hanoi, Vietnam.

Hines, M., S. Golombok, J. Rust, K. Johnston, J. Golding, and the Avon Longitudinal Study of Parents and Children Study Team. (2002). Testosterone during pregnancy and gender role behavior of preschool children: A longitudinal, population study. *Child Development.* Vol. 73, No. 6, 1678–87.

Hoefler, A. (2008). Dealing with the consequences of violent conflicts in Africa. Paper for the African Development Bank Report 2008. http://users.ox.ac.uk/~ball0144/consequences.pdf. Retrieved 12/29/2014.

Hollin, C. (2002). Does punishment motivate offenders to change? In Mary McMurran (ed.), *Motivating Offenders to Change: A Guide to Enhancing Engagement in Therapy.* New York: Wiley.

The Holy Bible (King James Version). (1964 edition). The National Publishing Co.

Hooks, B. (1984). *Feminist Theory: From Margin to Center.* Boston: South End Press.

Huffingtonpost.com. (2009). Obama Ghana speech: Full text. http://www.huffingtonpost.com/2009/07/11/obama-ghana-speech-full-t_n_230009.html. Retrieved 10/11/2009.

———. (2011). Caryl Stern: Famine in Africa: Why women and children need the most help. http://www.huffingtonpost.com/caryl-stern/famine-in-africa-why- wome_b_914562.html. Retrieved 1/9/2014.

———. (2014). U.S. nurse: We are treating Americans with Ebola because 'it's the right thing.' http://m.huffpost.com/us/entry/5663317. Retrieved 8/9/2014.

Hughes, R. (2005). The effects of divorce on children. Urbana, IL: *University of Illinois Extension.* Http//www.parenting247.0rg/article.cfm?ContentID=646. Retrieved 10/30/2012.

Hurd, E. (2010). Girls, 14, forced to marry in South Africa. http://www.News.sky.com/story/759246/girls-14-forced-to-marry-in-south-africa. Retrieved 8/5/2012.

UNA-GB Model UN. (n.d.). http://rmunatunagb.wikispaces.com/file/view/GA3-Forced+Marriage.pdf. Retrieved 7/26/2012.

Ibtimes.co.uk. (2013). http://www.ibtimes.co.uk/top-five-countries-highest-rates-maternal-mortality-1447398. Retrieved 5/25/2014.

Ikdahl, I., A. Hellum, R. Kaarhus, T. Benjaminsen, and P. Kameri-Mbote. (2005). Human rights, formalization and women's land rights in southern and eastern Africa. *Studies in Women's Law*, No. 57, Institute of Women's Law, University of Oslo, ISSN 1502–8127, 1–132.

International Justice Resource Center (Ijrcenter.org). (n.d.). Economic Community of West African States Court of Justice. http://www.ijrcenter.org/regional-communities/economic-community-of-west-african-states-court-of-justice/. Retrieved 9/8/2014.

Immigration and Refugee Board of Canada. (2006). Nigeria: Forced marriage among the Yoruba, Igbo, and Hausa-Fulani; prevalence, consequences for a woman or minor who refuses to participate in the marriage; availability of state protection (February 2006), 3rd March 2006, NGA101044, E, available at: http://www.unchcr.org/refworld/docid/45f1478a11.html [accessed 3 August 2012].

———. (2006). Nigeria: Levirate marriage practices among the Yoruba, Igbo and Hausa-Fulani; consequences for a man or woman who refuses to participate in the marriage; availability of state protection (February 2006), 16 March 2006, NGA101045-E, available at http://www.unhcr.org/refworldd/docid/45f147881.1html [accessed 8/02/2012].

Independent.co.uk. (2014). Ebola outbreak: Western drugs firms have not tried to find vaccine 'because virus only affects Africans says UK's top public health doctor. http://www.independent.co.uk/news/world/africa/west-accused-of-tardiness-over-ebola-outbreak-9644671.html. Retrieved 8/10/2014.

———. (2014). Plight of missing Nigerian schoolgirls highlights an underlying lack of regard for female education. http://www.independent.co.uk/news/world/Africa/plight-of-missing-nigerian-schoolgirls-highlights-an-underlying-lack-of-regard-for-female-education-9321374.html. Retrieved 5/29/2014.

International Food Policy Research Institute. (IFPRI) (2013). What's really causing water scarcity in Africa South of the Sahara? http://www.ifpri.org/blog/what-s-really-causing-water-scarcity-africa-south-sahara. Retrieved 2/4/2014.

International Labor Office (ILO). (2012). *Hard to see, harder to count.* 2nd ed. Geneva: International Labor Organization.

International Labor Organization. (1999). "Decent Work." Report of Mr. Juan Somavia, ILO Director-General, 87th session of the International Labor Conference.

———. (2011). Making the crisis recovery work for women! http://www.ilo.org/gender/events/WCMS_151285/lang--en/index.htm. Retrieved 7/26/2014.

International Strategy for Disaster Reduction (ISDR. (2007). Drought, Desertification and Water Scarcity, http://www.un.org/waterorlifedecade/pdf/2007_isdr_drought_desertification_and_water_scarcity_eng. Retrieved 8/7/2014.

IRIN Africa. (2007). http://www.irinnews.org/Report/74027/MALI-Child-marriage-neglected-problem. Retrieved 3/22/2012.

Jacob, M. (2005). William J. Wilson's "Ghetto-related behaviors," values and poverty: A test. In R. Dennis. *Marginality, Power, and Social Structure: Issues in Race, Class, and Gender Analysis*. Research in race and ethnic relations, Volume 12. Amsterdam: Elsevier, 253–70.

Jaulmes, C. (2007). Literacy empowers women and girls in Northern Nigeria. http://www.unicef.org/infobycountry/nigeria_39152.html. Retrieved 10/9/2011.

Jawahar, D., and S. Raghavendra. (2011). Perceptual Difference of Role-based Performance—A Gender Study. *International Journal of Business, Humanities & Technology*. Vol. 1 Issue 3, 175–86.

Jemphrey, M. (2011). The Levirate custom of inheriting widows among the Supyire people of Mali: Theological pointers for Christian marriage. Academia.edu. http://www.academia.edu/4363866/. Retrieved/1/1/2014.

Jina, R., and L. Thomas. (2012). Health consequences of sexual violence against women. Best Practice and research Clinical Obstetrics & Gynecology, Elsevier. www.sciencedirect.com/science/article/pii/S1521693412001344. Retrieved 10/08/2012.

Johannes, E. (2010). Women's education in sub-Saharan Africa: Obstacles facing women and girls access to education: The case of Kenya. *Kenya Studies Review*. Vol. 1, no.2, pp.57–71.

Johnstone, G., and D. Van Ness. (2007). The meaning of restorative justice. In G. Johnston and D. Van Ness. *Handbook of Restorative Justice.* Portland, Oregon: Willan Publishing, 5–23.

Jorda, C., and J. de Hamptinne. (2002). "The status and role of the victim." In A. Cassese et al. (eds.), *The Rome Statute of the International Criminal Court: A commentary*, Vol. 2, Oxford University Press, Oxford, 2002, 1387–97.

Kabore, W., Y. Yaro, and I. Dan-Koma. (2008). Background study of the inter-agency joint programme on violence against women, Burkina Faso. The Inter-Agency Network on Women and Gender Equality Task Force on Violence against Women. www.un.org/womenwatch/ianwge/taskforces/vaw/version_anglaise l_etude de baseVEF 2009-ud.docx. Retrieved 8/5/2012.

Kahan, D. (1996). What do alternative sanctions mean? *University of Chicago Law Review*, 63, 591.

Kamradt-Scott, A. (2012). Evidence-based medicine and the governance of pandemic influenza. *Global Public Health*, Vol. 7, 111–26.

Kaye, D., A. Mirembe, A. Ekstrom, G. Kyomuhendo, and A. Johansson. (2005). Implications of bride price on domestic violence and reproductive health in Wakiso District of Uganda. *African Health Sciences*. Vol. 5, Issue 4, 300–303.

Kelman, H. (1958). Compliance, identification, and internalization: Three processes of opinion change. *Journal of Conflict Resolution*, 2: 51–60.

Kennedy, F. (1972). *Pathology of Oppression.* Sound Recording. University of Iowa Lecture Series.

Kentor, J. (2001). The long term effects of globalization on income inequality, population growth, and economic development. *Social Problems*, Vol. 48, no. 4, 435–55.

Kes, A., and H. Swaminathan. (2006). Gender and Time Poverty in Sub-Saharan Africa. In C. Blackden and Q. Wodon, *Gender, Time Use, and Poverty in Sub-Saharan Africa*. World Bank Working Paper No. 73, Ch. 2, 13–26.

Kevlihan, R. (2013). Providing health services during a civil war: The experience of a garrison town in South Sudan. Overseas Development Institute, 2013 http://content.ebscohost.com.proxy.lib.odu.edu/ContentServer.asp? Retrieved 12/29/2014.

Kingue, S., L. Rosskamm, A. Bela, A. Adjidja, and L. Codjia. (2013). Strengthening human resources for health through multisectoral approaches and leadership: The case of Cameroon. *Bulletin of World Health Organization*, Vol. 91, 864–67.

Kinney, M., K. Kerber, R. Black, B. Cohen, F. Nkrumah, H. Coovadia, P. Nampala, and J. Lawn. (2010). Sub-Saharan Africa's mothers, newborns, and children: Where and why do they die? PLoS Med 7(6): e1000295.doi:10.137/journal.pmed.1000294.

Kiragu, J. (1996). Policy overview: HIV prevention and women's rights—Their promotion goes hand in hand. *AIDS Captions*, 8-14. Secondary Source ID: PIP/118343.

Kurfi, A. (2009). Leadership styles: The managerial challenges in emerging economies. *Euro Journals, Inc*. ISSN: 1451–243X, Issue 6.

LaFraniere, S. (2005). Forced to marry before puberty, African girls pay lasting price. The New York Times, www.nytimes.com, November 27, 2005. Retrieved 12/26, 2013.

Lako, W. (2004). Gender difference masquerading as a tool for women oppression in cultural discourse. *The Ahfad Journal*. Vol. 21, No. 1, 4–17.

Lambert, M., E. Perrino, and E. Barrera. (2012). Understanding the barriers to female education in Ghana. http://www.bluekitabu.org/blue-kitabu-research-instit/understanding_the_barriers_.pdf. Retrieved 8/2/2014.

Langston, D. (1988). Tired of playing monopoly? In J. W. Cochran, D. Langston, and C. Woodard (eds.), *Changing Our Power: An Introduction to Women's Studies* (100–110). Dubuque, IA: Kendall-Hunt.

Laufer, A., and Schechory-Bitton. (2013). Forced displacement and its implications for youth's distress and posttraumatic growth. In K. Jaishankar and N. Ronel, *Global Criminology: Crime and Victimization in a Globalized Era*. CRC Press/Taylor & Francis Group, Ch. 14, 253–68.

Lee, A. (2013). "Can you hear me now?" Making participatory governance work for the poor. *Harvard Law & Policy Review*, Vol. 7, 405–41.

Lee, M. (2007). *Human Trafficking*. Portland, Oregon: Willan Publishing.

Legalnaija, B2012). Legalnajia: Our fundamental human rights. http://www.legalnaija.blogspot.com. Retrieved 1/20/2014.

Legislation.Gov.uk. www.legislation.gov.uk/ukpga/2007/20contents (Forced Marriage (Civil Protection) Act 2007. Retrieved 6/20/2013.

Legislative Council Secretariat. (2006). Causes of Women's Poverty. http://www.legco.gov.hk/yr05–06/english/sec/library/0506fs07e.pdf Retrieved 1/14/2015.

Legotlo, M. (2014). *Challenges and Issues Facing the Education System in South Africa*. Africa Institute of South Africa (AISA): African Books Collective.

Leinhardt, G., A. Seewald, and M. Engel. (1979). Learning what's taught: Sex differences in instruction. *Journal of Education and Psychology*, 71:432–39.

Leserman, J. (2005). Sexual abuse history: Prevalence, health effects, mediators, and psychological treatment. *Journal of Biobehavioral Medicine*. Vol. 67, no. 6, 906–15.

Letsie, M., B. Schalk, and T. Modise. (2008). Women trafficking in South Africa: North West Provincial Legislature. *Lincoln Journal of Social & Political Thought*. Vol. 6, Issue 1, 57–69.

Li, M., V. Mardhekar, and A. Wadkar. (2012). Coping strategies and learned helplessness of employed and nonemployed educated married women from India. *Health Care for Women International*.Vol. 33, No. 5, 495–508.

Lionnet, F. (2005). Women's rights, voices, and identities: The limits of universalism and the legal debate around excision in France. In O. Nnaemeka, *Female Circumcision and the Politics of Knowledge*. Westport, CT: Praeger.

Lipsey, R. (1996). Economic growth, technological change, and Canadian economic policy. C.D. Howe Benefactors Lecture. Toronto: C.D. Howe Institute.

Litvack, J., and C. Bodart. (1993). User fees plus quality equals improved access to health care: Results of field experiment in Cameroon. *Social Science and Medicine*, Vol. 37, no. 3, 369–83.

Lorde, A. (1984). An open letter to Mary Daly. In *Sister Outsider: Essays and Speeches*, 66–71. Trumansburg, NY: Crossing Press.

Lott, B., and H. Bullock. (2010). Social class and women's Lives. *Psychology of Women Quarterly*. Vol. 34, 421–24.

Lutya, T. (2012). Human trafficking of young women and girls for sexual exploitation in South Africa. http://dx.doi.org/10.5772/39202. Retrieved 7/9/2014.

Maccoby, E., and C. Jacklin. (1974). *The Psychology of Sex Differences*. Stanford, CA: Stanford University Press.

Madori, M. (2013). Education: Problems and challenges in Nigeria, what to be done. http://sundaytrust.com.ng/index.php/comment-debate/12514-education-problems-and-challenges-in-nigeria-what-to-be-done. Retrieved 5/31/2014.

Mail Online. (28 May 2012). Young girls kidnapped and forced to marry HIV-positive men because sufferers believe VIRGINS are a cure for AIDS. www.dailymail.c.uk/news/article-215096/Virginal-young-girls-South-Africa. Retrieved 08/09/2012.

Mackey, D., and K. Levan. (2013). *Crime Prevention.* Burlington, Massachusetts: Jones & Bartlett.

Malmberg-Calvo, C. (1994). "Case study on the role of women in rural transport: Access of women to domestic facilities." SSARTP (Sub-Saharan Africa Transport Policy Program, World Bank and Economic Commission for Africa) Working Paper No. 11. Environmentally Sustainable Development Division, Technical Development, Africa Region, The World Bank. Washington, DC.

Maluleke, M. (2012). Culture, tradition, custom, law and gender equality. South African Legal Information Institute (SAFLII). http://www.saflii.org/za/journals/PER/2012/1.html. Retrieved 1/4/2014.

Malungo, J. (1999). Challenges to sexual behavioral changes in the era of HIV/AIDS: The case of sexual cleansing and levirate marriage in Zambia. *Resistances to Bahavioural Change to Reduce HIV/AIDS Infection*, Ch. 4, pp.41–57. http://www.htc.anu.edu.au/pdfs/resistances_ch4.pdf. Retrieve, 12/30/2013.

———. (2001). Sexual cleansing (*Kusalazya*) and levirate marriage (*Kunjilila mung'anda*) in the era of AIDS: changes in perceptions and practices in Zambia. *Social Science & Medicine*, Vol. 53, Issue 3, 371–82.

Mason, K., and Y. Lu. (1988). Attitudes towards women's familial roles: Changes in the United States, 1977–1985. *Gender and Society.* Vol. 2. 39–57.

Marini, M. (1990). Sex and gender: What do we know? *Sociological Forum*, Vol. 5, No. 1, 95–120.

Marquis, S., and E. Butler. (2001). *Practice Guidelines for Prenatal and Postnatal Outreach in British Columbia, Canada*. Victoria: BC Ministry for Children and Families.

Marshall, L. (2004). Unacceptable: The Impact of war on women and children. http://www.Commondreams.org/views04/1219–26.htm. Retrieved 1/13/2014.

Martens, J., M. Pieczkowski, and B. Vuunren-Smyth. (2003). *Seduction, Sale and Slavery: Trafficking in Women and Children for Sexual Exploitation in Southern Africa*, Pretoria: IOM Regional Office for Southern Africa.

McCall, G., and J. Simmons. (1978). *Identities and Interactions*. New York: Free Press.

McFerson, H. (2010). Poverty among women in Sub-Saharan Africa: A review of selected issues. *Journal of International Women's Studies*, Vol. 11, No. 4, 50–72.

McGarrity, J. (2014). US military says climate change could increase wars, conflict. http://www.rtcc.org/2014/03/06/us-military-says-climate-change-could-increase-wars- conflict. Retrieved 8/8/2014.

Mclntosh, M. (2009). *Yoruba Women, Work, and Social Change*. Indiana: Indiana University Press.

Mead, G. (1934). *Mind, Self, and Society*. Chicago: University of Chicago Press.

Meier, R., and W. Johnson. (1977). Deterrence as social control: The legal and extralegal production of conformity. *American Sociological Review*, Vol. 42, No. 2, 292–304.

Mihalakas, N. (2011). 'Intra-African Trade'—A renewed urgency for further regional integration by the AU. http://foreignpolicyblogs.com/2011/12/13/%E2%80%98intra-african-trade%E2%80%99-%E2%80%93-a-renewed-urgency-for-further-regional-integration-by-the=au/. Retrieved 6/6/2014.

Migration News (Russia). (Dec. 11, 1994).

Miles, D., B. Sinervo, L. Hazard, E. Svensson, and D. Costa. (2007). Relating endocrinology, physiology and behaviour using species with alternative mating strategies. *Functional Ecology*. Vol. 21, Issue 4, 653–65.

Miller, J., and C. Mullens. (2006). Taking stock: The status of feminist theories in Criminology. In F. T. Cullen, J. P. Wright, and K. R. Blevins (eds.), *Taking Stock: The Status of Criminological Theory—Advances in Criminological Theory.* Vol. 15, 217–49. New Brunswick, NJ: Transaction.

Miller, M., C. Schreck, and R. Tewksbury. (2008). *Criminological Theory: A Brief Introduction.* 2nd ed. Boston: Pearson and Allyn & Bacon.

Moghadam, V. (2005). "The 'Feminization of Poverty' and women's Human Rights," *Papers in Women's Studies and Gender Research*, No. 2, 1–39.

Monekosso, T. (2001). Africa's forced marriages. BBC News, http://news.bbc.co.uk/2/hi/africa/1209099.stm. Retrieved 5/10/2012.

Mongbo, S. (2007). Women and girls: Victims of the forces of the market and levirate marriage. *Women's Global Network for Reproductive Rights Newsletter*, 88/89, 24–26.

Muabu, G., and X. Ackerman. (2013). Focusing on Quality Education in sub-Saharan Africa. Brookings Institution. http://www.brookings.edu/blogs/education-plus-development/posts/2013/05/28-quality-education-sub-saharan-african-africa-mwabu-ackerman. Retrieved 05/14/2016.

Mulokozi, G. (2000). Improved Solar Drying of Vitamin A-rich Foods by Women's Groups in the Singida District of Tanzania. http://www.siteresources.worldbank.org. Retrieved 1/7/2014.

Munby, J. (2006). Re SA (Vulnerable adult with capacity: Marriage) [2005] EWHC 2942 (FAM), 1 *FLR*, 867–902.

Mwaba, A. (2000). Trade liberalization and growth: Policy options for African countries in a global economy. http://www.afdb.org/fileadmin/uploads/afdb/Documents/Publications/00157654-EN- ERP-60.PDF. Retrieved 6/6/2014.

Naisse, M., A. Afouda, A. Amani, and the World Conservation Union. (2004). Reducing West Africa's vulnerability to climate impacts on water resources, wetlands and desertification: Elements for regional strategy for preparedness and adaptation. IUCN.

News.yahoo.com. (2013). Fears of genocide in Central African Republic. http://news.yahoo.com/central-african-republic-risk-genocide. Retrieved 1/13/2014.

Negin, V., Abd. Z. Rashid, and H. Nikopour. (2010). The causal relationship between corruption and poverty: A panel data analysis (online) http://mpra.ub.uni-muenchen.de/24871/1/MPRA_paper_2487.pdf. Retrieved 10/15/2014.

Ngassa, V. (1998). *Gender Approach to Court Actions*. Cameroon: Friedrich Ebert Stiftung.

Ngassa, V., and C. Time. (1999). *Gender Law Report.* 1999 G.L.R., Vol. 1. Cameroon: Friedrich Ebert Stifung.

Nhanenge, J. (2014). Poverty's root cause and possible solution: Ending reductionism, and developing a holistic worldview. Paper presented at the 7th Annual Poverty and Social Protection Conference, Bangkok, Thailand, March 9–11, 2014.

Nordas, R., and N. Gleditsch. (2007). Climate change and conflict. *Political Geography*, Vol. 26, 627–38.

Nunzio, M. (2014). Thugs, spies and vigilantes: Community policing and street politics in inner city Addis Ababa. *The Journal of the International African Institute*. Volume 84, No. 3, 444–65.

Nussbaum, M. (2000). Women's capabilities and social justice. *Journal of Human Development*, Vol. 1, No. 2, 219–47.

Nwosa, C. (2005). Social Changes in Widowhood across Cultures. Lagos: Nigeria, Daily Champion, November 8, 2005. www.allafrica.com/stories/200511080141.html. Retrieved 6/20/2009.

Nyerere, J. (1970). Education for self-reliance. In W. Cartey and M. Kilson (eds.), *The Africa Reader: Independent Africa*. New York, NY: Vintage Books, 237–55.

Obiora, L. (2005). The anti-female circumcision campaign deficit. In O. Nnaemeka, ed. *Female Circumcision and the Politics of Knowledge*. Westport, CT: Praeger.

Odabassi, B. (2013). The effect of learned helplessness to success. *International Journal of Academic Research*. Vol. 5, No. 4, 125–33.

Oduyoye, M. (1995). *Daughters of Anowa: African Women and Patriarchy*. Maryknoll, NY: Orbis Books.

Oecd.org. (2013). EDIF 2013—No10 (eng)—v9 Final bis.pdf. http://www.oecd.org/edu/skills-beyond-school/EDIF%202013--N%C2%B010%20(eng)--v9%20FINAL%20bis.pdf. Retrieved 3/17/2014.

Okoro, M. (2009). "The role of leadership in a country's development: Obstacles, weaknesses and progresses," a paper presented at the College of Agriculture, Arkansas State University.

Okoth-Ogendo, HWO. (1989). Some issues of theory in the study of tenure relations in African Agriculture, 59 *Africa* 6 (1989).

Oliphant, L. (2009). Marriages mMade in Hell. City Press, 12 April, 25.

Olorunsanya, E., and O. Omotesho. (2014). A gender analysis of determinants of poverty among rural farming households in Nigeria. *Albanian Journal of Agricultural Sciences*. VP; 13, No. 2, 96–109.

Oluwole, S. (1993). *Womanhood in Yoruba Traditional Thought*. Bayreuth: Iwalewa-Haus.

Omwami, E. (2011). Relative-change theory: Examining the impact of patriarchy, paternalism, and poverty on the education of women in Kenya. *Gender and Education*. Vol. 23, No.1, 15–28.

One.Org. (2010). The Millennuim Development Goals: How is Africa Doing? https://www.one.org/us/policy/the-millenium-development-goals-how-is-africa-doing/ Retrieved 05/15/2016.

Onuoha, B. (2011). The State human trafficking and human rights issues in Africa. *Contemporary Justice Review*. Vol. 14, No. 2, 149–66.

Order of Truth. (2013). UK government wastes 1 billion of taxpayers' money on foreign aid to Nigeria. http://orderoftruth.wordpress.com/2013/08/09/uk-government-wastes-1-billion-of-taxepayers-money-on-foreign-aid-to-nigeria/. Retrieved 11/13/2013.

Otu, S. (2012). Corruption and governance: Dynamics, institutional reform, and strategies for controlling leadership-centered crimes. In C. Okafo, *Grounded Law: Comparative Research on State and Non-State Justice in Multiple Societies*. United Kingdom: Wildfire Publishing House, Ch. 17, 420–57.

Oumo, O. (2004). "Bride price and violence against women: The case of Uganda." Paper presented at the International Bride Price Conference, February, Kampala, Uganda.

Oxfam.com. Famine in Somalia: Causes and solutions/Oxfam International. http://www.oxfam.org/en/emergencies/east-africa-food-crisis/famine-somalia-what- needs-be-done. Retrieved 1/9/2014.

Oyebanji, M. (1981). Proposals for reform of marriage laws in Nigeria. In Aguda, T.A. (ed.), *The Marriage Laws of Nigeria* (p. 151). Lagos: The Nigerian Institute of Advanced Legal Studies.

Pagelow, M. (1984). *Family Violence*. New York: Greenwood Press.

Pandofelli, L., R. Meinzen-Dick, and S. Dohrn. (2008). Gender and collective action: Motivations, effectiveness and impact. *Journal of International Development*.Vol. 20, Issue 1, pp. 1–11.

Pandofelli, L., R. Meinzen-Dick, and S. Dohrn. (2007). Gender and collective action: A conceptual framework for analysis. *International Food Research Institute*. www.ifpri.org,CAPRIWP64.pdf. Retrieved 2/4/2014.

Park, A. (2006). "Other inhuman acts": Forced marriage, girl soldiers, and the special court for Sierra Leone. *Social & Legal Studies*, 15, 315–37.

Partnerships, Resource Mobilisation and Communications, NEPAD Agency (n.d.). "Africa can't develop through external aid" by Professor Richard Mkandawire. http://www.nepad/news/2347/%E2%80%9Cafrica-can%E2%80%99t-develop-through- external-aid%E2%80%9d. Retrieved 3/5/2015.

Pearson, G. (2011). Famine in Africa: What is the long-term solution? http://www.huffingtonpost.ca/glen-pearson/famine-africa_b_920065.html. Retrieved 12/27/2014.

Peters, D., A. Garg, G. Bloom, D. Walker, W. Brieger, and M. Rahman. (2008). Poverty and access to health care in developing countries. *Annals of the New York Academy of Sciences*. 1136, 161–71.

Peterson, C., S. Maier, and M. Seligman. (1993). *Learned Helplessness: A Theory of the Age of Personal Control*. New York: Oxford University Press.

PEW Charitable Trusts. (2010). Gender equality universally embraced, but inequalities acknowledged/Pew Research . . . http://www.pewglobal.org/2010/07/01/gender-equality. Retrieved 5/10/2013.

Phillips, R. (2009). Food security and women's health: A feminist perspective for international social work. *International Social Work*, Vol. 52, 485–98.

Pickhardt, C. (2011). The impact of divorce on young children and adolescents. www.psychologytoday.com/…childs…/the-impact-divorce-young-children. Retrieved 10/30/12

PlanInternational.org. (2012). Because I am a Girl: Progress and Obstacles to Girls Education in Africa. http://www.plan-international.org/girls/pdfs/progress%20and%20obstacles%20to%20girls%20education%20in%20Africa_ENG.pdf. Retrieved 8/2/2014.

Plan UK. Early and forced marriage—facts, figures and what you can do. www.plan-uk.org/early-and-forced-marriage/html. Retrieved 8/9/2012.

Plateau, J., A. Abraham, F. Gaspart, and L. Stevens. (2000). Traditional marriage practices as determinants of women's land rights: A review of research-articles prepared based on research by Jean-Philippe Plateau, Anita Abraham, Frederic Gaspart, and Luc Stevens. CRED Centre de Recherche en Economie du Developpment. University of Namur, Belgium. http://www.fao.org/docrep/008/a0297e/a0297e05.htm. Retrieved 1/2/2014.

Poverties.org. (2013). Famine in Africa: The failure of the world system. http://www.poverties.org/famine-in-africa.html. Retrieved 12/28/2014.

Prince, C. (2009). Parents sell girls as child brides. *Sunday Times*, 31 May.

Puechguirbal, N. (2010). Discourses on gender, patriarchy and resolution 1325: A textual analysis of UN Documents. *International Peacekeeping*. Vol. 17, No. 2, 172–87.

Rackley, E. (2005). Armed violence against women in Burundi. *Humanitarian Exchange Magazine*. http://www.odihpn.org/humanitarian-exchange-magazine/issue-31/armed-violence-against-women-in-burundi. Retrieved 1/30/2014.

———. (2005). Armed violence against women in Burundi. *Humanitarian Exchange*. No. 31, 34–36.

Ramey, E. (1973). Sex hormones and executive ability. *Annals of the New York Academy of Sciences*. Vol. 208, 237–45.

Rauschenbach, M., and D. Scalia. (2008). Victims and international criminal justice: A vexed question? *International Review of the Red Cross*. Vol. 90, No. 870, 441–59.

Ray, E., and K. Kilburn. (1970). Behavior modification techniques applied to community behavior problems. *Criminology*, Vol. 8, 173–84.

Reddy, R. (2008). Gender, culture and the law: Approaches to 'honour crimes' in the UK. *Feminist Legal Studies*, Vol. 16, 305–21.

Refworld.org. (2006). Ghana: Forced marriages; prevalence of such marriages; whether a woman can refuse such a marriage, and the consequences of the refusal; available state protection and redress (2004–2006). http://www.refworld.org/docid/45f1473720.html. Retrieved 12/29/2013.

———. (2012). http://www.unhcr.org/refworld/publisher,IRBC,,ML1,469cda0c,0.html. Retrieved 3/22/2012.

Reliefweb.int. (2012) Trends in maternal mortality 1990–2010. WHO, UNICEF, UNFPA and The World Bank estimates. http://reliefweb.int/sites/reliefweb.int/files/resources/Full_Report_3984.pdf. Retrieved 2/26/2014.

Rich, A. (1986). *Of Women Born, Motherhood as Experience and Institution*. New York: Norton.

Riddell, W. (2004). The social benefits of education: New evidence on an old question. Paper prepared for the conference "Taking public universities seriously," University of Toronto,

December 3–4. http://www.Utoronto.ca/president/04conference/downloads/riddell.pdf. Retrieved 2/6/2014.

Rogers, E. (1995). *Diffusion of Innovations*. New York: The Free Press/Macmillan Publishing Co., Inc.

Ronel, N. (2012). From criminal spin to positive criminology. In K. Jaishankar and N. Ronel (eds.), *Global Criminology: Crime and Victimization in a Globalized Era.* Boca Raton, FL: CRC Press/Taylor and Francis Group, LL.C, Ch. 18, 335–52.

Rose, P., and S. Al-Samarrai. (2001). Household constraints on schooling by gender: Empirical evidence from Ethiopia. *Comparative Educational Review*. Vol. 45, No.1, 6–63.

Roseboom, T., de Rooij, and R. Painter. (2006). The Dutch famine and its long-term consequences for adult health. *Early Human Development*. Vol. 82, 485–91.

Ruback, R., A. Gladfelter, and B. Lantz. (2014). Paying restitution: Experimental analysis of the effects of information and rationale. *Criminology and Public Policy.*Vol. 13, Issue 3, 405–34.

Sa'ah, J. (2007). Cameroon dances to Anti-graft beat. http://news.bbc.co.uk/2/hi/africa/7131637.stm. Friday, December 2007. Retrieved 6/18/2011.

Sachs, J., and S. Collins. (1989). *Developing Country Debt and Economic Performance*, Vol. 3: Country Studies—Indonesia, Korea, Philippines, Turkey. ISBN 0226733351, Chicago: University of Chicago Press.

Samuels, F., M. Gavrilovic, C. Harper, and M. Nino-Zarazua. (2011). Food, financial and fuel: The impacts of the triple F crisis in Nigeria, with a particular focus on women and children – Kano State focus. London, Overseas Development Institute. (http://www.odi.org.uk/resources/details.asp?id=6049&title=food-finance-fuel-crisis-women-children-nigeria. Retrieved 7/27/2014.

Sarsons, H. (2011). Rainfall and conflict. http://www.econ.yale.edu/conference/neudc11paperpers/paper_199.pdf. Retrieved 8/8/2014.

Saraladevi, N., P. Jacob, C. Roger, B. Tutt, and J. Eastwood. (2009). Shortage of healthcare workers in developing countries---Africa. *Ethnicity & Disease*, Vol. 19, 60–64.

Sawadogo, W. (2012). The challenges of transnational human trafficking in West Africa. *African Studies Quarterly*. Vol. 13, Issue 1, 95–115.

Sbs.com.au (2014). Child brides' big issue in Africa. http://www.sbs.com.au/news/article/2014/05/30/child-brides-big-issue-africa. Retrieved 7/4/2014.

Scalise E. (2012). Indigenous women's land rights: Case studies from Africa. *State of the World's Minorities and Indigenous People*, 53–59. http://minorityrights.org/download.php?id=1117. Retrieved 10/24/2014.

Scanzoni, L., and J. Scanzoni. (1981). *Men, Women, and Change*. 2nd ed. New York: McGraw-Hill Book Company.

Schmerler, K., M. Perkins, S. Phillips, T. Rinehart, and M. Townsend. (2006). A Guide to Reducing Crime and Disorder through Problem-Solving Partnerships. Community Oriented Policing Services (COPS) U.S. Department of Justice. http://www.cops.usdoj.gov/files/ric/publications/e05060069.pdf. Retrieved 10/6/2014.

Schulz, D. (2012). *Culture and Customs of Mali.* Books.google.com/books?isbn=031335913. http://www.google.com/search?q=levirate+marriages+in+mali&ie=UTF-8&oe=8&hl=en&client=safari#hl=en&q=inauthor:%22Dorothea+schulz%22&tbm=bks. Retrieved 1/1/2014.

Seavey, C., P. Katz, and S. Zalk. (1975). Baby X: The effect of gender labels on adult responses to infants. *Sex Roles*, 1:103–9.

Secretarait.thecommonwealth.org (2013). Women's land Rights handbook–Cameroon.pdf. http://www.secretarait.thecommonwealth.org/files/255932/filename/women'sLandRightsHandbook-Cameroon.pdf. Retrieved 2/15/2014.

Seligman, M. (1972). Learned helplessness. *Annual Review of Medicine*, Vol. 23, 407–12.

Sender, J., and S. Smith. (1986). *The Development of Capitalism in Africa.* London, England: Methuen.

Shelley, L. (2010). *Human Trafficking: A Global Perspective*. Cambridge: Cambridge University Press.

Siddiqui, H. (2003). "It was written in her kismet": Forced marriage. In *From homebreakers to jailbreakers: Southall Black Sisters*, ed. Rahila Gupta, 67–91. London: Zed Books.

Sidint.net (n.d.). Human trafficking in East Africa . http://sidint.net/content/human-trafficking-east-africa. Retrieved 2/5/2014.

Sil.Org. (2010). http://www.sil.org/literacy/wom.lit.htm. Women and Literacy. Retrieved 6/8/2011.

Sirleaf, J. (2014). 'Africa Rising'? Not really, unless we invest more in girls. http://edition.com/2014/06/16/world/africa/africa-rising-invest-girls-johnson-sirleaf/index.html. Retrieved 05/14/2016.

Sita, N. (2003). Trafficking in women and children: Situation and some trends in African countries. UNAFRI, May.

Siteresources.worldbank.org (2013). Cameroon-governance-in-the-education-sector.pdf. http://siteresources.worldbank.org/INTCAMEROON/Resources/cameroon-governance-in-the-education-sector.pdf. Retrieved 6/1/2014.

Smith, M., and J. Segal. (2012). Child Abuse and Neglect: Recognizing and preventing child abuse. Helpguide. www.helpguide.org/mental/child_abuse_physical_emotional_sexual_neglect.htm. Retrieved 10/01/2012.

The Spectator. (2014). Why foreign aid fails—and how to really help Africa by Daron Acemoglu and James Robinson. http://www.spectator.co.uk/features/9121361/why-aid-fails. Retrieved 3/5/2015.

Sorosoro.org. http://www.sorosoro.org/en/the-fate-of-widows. Retrieved 1/2/2014.

State.gov. U.S. Department of State, mobile. Niger. Bureau of Democracy, Human Rights, and Labor. 2010 Country Reports on Human Rights Practices. Report, April 8, 2011. http://www.m.state.gov/md154362.htm. Retrieved 12/28/2013.

Steffen, C. (2011). *Mutilating Khalid: The Symbolic Politics of Female Genital Cutting.* Trenten, New Jersey: The Red Sea Press, Inc.

Steffensmeier, D. (1980). Sex differences in patterns of adult crime, 1965–77. *Social Forces.*Vol. 58, 1080–109.

Stern, C. (2011). Famine in Africa: Why women and children need the most help. *Huffington Post*, October 1, 2011. www.huffingtonpost.com/caryl.stern/famine-in-africa-why-wome-b-914562. html. Retreived 7/6/2013.

Stets, J., and P. Burke. (2003). A sociological approach to self-identity. In M. Leary and J. Tangney (eds.), *The Handbook of Self and Identity*. New York: Guilford Press.

Stoprapeinconflict.org. Stop rape in Democratic Republic of Congo—The international campaign to stop rape and gender violence in conflict. http://www.stoprapeinconflict.org/dr_congo. Retrieved 2/3/2014.

Stopvaw.org (2010). Defining other forms of forced marriage: Wife inheritance, levirate and sororate marriages. http://www.stopvaw.org/defining_other_forms_of_forced_marriage_wife_inheritance+levirate_and_sororat_marriages. Retrieved 1/3/2014.

Strickland, R. (2004). To have and to hold: Women's property and inheritance rights in the context of HIV/AIDS in Sub-Saharan Africa. *International Center for Research on Women*, Washington, DC, 1–84.

Stryker, S. (2007). Identity theory and personality theory: Mutual relevance. *Journal of Personality*. Vol. 75, No. 6. 1083–102.

Sultana, A. (2010). Patriarchy and women's gender ideology: A socio-cultural perspective. *Journal of Social Science*. Vol. 6, No. 1, 123–26.

Sutherland, E. (1934). *Principles of Criminology*. 2nd. Ed. Philadelphia, PA, J.B. Lippincott.

Tawiah, E. (2007). Maternal health care in five sub-Saharan African countries. http://www.uaps2007.princeton.edu/papers/70586. Retrieved 2/22/2014.

Taylor, E. (2002). Trafficking in women and girls. Paper prepared for Expert Group Meeting on Trafficking in Women and Girls, Glen Cove, New York, 18–22 November.

Taylor, V. (2010). Emancipation and its failures. *Development.* Vol. 53, Issue 2, 164–68.

Temesgen, G. (2014). Root causes and solutions to human trafficking in Ethiopia. *International Journal of Sciences and Research*, Vol. 3, Issue 8, 1578–85.

Thirlwall, A. (2000). Trade, trade liberalisation and economic growth: The theory and evidence. http://www.afdb.org/fileadmin/uploads/afdb/Documents/Publications/00157660-FR-ERP-63.PDF. Retrieved 6/6/2014.

Thompson, C. (2011). Women hit hardest by East African Famine. Msmagazine.com http://www.msmagazine.com/blog/2011/07/31/women-hit-hardest-by-east-african-famine. Retrieved 1/12/2014.

Time, C. (2012). The Cameroonian woman and the law. In C. Okafo (ed), *Grounded Law: Comparative Research on State and Non-State Justice in Multiple Societies*. U.K.: Wildfire Publishing, ch. 18, 458–73.

Time, V. (2012). Failed justice and political extremism: Discussing the dilemma. In C. Okafo (ed.), *Grounded Law: Comparative Research on State and Non-State Justice in Multiple Societies*. UK: Wildfire Publishing, Ch. 6, 152–78.

———. (2013). Forced marriages, bride price, and levirate, domestic violence: Victimization of women and struggles for justice and equity in selected African countries. In K. Jaishankar and N. Ronel (eds.), *Global Criminology: Crime and Victimization in the Globalized Era.* January, CRC Press/Taylor and Francis Group, 271–88.

Trafficking-GB2ed-2005. http://www.unicef-irc.org/publications/pdf/trafficking-gb2ed-2005.pdf. Retrieved 3, 3/2014.

Transparency International. (2003). Corruption Surveys and Indexes. http://www.transparency.org/faq-corruption.html. Retrieved July 20, 2003.

———. (2006). Corruption Surveys and Indexes. http://www.transparency.org/faq-corruption.html. Retrieved May 5, 2006.

———. (2014). Overview of Corruption and Anti-Corruption in the Democratic Republic of Congo. http://www.transparency.org/files/content/corruptionquas/country_profile_DRC_2014.pdf. Retrieved 10/19/2014.

Toubia, N. (1995). *Female Genital Mutilation: A Call for Global Action.* RAINBO, New York.

Tsikata, D. (2003). Securing women's interests within land tenure reforms: Recent debates in Tanzania. *Journal of Agrarian Change,* Vol. 3, No. 1, 149–83.

Turner, T. (2008). *The Congo Wars: Conflict, Myth and Reality.* London/New York, NY: Zed Books.

Tyakume, V. (2009). Child protection, violence and abuse against children, ukuthwala practices, virginity testing, initiation: Department of Justice and Molo Songololo briefings. Pretoria: *Parliamentary Monitoring Group*.

Tyler, T. (2001). A psychological perspective on the legitimacy of institutions and authorities. In J. T. Jost and B. Major (eds.), *The Psychology of Legitimacy: Emerging Perspectives on Ideology, Justice, and Intergroup Relations*. Cambridge, U.K.: Cambridge University Press.

———. (2011). *Why people cooperate.* Princeton, N.J.: Princeton University Press.

Ufuk, G. (2013). Hope and despair for women in Islamic States. Organizations of Islamic Countries. http://www.oicun.org/71/20130508035638010.html. Retrieved 2/5/2015.

UNAIDS.org. (2012). Impact of the global economic crisis on women, girls and gender equality. http://ww.uniaids.org/en/media/uniaids/contentassests/documents/document/2012/discussionpapers/JC2368_impact-economic-crisis-women_en.pdf. Retrieved 3/29/2014.

———. (2013). Global Report 2013. http://www.unaids.org/en/media/unaids/contentassets/documents/epidemiology/2013/gr2013/unaids_global_report_2013_en.pdf. Retrieved 8/11/2014.

UNCCD.int. (n.d.). Addressing desertification, land degradation and drought in Africa. http://www.unccd.int/en/regional-access/Africa/pages/alltext.aspx. Retrieved 8/7/2014.

UNDESA United Nations Department of Economic and Social Affairs. (2012). International Decade for Action 'water for Life' 2005–2015, http://www.un.org/waterorlifedecade/scarcity.shtml. Retrieved 8/7/2014.

UNDP. (1995). *Human Development Report*. New York: UNDP.

———. (2013). Human Development Index. Https://www.data.undp.org/dataset/Table-1-Human- Development-Index-and-its-components/. Retrieved 2/7/2014.

———. (n.d.). Why the private sector is so important in alleviating poverty. http://web.undp.org/cpsd/documents/report/english/chapter1.pdf. Retrieved 1/4/2015.

UNESCO. (2012). World atlas of gender equality in education; 2012. http://www.uis.unesco.org/Education/Documents/unesco-world-atlas-gender-education-2012.pdf. Retrieved 3/29/2014.

UNFPA (2005). Child marriage/UNFPA-United Nations population fund. http://www.unfpa.org/child-marriage. Retrieved 6/7/ 2014.

———. (2001). The impact of armed conflict on women and girls: A consultative meeting on mainstreaming gender in areas of conflict and reconstruction. www.unfpa.org/upload/lib_pub_file/46_filename_armedconflict_women.pdf. Retrieved 1/22/2014.

UN.GIFT=United Nations Global Initiative to Fight Human Trafficking. (2009). Global report on trafficking in persons. Vienna: UN Office on Drugs and Crime.

UNHCR. http://allafrica.com/stories/201312180379.html?aa_source=useful-column.Retrieved 1/9/2014.

UNICEF. (2007). Investing in the Children of the Islamic World.

———. (n.d.). Impact of armed conflict on children: war hits home when it hits women and girls. http://www.unicef.org/graca/women.htm. Retrieved 1/29/2014.

United Nations, CEDAW Convention on the Elimination of all forms of Discrimination against Women. (2014). Joint general recommendation/general comment No.31 of the committee on the Elimination of Discrimination against Women and No. 18 of the Committee on the Rights of the Child on harmful practices. http://tbinternet.ohchr.org/Treaties/CEDAW/Shared%20Documents/1_Global/CEDAW_C_GC_31_CRC_C_GC_18_7557_E.doc. Retrieved 1/7/2015.

United Nations Human Rights. (2000). U.N. Protocol to Prevent, Suppress and Punish Trafficking in Persons, especially Women and Children (Palermo Protocol). http://www.ohchr.org/EN/Professionalinterest/Pages/ProtocolTraffickinginpersons.aspx. Retrieved 6/7/2014.

United Nations Inter-Agency Project on Human Trafficking. (UNIAP) (n.d.). Human trafficking background information. http://www.no-trafficking.org/resources-background-risks.html. Retrieved 7/7/2014.

UN Water Factsheet on Water Scarcity (Untitled). (2013). http://www.unwater.org/user_upload/unwater_new/doc/A4%20templates%20(water%20scarcity).pdf. Retrieved 7/7/2015.

USA Today. (2013).http://www.usatoday.com/story/news/world/2013/08/20/congo-civil- war/2624757. Retrieved 2/3/2014.

U.S. State Department. (2008). Trafficking in persons report: Country narrative–Cameroon. http://www.gvnet.com/humantrafficking/Cameroon-2.htm. Retrieved 6/22/2014.

Valian, V. (1998). *Why So Slow? The Advancement of Women*. Cambridge: MIT Press.

Veil, L. (1998). *The Issue of Child Domestic Labor and Trafficking in West and Central Africa*. Report prepared for the UNICEF sub-regional Workshop on Trafficking in Child Domestic Workers, particularly girls in domestic service, in West and Central Africa Region, Cotonu, 6–8 July.

Veit, P. (2009). Stopping the resource wars in Africa. *World Resource Institute*, http://www.wri.org/blog/2009/08/stopping-resource-wars-africa. Retrieved 12/29/2014.

Verhoeven, H. (2011). Climate change, conflict and development in Sudan: Global Neo-Malthusian narratives and local power struggles. *Development and Change,* Vol. 42, no. 3, 679–707.

Vickery, C. (1977). "The Time-Poor: A New Look at Poverty." *Journal of Human Resources*, Vol. 12, no. 1, 27–48.

Virani, S (2007). *The Islamillis in the Middle Ages: A History of Survival, A search for Salvation*. New York: Oxford University Press.

Voanews.com. (2010). Ethiopian women seek improved access to pre-natal care. http://www.voanews.com/content/ethiopian-women-seek-improved-accesss-to-pre-natal-care-104958679/156071.html. Retrieved 2/21/2014.

Walker, C. (2003). Piety in sky? Gender policy and land reform in South Africa. *Journal of Agrarian Change*, Vol. 3, no. 1, 113–47.

Walker, L. (1979). *The Battered Woman*. New York: Harper & Row.

Warren, B. (1980). *Imperialism: Pioneer of Capitalism.* London, England: New Books.

Water for Life Decade. (2014). Water Scarcity/International Decade for Action 'Water for Life' 2005–2015. http://www.un.org/waterforlifedecade/scarcity.shtml. Retrieved 10/7/2015.

Watkins, K. (2013). Too little access, not enough learning: Africa's twin deficit. http://www.brookings.edu/research/opinions/2013/01/16-africa-learning-watkins. Retrieved 2/9/2014.

Welch, G. and A. Sachs. (1987). The bride price, revolution, and the liberation of women. *International Journal of Sociology of Law*, Vol. 15, No. 4, 369–93.

Welchman, L., and S. Hossain. (2005). *'Honour': Crimes, paradigms and violence against women*, ed. Lynn Welchman and Sara Hossain, 1–21. London: Zed Books.

Welsh, M. (2014). African, farming and solutions. *The Cairo Review of Global Affairs,* http://www.aucegypt.edu/GAPP/CairoReview/pages/articleDetails.aspx?aid=96. Retrieved 12/27/2014.

Welstead, M. (2009). Forced Marriage: Bifurcated values in the U.K. *Denning Law Journal*, Vol. 21, 49–65.

Wilson, W. (1997). "Ghetto-related behavior and the structure of opportunity." In *When Work Disappears*. new York: Alfred A. Knopf, 51–86.

Women for Women's Human Rights—New Ways: Sexuality and Human Rights in Muslim Societies. Inonu Caddesi, 29/6 Saadet Apt. Gumusuyu, 34437 Instabul. http://www.humanrights.net/wwwhr.org. Retrieved 10/26/2013.

World Bank. (2013). An analysis of issues shaping Africa's economic future, *Africa's Pulse,* Volume 8, pp 1–40. http://www.worldbank.org/content/dam/worldbank/document/Africa/Report/Africas-pulse-brochure_Vol8.pdf. Retrieved 6/3/2014.

———. (2013). Maternal mortality ratio (modeled estimate, per 100,000 live births) [Data] Table. http://data.worldbank.org/indicator/SH.STA.MMRT. Retrieved 5/28/2014.

World Economic Forum. (2013). *The Global Gender Gap Report 2012*. Switzerland.

World Health Organization. (2011). Impact of economic crises on mental health. http://www.euro.who.int/__data/assets/pdf_file/0008/134999/e94837.pdf. Retrieved 7/29/2014.

Worldrevolution.org. (n.d.). Women and war. http://www.worldrevolution.org/guidepage/womenandwar/intro. Retrieved 2/3/2014.

WorldSavvy.org. (2009). Global status of women: How is the current global economic crisis expected to affect women? http://worldsavvy.org/monitor/index.php? Retrieved 7/25/2014.

Worldwithoutgenocide.org. (2008–2009). Democratic Republic of Congo/World without genocide. http://worldwithoutgenocide.org/genocides-and-conflicts/congo. Retrieved 2/3/2014. www2.gnb.ca.

What is poverty?—Economic and social inclusion corporation. http://www2.gnb.ca/content/gnb/en/departments/esic/overview/contnt/what-is-poverty.html. Retrieved 2/14/2014.

Yuan, N., M. Koss, and M. Stone. (2006). The psychological consequences of sexual trauma. Harrisburg, PA: VAWnet, a project of the *National Resource Center* on Domestic Violence/Pennsylvania Coalition against Domestic Violence. Retrieved 9/29/2012, from http://www.vawnet.org

Yusuf, M., C. Malarvizhi, M. Mazumder, and Z. Su. (2014). Corruption, poverty, and economic growth relationship in the Nigerian economy. *Journal of Developing Areas*, Vol. 48, No. 3, 95–107.

Zaman, F. (2006). The nature of political empowerment and gender in local governance: A comparative study of Dhaka city Corporation and Narayangonj municipality.

Zelikovsky, S. (2014). How about some commonsense on Ebola? *Washington Times*, News Bank, Access World News. http://infoweb.newsbank.com.proxy.lib.odu.edu/iw-search/we/infoweb? Retrieved 12/30/2014.

Zoundi, S. (2011). Famine in East Africa: Solutions exist in Africa. http://oecdinsights.org/2011/08/19/famine-in-east-africa-solutions-exis-in-africa. Retrieved 12/27/2014.

CASES

AE/K Estate of Ndjouchuit (n.d.) Unreported. In Ngassa (1998). *Gender Approach to Court Actions*. Cameroon, Friedrich Stiftung, 46.

Bhe v. Magistrate, Khavelitsha & others (2004). Constitutional Court Case CCT49/03.

David Tchakokam v. Keou Magdaleine (High Court of Meme Division, Holden in Kumba)—HCK/AE/K.38/97/32/92 (1998).
Ephraim v. Pastory & another (1990) High Court Application No. 70/89 (unreported) Delivered on February 22, 1990.
Hadijatou Mani Koraou v. The Republic of Niger (ECW/CCJ/JUD/06/08 of 27 October 2008.
I v. I (1971) East African Law Reports 278.
Maya Ikome v. Manga Ekemason CASWP/CC76/85 (unreported).
Ndenno c/Mme Guamgne Alphonsine (no.36 of 27th June 1996.
Ngeh v. Ngome (1963). West Cameroon Law Report page 32–33.
Ogunkoya v. Ogunkoya (1988: 6). Nigerian Court of Appeals (Alewo and Olong, 2012)
Prosecutor v. Brima, Kamara, and Kanu (2004) SCSL-04–16-T.
Re SA (Vulnerable Adult with capacity: Marriage) [2005] EWHC 2942 (FAM) 1 FLR 2006.
SERAP v. Federal Republic of Nigeria and Universal Basic Education Commission ECW/CCJ/APP08/08.

Index of Names

Index of Subjects

About the Author

Victoria M. Time is a university professor and professor of criminal justice in the Department of Sociology and Criminal Justice at Old Dominion University in Norfolk, Virginia, U.S.A. Her education comprises two law degrees from the University of Cameroon; a masters in comparative law from George Washington University Law School; a masters in justice, law and society from American University in Washington, DC; and a PhD in criminology from Indiana University of Pennsylvania.

She has geared her research endeavors to capture her various interests in comparative justice systems, human rights, nation building, crimes of culture, and contemporary legal issues. She has published extensively and some of her works can be found in the *Journal of Criminal Justice, International Journal of Comparative and Applied Criminal Justice, Women and Criminal Justice, Social Justice, Journal of Ethnicity in Criminal Justice*, *Asian Journal of Criminology*, and a host of other journals. Her works are also published as book chapters in several books, and her first book titled *Shakespeare's Criminals: Criminology, Fiction, and Drama*, also portrays her interest in the English classics and criminological theory.

Victoria M. Time has traveled extensively in the United States and worldwide to present her research at conferences and symposiums or to teach at foreign universities such as University of Kitakyushu, Japan, and Zhejiang University Guanghua Law School, China.